AF668414

Chicken Farming

ABOUT THE AUTHOR

Narender Kumar Vyas, born on May 1974, He is professor of Zoology in Patna University. He has 24 years of experience as an outstanding teacher and researcher. He received M.Sc. (Zoology) and P. Hd in Dairy Science from Bhasgalpur, Bihar. He did many works in the field of Aquatic Insects Ecology, Limnolgy and Conversation ecology. He published more than 24 research articles in reputed National and International Journals. He edited and as an Author in more than 13 books in his carrier.

ABOUT THE BOOK

A poultry farm is where domesticated birds are raised. Poultry include chickens, turkey, ducks, and geese. These animals are raised for their meat and eggs. Chickens are the most common bird raised for both meat and eggs. Chickens that are raised for their meat are called broilers. Chickens that are raised for their eggs are called laying hens or layers. Some special breeds of poultry are raised for shows and competitions. Poultry farming, raising of birds domestically or commercially, primarily for meat and eggs but also for feathers. Chickens, turkeys, ducks, and geese are of primary importance, while guinea fowl and squabs (young pigeons) are chiefly of local interest. This article treats the principles and practices of poultry farming. For a discussion of the food value and processing of poultry products, see egg and poultry processing. Poultry is one of the fastest growing segments of the agricultural sector in India today. While the production of agricultural crops has been rising at a rate of 1.5 to 2 percent per annum, that of eggs and broilers has been rising at a rate of 8 to 10 percent per annum. As a result, India is now the world's fifth largest egg producer and the eighteenth largest producer of broilers. The book is intended to be a guide for under graduate and post graduate students of veterinary and animal science, broiler farm managers and entrepreneurs, and farming aspirants.

Chicken Farming

NARENDER KUMAR VYAS

AMIGA PRESS INC.
Delhi-110051

AMIGA PRESS INC.
H.O :- 28-A, Indra Park, St.No. 9
Near-Chander Nagar, Krishna Nagar
Delhi: - 110051 (India)
Tel: - 011-22504028, +91-98736-57000
Email :- amigapress@gmail.com
info@amigapress.co.in
amigaeditorial@gmail.com
amigapub@gmail.com

Website: - www.amigapress.co.in

This edition is published by Amiga Press Inc.

ISBN : 978-93-84533-52-6

Copyright© Reserved
First Published 2020

Publisher's note:
All rights reserved, no part of this publication may be reproduced, stored in a retrieval system or transmitted in any form or by any means, electronic, mechanical, photocopying, recording or otherwise without the prior written permission of the publisher or the copyright holder.

This book contains information obtained from authentic and highly regarded sources. Reasonable efforts have been made to publish reliable data and information, but the author's, editor/s and publisher cannot assume responsibility for the validity of all materials or the consequences of their use. The author/s, editor/s and publishers have attempted to trace and acknowledge the copyright holders of all materials reproduced in this publication and apologize to copyright holders, if permission and acknowledgements to publish in the form have not been taken. If any copyright material has not been acknowledge please write and let us know so we may rectify it, in subsequent reprints.

Publisher Notice: - Presentations, Logos (the way they are written/ Presented), in this book are under the copyright of the publisher and hence, if copied/resembled the copier will be prosecuted under the law.

Printed and bound in India by Replika Press Pvt. Ltd.

Preface

A poultry farm is where domesticated birds are raised. Poultry include chickens, turkey, ducks, and geese. These animals are raised for their meat and eggs. Chickens are the most common bird raised for both meat and eggs. Chickens that are raised for their meat are called broilers. Chickens that are raised for their eggs are called laying hens or layers. Some special breeds of poultry are raised for shows and competitions.

Poultry farming is the practice of raising poultry, such as chickens, turkeys, ducks, and geese, as a subcategory of animal husbandry, for the purpose of farming meat or eggs for food. More than 50 billion chickens are reared annually as a source of food, for both their meat and their eggs. Chickens farmed for meat are called broilers, whilst those farmed for eggs are called egg-laying hens. In total, the UK alone consumes over 29 million eggs per day. Some hens can produce over 300 eggs a year. Chickens will naturally live for 6 or more years. After 12 months, the hen's productivity will start to decline. This is when most commercial laying hens are slaughtered. The vast majority of poultry are raised using intensive farming techniques. According to the Worldwatch Institute, 74 percent of the world's poultry meat, and 68 percent of eggs are produced this way. One alternative to intensive poultry farming is free range farming.

Chicken breeding is an outstanding example of the application of basic genetic principles of inbreeding and crossbreeding as well as of intensive mass selection to effect faster and cheaper gains in meat and maximum egg production for the egg-laying strains. Maximum use of heterosis, or hybrid vigour, through incrosses and crossbreeding has been made. Rapid and efficient weight gains and high-quality, plump, meaty carcasses have been achieved thereby.

Poultry are quite susceptible to a number of diseases; some of the more common are fowl typhoid, pullorum, fowl cholera, chronic respiratory disease, infectious sinusitis, infectious coryza, avian infectious hepatitis, infectious synovitis, bluecomb, Newcastle disease, fowl pox, avian leukosis complex, coccidiosis, blackhead, infectious laryngotracheitis, infectious bronchitis, and erysipelas. Strict sanitary precautions, the intelligent use of antibiotics and vaccines, and the widespread use of cages for layers and confinement rearing for broilers have made it possible to effect satisfactory disease control.

Broiler breeder farms raise parent stock which produce fertilized eggs. A broiler hatching egg is never sold at stores and is not meant for human consumption. The males and females are separate genetic lines or breeds. The chicks they produce will therefore be hybrids or 'crosses'. Since the birds are bred mainly for efficient meat production, producing eggs can be a challenge. In Canada, the average producer houses 15,000 birds that begin laying hatching eggs at 26 weeks of age. Each bird will lay about 150 hatching eggs for the next 34 to 36 weeks. This cycle is then repeated when the producer puts another flock of 26 week-old birds into his barns to begin the process again. As a general rule, each farmer produces enough broiler hatching eggs to supply chicks for 8 chicken producers.

Among the world's agricultural industries, chicken breeding in the U.S. is one of the most advanced. Intensive nutritional research and application, highly improved breeding stock, intelligent management, and scientific disease control have gone into the effort to give a modern broiler (meat chicken) of uniformly high quality produced at ever-lower cost. A modern broiler chick can reach a 2.3-kg (5-pound) market weight in five weeks, compared with the four months that were required in the mid-20th century. Additionally, annual egg production per hen has increased from about 100 in 1910 to over 300 in the early 21st century.

The book is intended to be a guide for under graduate and post graduate students of veterinary and animal science, broiler farm managers and entrepreneurs, and farming aspirants.

—Editor

Contents

1

Chicken: An Introduction

The chicken (*Gallus gallus domesticus*) is a domesticated fowl. As one of the most common and widespread domestic animals, and with a population of more than 24 billion in 2003, there are more chickens in the world than any other bird. Humans keep chickens primarily as a source of food, consuming both their meat and their eggs.

Conventional wisdom has held that the chicken was domesticated in India, but recent evidence suggests that domestication of the chicken was already under way in Vietnam over 10,000 years ago. From India the domesticated fowl made its way to the Persianized kingdom of Lydia in western Asia Minor, domestic fowl were imported to Greece by the fifth century BC. Fowl had been known in Egypt since the 18th Dynasty, with the "bird that lays every day" having come to Egypt from the land between Syria and Shinar, Babylonia, according to the annals of Tutmose III.

TERMINOLOGY

In the UK, Ireland and Canada adult male chickens are primarily known as *cocks,* whereas in America and Australia they are better known as *roosters.* Males under a year old are *cockerels.* Castrated roosters are called *capons* (though both surgical and chemical castration are now illegal in some parts of the world). Females over a year old are known as *hens,* and younger females are *pullets.* In Australia and New Zealand (also sometimes in Britain), there is a generic term *chook* to describe all ages and both sexes. Babies are called *chicks,* and the meat is called *chicken.*

"Chicken" was originally the word only for chicks, and the species as a whole was then called *domestic fowl,* or just *fowl.* This use of "chicken" survives in the phrase "Hen and Chickens", sometimes used as a British public house or theatre name, and to name groups of one large and many small rocks or islands in the sea.

General Biology and Habitat

Chickens are omnivores. In the wild, they often scratch at the soil to search for seeds, insects and even larger animals such as lizards or young mice.

Chickens may live for five to eleven years, depending on the breed. In commercial intensive farming, a meat chicken generally lives only six weeks before slaughter. A free range or organic meat chicken will usually be slaughtered at about 14 weeks. Hens of special laying breeds may produce as many as 300 eggs a year. After 12 months, the hen's egg-laying ability starts to decline, and commercial laying hens are then slaughtered and used in baby foods, pet foods, pies and other processed foods. The world's oldest chicken, according to the Guinness Book of World Records, died of heart failure when she was 16 years old.

Roosters can usually be differentiated from hens by their striking plumage, marked by long flowing tails and shiny, pointed feathers on their necks and backs (the *hackles* and *saddle*)—these are often colored differently from the hackles and saddles of females.

However, in some breeds, such as the Sebright, the cock has only slightly pointed neck feathers, the same colour as the hen's. The identification must be made by looking at the comb, or eventually from the development of spurs on the male's legs (in a few breeds and in certain hybrids the male and female chicks may be differentiated by colour). Adult chickens have a fleshy crest on their heads called a *comb or cockscomb,* and hanging flaps of skin either side under their beaks called *wattles.* Both the adult male and female have wattles and combs, but in most breeds these are more prominent in males.

A *muff* or *beard* is a mutation found in several chicken breeds which causes extra feathering under the chicken's face, giving the appearance of a beard.

Domestic chickens are not capable of long distance flight, although lighter birds are generally capable of flying for short distances, such as over fences or into trees (where they would naturally roost). Chickens will sometimes fly to explore their surroundings, but usually do so only to flee perceived danger.

Chickens are gregarious birds and live together as a flock. They have a communal approach to the incubation of eggs and raising of young. Individual chickens in a flock will dominate others, establishing a "pecking order", with dominant individuals having priority for access to food and nesting locations. Removing hens or roosters from a flock causes a temporary disruption to this social order until a new pecking order is established. Adding hens—especially younger birds—to an existing flock, can lead to violence and injury.

Hens will try to lay in nests that already contain eggs, and have been known to move eggs from neighbouring nests into their own. Some farmers use fake eggs made from plastic or stone (or golf balls) to encourage hens to lay in a particular location.

The result of this behaviour is that a flock will use only a few preferred locations, rather than having a different nest for every bird. Hens can also be extremely stubborn about always laying in the same location.

It is not unknown for two (or more) hens to try to share the same nest at the same time. If the nest is small, or one of the hens is particularly determined, this may result in chickens trying to lay on top of each other.

Skull of a chicken three weeks old. Here the opisthotic bone appears in the occipital region, as in the adult Chelonian. bo = Basi-occipital, bt = Basi-temporal, eo = Opisthotic, f = Frontal, fm = Foramen magnum, fo = Fontanella, oc = Occipital condyle, op = Opisthotic, p = Parietal, pf = Post-frontal, sc = Sinus canal in supra-occipital, so = Supra-occpital, sq = Squamosal, 8 = Exit of vagus nerve.

Roosters crowing (a loud and sometimes shrill call) is a territorial signal to other roosters. However, crowing may also result from sudden disturbances within their surroundings. Hens cluck loudly after laying an egg, and also to call their chicks.

In 2006, scientists researching the ancestry of birds "turned on" a chicken recessive gene, *talpid2*, and found that the embryo jaws initiated formation of teeth, like those found in ancient bird fossils. John Fallon, the overseer of the project, stated that chickens have "...retained the ability to make teeth, under certain conditions..."

Courting

When a rooster finds food, he may call the other chickens to eat it first. He does this by clucking in a high pitch as well as picking up and dropping the food. This behaviour can also be observed in mother hens, calling their chicks. In some cases the rooster will drag the wing opposite the hen on the ground, while circling her. This is part of chicken courting ritual and has been called a "dance". The dance triggers a response in the hen's brain, and when the hen responds to his "call", the rooster may mount the hen and proceed with the fertilization.

CHICKEN AS FOOD

Chicken is the most common type of poultry in the world. In developed countries, chickens are usually subject to intensive farming methods.

History

The modern chicken is a descendant of red junglefowl hybrids along with the grey junglefowl first raised thousands of years ago in the northern parts of the Indian subcontinent.

Chicken as a meat has been depicted in Babylonian carvings from around 600 BC. Chicken was one of the most common meats available in the Middle Ages. It was eaten over most of the Eastern hemisphere and a number of different kinds of chicken such as capons, pullets and hens were eaten. It was one of the basic ingredients in the so-called white dish, a stew usually consisting of chicken and fried onions cooked in milk and seasoned with spices and sugar.

In the 1800's chicken was more expensive than other meats and it was "sought by the rich because [it is] so costly as to be an uncommon dish." Chicken consumption in the United States increased during World War II due to a shortage of beef and pork.In Europe, consumption of chicken overtook that of beef and veal in 1996, linked to consumer awareness of Bovine spongiform encephalopathy (mad cow disease).

CLASSIFICATIONS OF CHICKENS

The breeds and varieties of domestic chickens known today are generally believed to have descended mainly from the Red Jungle Fowl (Gallus bankiva, also called Gallus gallus) of Southeast Asia where it still exists in the wild. Domesticated chickens may have been kept in India as long ago as 3,200 B.C., and records indicate they were kept in China and Egypt as early as 1,400 B.C. The earliest domestications of fowl were mainly for cockfighting rather than for food. Cockfighting was suppressed in the Western World and replaced by poultry exhibition before the 18th Century. Poultry exhibitions started in America in 1849. Interest in these shows grew and numerous breeds and varieties were and continue to be developed, leading to the large number of varieties now in existence.

There are approximately 175 varieties of chickens grouped into 12 classes and approximately 60 breeds. A class is a group of breeds originating in the same geographical area. The names themselves — Asiatic, American, Mediterranean, and so on — indicate the region where the breeds originated.

Breed means a group which possesses a given set of physical features, such as body shape, skin color, carriage or station, and number of toes. Variety is a category of breed and is based on feather color, comb, or presence of a beard and muff. Thus, the Plymouth Rock may be Barred, White, Buff, or one of several other colors. The Rhode Island Red may have either a single or rose comb. In each case, the body shape and physical features should be identical. Breed and variety tell little about the qualities of good producing stock.

Strain, however, does. A strain is a group or breeding population within a variety or cross that has been bred and developed by a person or organization to possess certain desirable characteristics. Many commercial strains exist, such as Babcock, DeKalb, Hyline, and Shaver, that have been bred for specific purposes.

Chickens are classified by sex and age, too. Although these terms tend to vary considerably, depending upon whether they are being applied to exhibitions, or commercial poultry production. Cockerel is a male chicken under one year of age; cock or rooster is a male more than one year old; pullet is a female under one year, and hen is a female over one year of age. When chicks are first hatched, they may be separated by sexes and are then called sexed chicks. If they have not been separated, they are known as straight-run chicks.

In market terms, a broiler or fryer is a young meat-type chicken that can be cooked tender by broiling or frying and usually weighing between 2 1/2 and 3 1/2 pounds. A roaster is a young meat-type chicken that can be cooked tender by roasting and usually weighing 4 pounds or more. A stewing chicken, hen, or fowl is a mature female chicken, often the by-product of egg production, with meat less tender than that of a roaster and can be cooked tender by stewing or a similar method.

CHICKENS IN RELIGION AND MYTHOLOGY

In Indonesia the chicken has great significance during the Hindu cremation ceremony. A chicken is considered a channel for evil spirits which may be present during the ceremony. A chicken is tethered by the leg and kept present at the ceremony for its duration to ensure that any evil spirits present during the ceremony go into the chicken and not the family members present. The chicken is then taken home and returns to its normal life.

In ancient Greece, the chicken was not normally used for sacrifices, perhaps because it was still considered an exotic animal. Because of its valour, the cock is found as an attribute of Ares, Heracles, and Athena. The alleged last words of Socrates as he died from hemlock poisoning, as recounted by Plato, were "Crito, I owe a cock to Asclepius; will you remember to pay the debt?", signifying that death was a cure for the illness of life.

The Greeks believed that even lions were afraid of cocks. Several of Aesop's Fables reference this belief.

In the New Testament, Jesus prophesied the betrayal by Peter: "Jesus answered, 'I tell you, Peter, before the rooster crows today, you will deny three times that you know me.'" (Luke 22:34) Thus it happened (Luke 22:61), and Peter cried bitterly. This made the cock a symbol for both vigilance and betrayal.

Earlier, Jesus compares himself to a mother hen when talking about Jerusalem: "O Jerusalem, Jerusalem, you who kill the prophets and stone those sent to you, how often I have longed to gather your children together, as a hen gathers her chicks under her wings, but you were not willing." In many Central European folk tales, the devil is believed to flee at the first crowing of a cock.

In traditional Jewish practice, a kosher animal is swung around the head and then slaughtered on the afternoon before Yom Kippur, the Day of Atonement, in a ritual called kapparos. A chicken or fish is typically used because it is commonly available (and small enough to hold). The sacrifice of the animal is to receive atonement, for the animal symbolically takes on all the person's sins in kapparos. The meat is then donated to the poor. A woman brings a hen for the ceremony, while a man brings a rooster. Although not actually a sacrifice in the biblical sense, the death of the animal reminds the penitent sinner that his or her life is in God's hands.

The Talmud speaks of learning "courtesy toward one's mate" from the rooster. This might refer to the fact that when a rooster finds something good to eat, he calls his hens to eat first.

The chicken is one of the Zodiac symbols of the Chinese calendar. Also in Chinese religion, a cooked chicken as a religious offering is usually limited to ancestor veneration and worship of village deities. Vegetarian deities such as the Buddha are not one of the recipients of such offerings. Under some observations, an offering of chicken is presented with "serious" prayer (while roasted pork is offered during a joyous celebration). In Confucian Chinese

Weddings, a chicken can be used as a substitute for one who is seriously ill or not available (e.g. sudden death) to attend the ceremony. A red silk scarf is placed on the chicken's head and a close relative of the absent bride/groom holds the chicken so the ceremony may proceed. However, this practice is rare today.

A cockatrice was supposed to have been born from an egg laid by a rooster.

Chickens in History

The first pictures of chickens in Europe are found on Corinthian pottery of the 7th century BC. The poet Cratinus (mid-5th century BC, according to the later Greek author Athenaeus) calls the chicken "the Persian alarm". In Aristophanes's comedy *The Birds* (414 BC) a chicken is called "the Median bird", which points to an introduction from the East. Pictures of chickens are found on Greek red figure and black-figure pottery.

In ancient Greece, chickens were still rare and were a rather prestigious food for symposia. Delos seems to have been a centre of chicken breeding.

An early domestication of chickens in Southeast Asia is probable, since the word for domestic chicken (**manuk*) is part of the reconstructed Proto-Austronesian language. Chickens, together with dogs and pigs, were the domestic animals of the Lapita culture, the first Neolithic culture of Oceania.

Chickens were spread by Polynesian seafarers and reached Easter Island in the 12th century AD, where they were the only domestic animal, with the possible exception of the Polynesian Rat (*Rattus exulans*). They were housed in extremely solid chicken coops built from stone.

The Romans used chickens for oracles, both when flying ("ex avibus", Augury) and when feeding ("auspicium ex tripudiis", Alectryomancy). The hen ("gallina") gave a favourable omen ("auspicium ratum"), when appearing from the left (Cic.,de Div. ii.26), like the crow and the owl.

For the oracle "ex tripudiis" according to Cicero (Cic. de Div. ii.34), any bird could be used, but normally only chickens ("pulli") were consulted. The chickens were cared for by the pullarius, who opened their cage and fed them pulses or a special kind of soft cake when an augury was needed. If the chickens stayed in their cage, made noises ("occinerent"), beat their wings or flew away, the omen was bad; if they ate greedily, the omen was good.

In 249 BC, the Roman general Publius Claudius Pulcher had his chickens thrown overboard when they refused to feed before the battle of Drepana, saying "If they won't eat, perhaps they will drink." He promptly lost the battle against the Carthaginians and 93 Roman ships were sunk. Back in Rome, he was tried for impiety and heavily fined.

In 161 BC, a law was passed in Rome that forbade the consumption of fattened chickens. It was renewed a number of times, but does not seem to have been successful. Fattening chickens with bread soaked in milk was thought to give especially delicious results. The Roman gourmet Apicius offers 17 recipes for chicken, mainly boiled chicken with a sauce. All parts of the animal are used: the recipes include the stomach, liver, testicles and even the pygostyle (the fatty "tail" of the chicken where the tail feathers attach).

The Roman author Columella gives advice on chicken breeding in his eighth book of his treatise on agriculture. He identifies Tanagrian, Rhodic, Chalkidic and Median (commonly misidentified as Melian) breeds, which have an impressive appearance, a quarrelsome nature and were used for cockfighting by the Greeks. For farming, native (Roman) chickens are to be preferred, or a cross between native hens and Greek cocks. Dwarf chickens are nice to watch because of their size but have no other advantages.

Per Columella, the ideal flock consists of 200 birds, which can be supervised by one person if someone is watching for stray animals. White chickens should be avoided as they are not very fertile and are easily caught by eagles or goshawks. One cock should be kept for five hens. In the case of Rhodian and Median cocks that are very heavy and therefore not much inclined to sex, only three hens are kept per cock. The hens of heavy fowls are not much inclined to brood; therefore their eggs are best hatched by normal hens. A hen can hatch no more than 15-23 eggs, depending on the time of year, and supervise no more than 30 hatchlings. Eggs that are long and pointed give more male, rounded eggs mainly female hatchlings.

Per Columella, chicken coops should face southeast and lie adjacent to the kitchen, as smoke is beneficial for the animals. Coops should consist of three rooms and possess a hearth. Dry dust or ash should be provided for dust-baths.

According to Columella, chicken should be fed on barley groats, small chick-peas, millet and wheat bran, if they are cheap. Wheat itself should be avoided as it is harmful to the birds. Boiled ryegrass (*Lollium* sp.) and the leaves and seeds of alfalfa (*Medicago sativa* L.) can be used as well. Grape marc can be used, but only when the hens stop laying eggs, that is, about the middle of November; otherwise eggs are small and few. When feeding grape marc, it should be supplemented with some bran. Hens start to lay eggs after the winter solstice, in warm places around the first of January, in colder areas in the middle of February. Parboiled barley increases their fertility; this should be mixed with alfalfa leaves and seeds, or vetches or millet if alfalfa is not at hand. Free-ranging chickens should receive two cups of barley daily.

Columella advises farmers to slaughter hens that are older than three years, because they no longer produce sufficient eggs. Capons were produced by burning out their spurs with a hot iron. The wound was treated with potter's chalk.

CHICKEN FREEZING

Raw chicken maintains its quality longer in the freezer as compared to when having been cooked because moisture is lost during cooking. There is little change in nutrient value of chicken during freezer storage. For optimal quality, however, a maximal storage time in the freezer of 12 months is recommended for uncooked whole chicken, 9 months for uncooked chicken parts, 3 to 4 months for uncooked chicken giblets, and 4 months for cooked chicken. Freezing doesn't usually cause color changes in poultry, but the bones and the meat near them can become dark. This bone darkening results when pigment seeps through the porous bones of young poultry into the surrounding tissues when the poultry meat is frozen and thawed.

It is safe to freeze chicken directly in its original packaging, however this type of wrap is permeable to air and quality may diminish over time. Therefore, for prolonged storage, it is recommended to overwrap these packages. It is recommended to freeze unopened vacuum packages as is. If a package has accidentally been torn or has opened while food is in the freezer, the food is still safe to use, but it is still recommended to overwrap or rewrap it. Chicken should be away from other foods, so if they begin to thaw, their juices won't drip onto other foods. If previously frozen chicken is purchased at a retail store, it can be refrozen if it has been handled properly.

Chicken can be cooked or reheated from the frozen state, but it will take approximately one and a half times as long to cook, and any wrapping or absorbent paper should be discarded. There are three generally accepted safe methods of reheating frozen chicken: in the refrigerator, in cold water, or using a microwave oven. These methods are endorsed by the FDA as safe, as they minimize the risk of bacterial growth. Bacteria survives but does not grow in freezing temperatures. However, if frozen cooked foods are not defrosted properly and are not reheated to temperatures that kill bacteria, chances of getting a foodborne illness greatly increase.

SLEEPING CHICKENS

When chickens sleep, they really sleep. Total darkness makes chickens go into a kind of stupor. They're an easy mark for predators at this point; they don't defend themselves or try to escape.

Because they're vulnerable when they sleep, chickens prefer to *roost* (perch) as high off the ground as they can when sleeping. The more "street-savvy" birds also pick a spot with overhead protection from the weather and owls. Chickens like to roost in the same spot every night, so when they're used to roosting in your chicken coop, they'll try to go back home at nightfall even if they've managed to escape that day or are allowed to roam.

Socializing Behaviours

With chickens, it's all about family. If you don't provide chickens with companions, they will soon make you part of the family. But chickens have very special and firm rules for all family or flock members. Chickens in the wild form small flocks, with 12 to 15 birds being the largest flock. Each wild flock has one rooster.

Ranking begins from the moment chicks hatch or whenever chickens are put together. Hens have their own ranking system, separate from the roosters. Every member of the flock soon knows its place, although some squabbling and downright battles may ensue during the ranking process. Small flocks make chicken life easier. In large flocks of 25 or more chickens and more than one rooster, fighting may periodically resume as both hens and roosters try to maintain the "pecking order."

The dominant hen eats first, gets to pick where she wants to roost or lay eggs, and is allowed to take choice morsels from the lesser-ranked hens. The second-ranked hen bows to none but the first, and so on. In small, well-managed flocks with enough space, the hens are generally calm and orderly as they go about their daily business.

Roosters establish a ranking system, too, if there's more than one in a flock. A group of young roosters without hens will fight, but generally an uneasy truce based on rank will become established. Roosters in the presence of hens fight much more intensely, and the fight may end in death for one of the roosters.

If more than one rooster survives in a mixed-sex flock, he becomes a hanger-on — always staying at the edge of the flock and keeping a low profile. If you have a lot of hens and a lot of space, such as in a free-range situation, each rooster may establish his own separate flock and pretty much ignore the other rooster except for occasional spats. How aggressive a rooster is depends on both the breed and the individuals within a breed. When a rooster becomes aggressive toward humans, the best option is the soup pot.

A rooster always dominates the hens in his care. Sorry, no women's lib in the chicken world. He gets what he wants when he wants it. And what he doesn't want is a lot of squabbling among his flock. When he's eating, all the hens can eat with him, and no one is allowed to pull rank. If squabbling among hens gets intense at other times, he may step in and resolve the problem.

A rooster can be much smaller and younger than the hens in the flock, but as long as he's mature, he's the ruler of the coop. But it's not all about terrorizing the ladies. The rooster is also their protector and guide, as well as their lover. He stands guard over them as they feed, shows them choice things to eat (usually letting them have the first bites), and even guides them to good nesting spots.

Roosters tend to have a favorite hen — usually, but not always, the dominant hen in the flock — but they treat all their ladies pretty well. They may mate more frequently with the favorite, but all hens get some attention.

Romance Between Roosters And Hens

Roosters have a rather limited courtship ritual, compared to some birds, and the amount of "romancing" varies among individuals, too. When a rooster wants to mate with a hen, he usually approaches her in a kind of tiptoelike walk and may strut around her a few times. Usually a hen approached this way crouches down and moves her tail to one side as a sign of submission.

The rooster jumps on the hen's back, holds on to the back of her neck with his beak, and rapidly thrusts his cloaca against hers a few times. He then dismounts, fluffs his feathers, and walks away. Boastful crowing may also take place soon after mating, although crowing is not reserved just for mating. The hen stands up, fluffs her feathers, and walks away as well. Both may preen their feathers for a few minutes after mating.

A young rooster may mate several hens within a few minutes of each other, but usually mating is spread out throughout the day. A rooster may mate a hen even if he's infertile: Fertility drops as roosters age, and cold weather also causes a drop in fertility.

The Celibate Hen — Living Without A Rooster

Hens don't need a rooster to complete their lives — or even to lay eggs, for that matter. A hen is hatched with all the eggs she's ever going to have, and she'll lay those eggs for as long as the hen lives (or until she's out of eggs), whether a rooster is around or not. The number of eggs a hen lays over her lifetime varies by breed and the individual. After the third year of life, though, a hen lays very few eggs.

Of course, without a rooster, no babies will be hatched from those eggs, but the eggs that you eat for breakfast don't need to be fertilized to be laid. Hormones control the egg cycle whether a rooster is present or not. And fertilized eggs don't taste differently — nor are they more nutritious — than unfertilized eggs. Is a hen happier with a rooster around? She probably is because it fits the more natural family lifestyle of chickens. But hens are pretty self-sufficient, and if they've never known life with a rooster, they really don't know what they're missing.

Bath Time For Chickens

Another interesting behaviour of chickens is their bathing habits. They hate getting wet, but they sure do love a dust bath. Wherever the coop has loose soil — or even loose litter — on the floor, you will find chickens bathing.

Chickens scratch out a body-sized depression in the soil and lie in it, throwing the soil from the hole into their fluffed-out feathers and then shaking to remove it. They seem very happy when doing this, so it must feel good. In nature, this habit helps to control parasites.

In the garden or lawn, these dust-bath bowls can be quite damaging, but you can't do much about it except put up a fence. If your chickens are confined all the time, they'll really appreciate a box of sand to bathe in.

LAYING STRAINS OF CHICKENS

Furnished cages are available to house large, medium, and small group sizes. The European Commission offers standards for furnished cages that include perching space for all hens and a nest and dust bath area, with minimum available space per hen of 750 cm^2 per bird.

Appleby suggests that group sizes of 8 hens or more in furnished cages should have 800 cm^2/hen and that smaller groups of 3 or less should have 900 cm^2/hen, plus an area with litter. In these systems, claw-shortening devices are helpful to maintain short claws, and perches can help to increase leg strength. Problems observed in this type of housing include increased keel bone deformities associated with high perch use and should be monitored.

Aviaries or Multi-tier Systems for Egg-laying Strains of Chickens

Aviaries, designed to use vertical space, consist of a ground floor plus one or more tiers consisting of perforated or slatted floors or platforms with manure belts underneath. Providing a littered area allows for dust bathing and reduces the incidence of cannibalism and feather pecking. The scratch area also allows the hens to keep their claws trimmed. The litter should cover enough area to allow for proper mixing of manure and avoid excessive manure and moisture accumulation.

The depth of the litter should be sufficient to prevent hens from coming in contact with the floor. Likewise, the depth of the litter should not be so deep that it encourages the laying of eggs on the floor. Opening and closing the littered areas for specified periods can be used as a management tool to prevent the laying of floor eggs. The European Commission recommends that the littered areas cover at least 30% of the useable floor area of the house.

The recommended floor space per hen for aviaries excludes nest space. Only the floor area and the tiers can be counted as usable space when calculating stocking density for hens in aviaries. Hens housed in aviaries have a high incidence of bone fractures during the laying cycle because of crash landings or failing to jump gaps effectively. Each tier should allow hens to safely access other vertical tiers, including the littered floor. For example, a ramp can be used to allow birds to move from the littered floor area to the first raised tier.

If ramps are used, they should be designed to prevent droppings from falling on the birds below. Hens should have access to the entire littered floor area, including the area under the raised tiers. Raised tiers need a system for frequent removal of manure. To reduce the incidence of hen injury, including broken bones, the highest tier should not exceed 2 m.

Vertical distance between tiers, which also includes the floor to the first tier, is recommended to be between 0.5 and 1.0 m. Measurements may be taken from the top of the littered floor or slat area to the underside of the manure belt. When adjacent tiers are staggered to allow for diagonal access to tiers of different heights, the hen's angle of descent should not exceed 45°.

The horizontal distance between tiers should not be more than 0.8 m. Where design discourages horizontal movement between different tiers, there should be a minimum distance between tiers of 2 m. For flock sizes that exceed 3,000 hens in a room, no more than 2 raised tiers above the floor are recommended. Smaller flock sizes of 3,000 or less can have up to 3 raised tiers in a room.

Birds that are to be housed in aviaries as adults should be reared as pullets in similar aviaries to facilitate adaptation to perches and nests. Typically, day-old chicks are housed in a central tier the first 10 d of age and then about half of the pullets can be distributed to the lower tier to provide more space as they age.

In this manner, the pullets quickly find the feed and water and are provided proper brooding temperatures during the early stages of growth. By 15 to 21 d of age, pullets are given full access to the aviary. Ramps are provided to allow pullets easy access to all levels of the aviary. Perch space per pullet is recommended to be 8 cm/pullet during the first 10 wk of age and 11 cm/pullet after 10 wk of age. Welfare standards for pullet aviaries are still in the investigational stage.

Outdoor Access or Free Range

Poultry may also be raised with access to the outdoors. Poultry raised under an organic protocol require outdoor access, which can be a range or a semi-enclosed yard often referred to as a veranda or winter garden. During inclement weather or for health-related reasons, birds should remain indoors or in shelters until such conditions are improved. A range is an outside fenced area. Fence height and fencing material should be of appropriate mesh size to retain domesticated poultry and prevent predator entry.

A permanent fence can be extended underground to a minimum depth of 0.25 m to prevent ground predator entry. The fence can be surrounded by an electric wire 25 to 45 cm above the ground and 0.6 to 1.0 m away from the primary fence. Overhead fine netting, as used for game birds, can be used to protect domestic poultry from wild avian predators and minimize disease transmission from wild species to domesticated poultry.

Ranges should be free of debris such as large rocks and fallen trees, environmental contaminants, and be designed to prevent muddy areas, to avoid injuries and foot problems, and to promote overall bird health. Vegetation should be used for ranges or sections of the range where soil erosion is problematic. Range rotation is one tool for minimizing the threat of a disease outbreak and to provide opportunity for land to recover from bird activity.

A covered veranda provides shade and is connected to the house and is made available to the hens during the daylight hours. The floor of the veranda can be solid and may be covered with litter. To minimize the probability of cannibalism, natural light or high-intensity artificial light can be used during early stages of rearing to facilitate the transition of birds from indoor to outdoor lighting conditions. Free-ranged birds without access to a permanent building should have covered shelters that provide shade, protection from inclement weather, litter, food, and water.

The sheltered area should provide space to allow all ranged birds to rest together without risk of heat stress. Mobile shelters should be moved on a regular basis or managed to minimize the probability of a disease outbreak or muddy conditions. Elevated perches designed for poultry can be provided on the range or inside the indoor shelter. All range, veranda, or any other type of outdoor access should be managed so that birds are protected from potential predators.

Weather permitting, birds should be given access to the outside as soon as they have full feather coverage to encourage ranging behaviour. Vegetation such as small bushes, crops such as corn, or cover panels that provide a sense of protection in the outdoor area can be used to encourage the use of the range. When indoor birds are allowed free access to the outdoors, they should have appropriately sized openings of sufficient number to facilitate bird exit from and entrance into the building; alternatively, the doors of the house can be opened to allow birds freedom of movement.

The size of each pophole should allow for easy passage of a bird to and from the outside. The number of popholes provided should allow birds to comfortably access the outside or inside without significant congregation of birds on either side of the pophole. A roof can be placed over a pophole to provide protection and baffles installed to reduce entry of wind into the house.

Slats can also be used to prevent the formation of muddy areas around the popholes. For whole house configuration without individual pens, popholes should be evenly distributed down the entire length of the building to prevent birds from blocking the access in and out of the building. On windy days, it may be wise to open popholes only on the leeward side, so providing more than the minimum number of popholes is advisable.

Egg-laying Strains of Chickens

The approximate age that egg-laying strains of chickens are allowed access to the range is about 12 wk of age. Before 12 wk of age, they are brooded in confinement. To allow for range rotation, provide each hen with 4 m^2 of outdoor access. Shade should be evenly distributed in the outdoor area and provided at a minimum of 8 m^2 per 1,000 hens.

Meat-type Chickens

Fast-growing strains of broilers should have access to a minimum of 1 m^2 of outdoor access, whereas slower growing strains require 2 m^2 of outdoor access.

Turkeys

The age that turkeys are given access to outdoors may vary from 5 to 12 wk depending on weather conditions and predator risk, with 8 wk being the most common age. A flock can gradually be transitioned to range by moving one-third of the flock the first morning and then moving the remainder of the flock a day or two later. The following formula can be used to calculate the minimum amount of shelter recommended: area, m^2 = [W]/D, where n is the number of birds in the flock, W is the expected average weight at depopulation, and D is the maximum stocking density in kg/m^2. Growing turkeys are allowed a minimum space allocation of 6 m^2/bird of free range.

Ducks

Information for porches or winter gardens for ducks is not available. When growing ducks are first introduced to the range, they need to be shown the location of the feeders, drinkers, and shelters. The outdoor feeders and drinkers should be surrounded by slatted or solid flooring to prevent the ground in the immediate area from becoming muddy. Free-ranged growing ducks are allowed a minimum of 2.5 m^2/bird when reared on well-maintained ranges with ground cover.

If the vegetation is poor, then a minimum of 4 m^2/growing duck should be provided. If ponds are available, they should be well maintained so as to avoid stagnant water containing decaying vegetation. Botulism in ducks can be a problem when pond water is not well aerated or not filtered to remove plant debris. Developing breeders may be raised outdoors on well-drained soil with open shelter. A minimum of 1,290 cm^2 of shelter area/bird is recommended for developing breeders.

2

Poultry Farming

Poultry farming is the practice of raising poultry, such as chickens, turkeys, ducks, and geese, as a subcategory of animal husbandry, for the purpose of farming meat or eggs for food. More than 50 billion chickens are reared annually as a source of food, for both their meat and their eggs. Chickens farmed for meat are called broilers, whilst those farmed for eggs are called egg-laying hens. In total, the UK alone consumes over 29 million eggs per day. Some hens can produce over 300 eggs a year. Chickens will naturally live for 6 or more years. After 12 months, the hen's productivity will start to decline. This is when most commercial laying hens are slaughtered. The vast majority of poultry are raised using intensive farming techniques. According to the Worldwatch Institute, 74 percent of the world's poultry meat, and 68 percent of eggs are produced this way. One alternative to intensive poultry farming is free range farming.

Friction between these two main methods has led to long term issues of ethical consumerism. Opponents of intensive farming argue that it harms the environment and creates health risks, as well as abusing the animals themselves. Advocates of intensive farming say that their highly efficient systems save land and food resources due to increased productivity, stating that the animals are looked after in state-of-the-art environmentally controlled facilities. A few countries have banned cage system housing, including Sweden and Switzerland. Consumers can still purchase lower cost eggs from other countries' intensive poultry farms.

FARMING

More than 50 billion chickens are reared annually as a source of food, for both their meat and their eggs. The vast majority of poultry are raised in factory farms. According to the Worldwatch Institute, 74 percent of the world's poultry meat and 68 percent of eggs are produced this way. One alternative to intensive poultry farming is free range farming.

Friction between these two main methods has led to long-term issues of ethical consumerism. Opponents of intensive farming argue that it harms the environment, creates human health risks and is inhumane. Advocates of intensive farming say that their highly efficient systems save land and food resources owing to increased productivity, and that the animals are looked after in state-of-the-art environmentally controlled facilities.

In part due to the conditions on intensive poultry farms and recent recalls of large quantities of eggs, there is a growing movement for small-scale micro-flocks or 'backyard chickens'. This involves keeping small numbers of hens (usually no more than a dozen) in suburban or urban residential areas to control bugs, to utilize chicken waste as fertilizer in small gardens, and of course for the high-quality eggs and meat that are produced.

Reared for meat

Chickens farmed for meat are called broiler chickens. Chickens will naturally live for six or more years, but broiler chickens typically take less than six weeks to reach slaughter size. A free range or organic meat chicken will usually be slaughtered at about 14 weeks of age.

Reared for eggs

Chickens farmed for eggs are called egg-laying hens. In total, the UK alone consumes over 29 million eggs per day. Some hens breedscan produce over 300 eggs per year, with "the highest authenticated rate of egg laying being 371 eggs in 364 days".

After 12 months of laying, the commercial hen's egg-laying ability starts to decline to the point where the flock is unviable. Hens, particularly from battery cage systems, are sometimes infirm or have lost a significant amount of their feathers, and their life expectancy has been reduced from around seven years to less than two years. In the UK and Europe, laying hens are then slaughtered and used in processed foods or sold as "soup hens". In some other countries, flocks are sometimes force moulted, rather than being slaughtered, to reinvigorate egg-laying. This involves complete withdrawal of food (and sometimes water) for 7–14 days or sufficiently long to cause a body weight loss of 25 to 35%, or up to 28 days under experimental conditions. This stimulates the hen to lose her feathers, but also reinvigorates egg-production. Some flocks may be force moulted several times. In 2003, more than 75% of all flocks were moulted in the US.

Artificial incubation

Incubation can successfully occur artificially in machines that provide the correct, controlled environment for the developing chick.The average incubation period for chickens is 21 days but may depend on the temperature and humidity in the incubator. Temperature regulation is the most critical factor for a successful hatch.

Variations of more than 1 °C (1.8 °F) from the optimum temperature of 37.5 °C (99.5 °F) will reduce hatch rates. Humidity is also important because the rate at which eggs lose water by evaporation depends on the ambient relative humidity. Evaporation can be assessed by candling, to view the size of the air sac, or by measuring weight loss. Relative humidity should be increased to around 70% in the last three days of incubation to keep the membrane around the hatching chick from drying out after the chick cracks the shell. Lower humidity is usual in the first 18 days to ensure adequate evaporation. The position of the eggs in the incubator can also influence hatch rates. For best results, eggs should be placed with the pointed ends down and turned regularly (at least three times per day) until one to three days before hatching. If the eggs aren't turned, the embryo inside may stick to the shell and may hatch with physical defects. Adequate ventilation is necessary to provide the embryo with oxygen. Older eggs require increased ventilation.

Many commercial incubators are industrial-sized with shelves holding tens of thousands of eggs at a time, with rotation of the eggs a fully automated process. Home incubators are boxes holding from 6 to 75 eggs; they are usually electrically powered, but in the past some were heated with an oil or paraffin lamp.

CHICKENS

For hundreds of years, chickens were kept in small flocks for home consumption of eggs and meat, with any surplus sold or exchanged for other produce. Not until the 20th century did poultry farming become commercialized. The production of eggs came first; for years the production of broilers was merely an offshoot, the male chickens being raised until 10 to 16 weeks old and then sold for meat.

Today most of the laying hens are housed in wire cages containing from two to ten hens each. The cages may be in a single tier or in tiers of up to five cages. Most of these are automated to provide a constant supply of feed and water and to maintain control of the environment. By comparison with litter floors, where the birds were constantly in contact with one another and with feces, the wire cages increase production efficiency, reduce the incidence of disease, and help keep costs down. A modern poultry farm may have several hundred thousand or even more than a million laying hens.

The Indian. poultry industry comprises somewhat fewer than 300 million such hens, but with modern production techniques they are supplying the nation with more eggs than did a larger hen population some years ago. A dozen eggs can be produced with less than 1.8 kg (less than 4 lb) of feed. Whereas egg-producing hens once produced about 100 eggs each year, such hens can now produce an average of more than 250 eggs each year.

In the mid-1990s the worldwide population of chickens was estimated at 12.7 billion. The annual production of hen eggs exceeded 41.5 million metric tons; China produced about 30 percent of the total. The U.S. is also a leader of the worldwide poultry industry, supplying more than 10 percent of the total egg output. Within the U.S., California produced nearly 9 percent of the nation's 74.3 billion eggs, followed by Ohio, Pennsylvania, Indiana, Georgia, and Iowa.

The modern broiler industry started on a commercial scale on the Delmarva (Delaware-Maryland-Virginia) Peninsula and then spread farther south and southwest. By the mid-1990s the industry was producing more than 7 billion broilers a year, most of them in the southern U.S., with an efficiency such that one unit weight of broiler was being produced with fewer than two unit weights of feed. Nearly all broilers are now the offspring of white Plymouth Rock females and dominant white Cornish males. The leading broiler-producing states are Arkansas, Georgia, Alabama, and North Carolina.

ADVANTAGES AND DISADVANTAGES

Free Range

Advantages

Free range poultry farming has the advantage of enabling the poultry to move around, foraging for their natural diet and living in cleaner conditions than in battery farming. In some farms, the manure from free range poultry can be used to benefit crops.

Disadvantages

The practical construction of a free range poultry farm can present more problems than the battery alternative. Finding suitable land with adequate drainage to minimise worms and coocidial oocysts, suitable protection from prevailing winds, good ventilation, access and protection from predators can be difficult. Excess heat, cold or damp can have a harmful effect on the animals and their productivity. Unlike battery farms, free range farmers have little control over the food their animals come across which can lead to unreliable productivity.

Free range farming in the UK, which accounts for 26 per cent of production, has come under similar criticism as battery farming in terms of animal welfare. This is due to the social abnormalities of having large numbers of birds in an outdoor space. Beak trimming due to cannibalism and infighting is common in this form of poultry farming as well as in batteries. Diseases are common and the animals are vulnerable to predators. In South-East Asia, a lack of disease control in free range farming has been associated with outbreaks of avian influenza.

Factory Farming

Advantages

The small cages restrict movement, and allow for more birds per unit area, and this allows for greater productivity and lower space and food costs, with more efforts put into egg laying. Battery farming is quicker, more economical and practical, and growth and output can be specifically controlled. The poultry are at less risk from predators and outdoor elements such as cold, heat, wind or damp, all of which can have significant impact on yield and health of the animals.

Disadvantages

The small environments reduce stimulation of the poultry, which often results in pecking each other or themselves whereas in the outdoors they would have other stimulation. A study by the Agricultural and Food Research Council in 1992 also found that 50 per cent of battery farmed poultry had bone disorders such as osteoporosisor breakages. Battery farms are also at greater risk of fire, due to the amount of electrical equipment and the likelihood of rodents chewing through the wiring. Battery farming is also the subject of much criticism and the products are often less popular than free-range alternatives, and the mislabling of one as the other has led to outrage in some consumer groups.

The use of gas to kill the birdsprior to harvesting was also criticized by Dr. Mohan Raj of United Poultry Concern who stated that current use of carbon dioxide fails to cleanly kill the birds, causing a "a painfully slow death of suffocation" VEGA states that "millions" of male chicks are killed in this way as they do not produce eggs. Debeaking is also heavily criticised due to the psychological effects and pain involved. The act of forced staravtion to reduce periods of off-lay is also unpopular.

Health concerns are not limited to the animals in battery farming, however. The US Department of Health released a list of risks to humans working in poultry battery farms and those living nearby, which included respiratory illnesses and musculoskeletal injuries, infections, odors and flies and chemical and infectious compounds in the soil which included the mixtures of antibodies, pathogens, nutrients, pesticides, hormones and other chemicals that are found in or are administered to battery poultry. Trace elements of copper or arsenic were also found.

Outbreaks of Avian influenza have also been blamed on battery farming in South-East Asia. Battery farming is prohibited in a number of countries, including Switzerland and Sweden, with movements in favour of banning active in the United Kingdom, Australia and Denmark.

ECONOMICS OF COMMERCIAL BROILER FARMING

There was wide a gap in demand and supply of poultry products especially during the tourist season.

The local production of broiler was insufficient to fulfil the demand. Therefore, the poultry products were being supplied from plains of Uttarakhand and NCR Delhi.

The high transportation cost and profit margin inflate the prices of eggs and meat. Keeping in view the high demand and escalating prices of poultry, farmers have initiated commercial production of broilers in the hill villages adjacent to towns/cities. They have started rearing broilers *"Vencobb white"* with farm production capacity of 500-4000 birds per batch..

The average mortality of day-old chicks during brooding was 7.75 per cent. The feed cost had a lion's share of nearly 72.2 per cent, followed by of DOCs cost (21.5 %). The gross return, total cost and net returns were ' 110, ' 99 and ' 11/broiler, respectively. The study has concluded that the commercial production of broilers has very thin margin as is evident from the B-C ratio. The farmers were unable to reap economic returns from broilers production because of wide fluctuations in prices of poultry feed and DOCs. The respondent-farmers suggested that the government should provide subsidy on poultry feed, ensure regular supply of good quality DOCs and develop infrastructural facilities to boost poultry entrepreneurship and broiler production in this region.

Constraints in Adoption of Integrated Poultry-Fish Farming System in Kumaon hills

The constraints being faced by the respondents, presented in Table 4, reveal that the high cost of DOCs and poultry feed was the main constraint in promotion of integrated poultry-fish farming in the hill region (RBQ value 70.13), followed by the poor quality DOCs which causes high mortality during early brooding under hill villages (RBQ value 69.48).

The management of small poultry feed-making units by SHG women-members shows concerns for inferior feed ingredients and non-availability of mineral mixture. The distance of veterinary hospital from villages and high consultation fee, unwillingness of para-vet staff to vaccination and delivery of poultry medicines at farmers door step were ranked 4th and 5th, respectively. Lack government subsidy and paucity of funds for construction of suitable poultry houses was another constraint in adoption of integrated poultry-fish farming system in the Kumaon region. Keeping in view, the weak financial status of farmers, there is the need for special government subsidy for sustainable development of integrated poultry-fish farming in the Kumaon hills. The study has concluded that government may address the issues of income and employment generation, malnutrition, poverty, hunger and women empowerment for livelihood security of rural poor in the Kumaon hills of Uttarakhand.

POULTRY DEVELOPMENT IN INDIA

The stage of poultry farming in different states/ UTs was examined by constructing developmental indices on parameters such as layer parent stock, number of improved birds relative to the total poultry population, number of hatcheries (both in private and public sector), and performance (i.e., number of eggs produced/year).This technique was used to build indices for major poultry producing states/UTs in the country.

The Poultry Development Index was constructed for the major poultry producing states of Indian Union.The states were classified in ascending order of WPDI. This implies that the state with the lowest WPDI was the first mentioned and so on. Assam & N.E. States were found in first place in the order, i.e., poultry farming is the least developed in these states, followed by Bihar, Orissa, and Himachal Pradesh, etc. Andhra Pradesh presented the most developed poultry production in India. In order to classify all states into two WPDI groups, the 0.52 level was arbitrarily chosen as the cut-off of different states classifying all states in two groups on the basis of low/high poultry farming development.

Growth in production

Poultry products had shown a massive growth in the country after 1961. Egg production in that year was 2,881 million, which increased to about 30,000 millions in the year 1996. Broiler production starting from zero increased 400 million birds in the year 1996. Similarly, poultry meat, which was about 81 thousand tones in the year 1961, increased to 659 thousand tones in that same period. The increased production increased the availability of poultry products for consumption.

Growth in Egg Production

Growth in egg production in the major producing states of different regions of the country was examined during the period of 1980-98. The period was further divided in to two periods, i.e., 1980-89 and 1990-98. Compound growth and simple growth rates were calculated for the three periods and four regions.

- Northern Region- There was a significant growth in egg production in all the egg-producing states of the region. Punjab presented a maximum growth rate of 3.12%/year during first period and 3.03%/year in the intermediate period, followed by Himachal Pradesh (3.03, 2.94) Haryana (2.98, 2.96) and U.P. (2.80, 2.86). The period of 2002-03 had the lowest growth rate in egg production in the region.
- Western Region – The major egg producing states in the region showed the most significant growth in egg production during first period, except for Rajasthan, where the second period had shown a much faster growth, wtih 2.99%/year. The overall growth in the states of Gujarat, Madhya Pradesh, Maharashtra and Goa remained at 2.90, 2.89, 2.83 and 2.82%/year, respectively.
- Southern Region: In this region, a maximum and highly significant growth rate of 3.14%/year was observed in Tamil Nadu during the first period, 2.79%/year in the second period and 2.96%/year in both periods, followed by Andhra Pradesh, with 2.97, 2.92 and 2.91%/year, respectively., Karnataka grew 2.88, 2.83 and 2.84%/year and Kerala had 2.86, 2.82, 2.83%/year, respectively, in the first, second and entire period of study.
- Eastern Region: In the Eastern Region, Sikkim presented maximum growth egg production rates of 3.20, 2.85 and 3.04%/year, in first, second and entire period, followed by West Bengal with 3.15, 2.78, 2.92% year, Nagaland with 2.99, 2.79 and 2.95%/year, Meghalaya with 2.99, 2.80 and 2.86%/year, Manipur with 2.87, 2.68 and 2.85%/year, Bihar with 2.93, 2.12 and 2.82%/year, and Assam with 2.87, 2.77 and

2.81%/year. At national level, egg production growth rate was higher in first period, with 2.96%/year. In the second period, it was 2.84%/year and in entire period the growth was 2.90%/year.

Growth in Productivity

Productivity of Desi (Local) and improved birds in different regions was examined for the period of 1987-88 to 1994-95. The mean productivity level of Desi (Local) birds was maximum, i.e., 156 eggs/year, in Himachal Pradesh, in Northern region, and minimum, with 62 eggs/year, in Manipur, in Eastern Region. In case of improved birds, the maximum productivity of 278 eggs/ year was reported in Andhra Pradesh, in the Southern region, and minimum of 109 eggs/year, in Manipur State, in the Eastern Region.

TECHNIQUES

Organic System

In organic systems, chickens are also free-range. Organic chickens are slower growing, more traditional breeds and live typically for around 81 days. They grow at half the rate of intensive chickens. They have a larger space allowance outside (at least 2 square metres and sometimes up to 10 square metres per bird).

Indoor with Higher Welfare

Chickens are kept indoors but with more space (around 12 to 14 birds per square metre). They have a richer environment for example with natural light or straw bales that encourage foraging and perching. The chickens grow more slowly and live for up to two weeks longer than intensively farmed birds. The benefits of higher welfare indoor systems are the reduced growth rate, less crowding and more opportunities for natural behaviour.

Free-range

Free range poultry farming consists of poultry permitted to roam freely instead of being contained in any manner. In the UK, the Department for Environment, Food and Rural Affairs says that a free range chicken must have daytime access to open-air runs during at least half of their life. Unlike in the United States, this definition also applies to eggs.

The European Union regulates marketing standards for egg farming which specifies a minimum condition for Free Range Eggs states that "hens have continuous daytime access to open-air runs, except in the case of temporary restrictions imposed by veterinary authorities".

In free-range broiler systems, the chickens are given continuous access to an outdoor range during the daytime and sheds where they are housed at night. Free-range chickens grow more slowly than intensive chickens. They live at least 56 days. In the EU each chicken must have one square metre of outdoor space.

Free range poultry production requires that the poultry have access to the outside. In some cases this means the poultry are raised on pasture, enabling the poultry to move around, forage for their natural diet and live in cleaner conditions than those in batteries. In some farms, the manure from free range poultry can be used to benefit crops.

The benefits are also a reduced growth rate and opportunities for natural behaviour such as pecking, scratching, foraging and exercise outdoors, as well as fresh air and daylight. Because they grow slower and have opportunities for exercise free-range chickens have better leg and heart health and a much higher quality of life.

Finding suitable land with adequate drainage to minimise worms and coccidial oocysts, suitable protection from prevailing winds, good ventilation, access and protection from predators can be difficult. Excess heat, cold or damp can have a harmful effect on the animals and their productivity. Unlike battery farms, free range farmers have little control over the food their animals come across which can lead to unreliable productivity.

Some free range farming in the UK, which accounts for 26% of production, has also come under criticism concerning animal welfare.

This is due to some large scale free range farms where social abnormalities arise due to having large numbers of birds in an outdoor space. Beak trimming due to cannibalism and infighting is common in this form of poultry farming as well as in batteries.

Diseases are common and the animals are vulnerable to predators. In South-East Asia, a lack of disease control in free range farming has been associated with outbreaks of Avian influenza.

Yarding

While often confused with free-range farming, yarding is actually a separate method of poultry culture by which chickens and cows are raised together. The distinction is that free-range poultry are either totally unfenced, or the fence is so distant that it has little influence on their freedom of movement. Yarding is common technique used by small farms in the Northeastern US.

Daily releases out of hutches or coops allows for instinctual nature for the chickens with protections from predators. The hens usually lay eggs either on the ground of the coop or in baskets if provided by the farmer. This technique can be complicated if used with roosters though, mostly because of difficulty getting them into the coop and to clean the coop while it is inside. This territorial nature is apparent while outside in which they have a brood of hens and sometimes even informal land claims. This can endanger people unaware of the existence of the territories who are attacked by the larger birds.

Intensive Chicken Farming

In egg-producing farms, birds are typically housed in rows of battery cages. Environmental conditions are automatically controlled, including light duration, which mimics summer daylength. This stimulates the birds to continue to lay eggs all year round. Normally, significant egg production only occurs in the warmer months. Critics argue that year-round egg production stresses the birds more than normal seasonal production.

Meat chickens, commonly called broilers, are floor-raised on litter such as wood shavings or rice hulls, indoors in climate-controlled housing. Poultry producers routinely use nationally-approved medications, such as antibiotics, in feed or drinking water, to treat disease or to prevent disease outbreaks arising from overcrowded or unsanitary conditions. In the U.S., the national organization overseeing chicken production is the Food and Drug Administration (F.D.A.). Some F.D.A.-approved medications are also approved for improved feed utilization. In the U.S., federal law prohibits the use of hormones or steroids in poultry production.

In egg-producing farms, cages allow for more birds per unit area, and this allows for greater productivity and lower space and food costs, with more efforts put into egg-laying. In the U.S., for example, the current recommendation by the United Egg Producers is 67 to 86 in^2 (430 to 560 cm^2) per bird, which is about 9 inches by 9 inches. Modern poultry farming is very efficient and allows meat and eggs to be available to the consumer in all seasons at a lower cost than free range production, and the poultry have no exposure to predators. The cage environment of egg producing does not permit birds to roam. The closeness of chickens to one another frequently causes cannibalism. Cannibalism is controlled by de-beaking (removing a portion of the bird's beak with a hot blade so the bird cannot effectively peck). Another condition that can occur in prolific egg laying breeds is osteoporosis. This is caused from year-round rather than seasonal egg production, and results in chickens whose legs cannot support them and so can no longer walk. During egg production, large amounts of calcium are transferred from bones to create eggshell. Although dietary calcium levels are adequate, absorption of dietary calcium is not always sufficient, given the intensity of production, to fully replenish bone calcium.

Under intensive farming methods, a meat chicken will live less than six weeks before slaughter. This is half the time it would take traditionally. This compares with free-range chickens which will usually be slaughtered at 8 weeks, and organic ones at around 12 weeks.

In intensive broiler sheds, the air can become highly polluted with ammonia from the droppings. This can damage the chickens' eyes and respiratory systems and can cause painful burns on their legs (called hock burns) and feet. Chickens bred for fast growth have a high rate of leg deformities because they cannot support their increased body weight. Because they cannot move easily, the chickens are not able to adjust their environment to avoid heat, cold or dirt as they would in natural conditions. The added weight and overcrowding also puts a strain on their hearts and lungs. In the U.K., up to 19 million chickens die in their sheds from heart failure each year.

Issues with Poultry Farming

Humane Treatment

Animal welfare groups have frequently criticized the poultry industry for engaging in practices which they believe to be inhumane. Many animal rights advocates object to killing chickens for food, the "factory farm conditions" under which they are raised, methods of transport, and slaughter. Compassion Over Killing and other groups have repeatedly conducted undercover investigations at chicken farms and slaughterhouses which they allege confirm their claims of cruelty.

Conditions in intensive chicken farms may be unsanitary, allowing the proliferation of diseases such as salmonella and E coli. Chickens may be raised in total darkness; hens are most often kept in crowded wire battery cages with space less than that of a sheet of paper per hen, as opposed to cage-free or free range. Rough handling and crowded transport during various weather conditions and the failure of existing stunning systems to render the birds unconscious before slaughter have also been cited as welfare concerns.

Another animal welfare concern is the use of selective breeding to create heavy, large-breasted birds, which can lead to crippling leg disorders and heart failure for some of the birds. Concerns have been raised that companies growing single varieties of birds for eggs or meat are increasing their susceptibility to disease.

A common practice among hatcheries is the mass-slaughter of newly-born male chicks of egg laying breeds, since they don't lay eggs, and do not grow fast enough to be profitable for meat. Once separated from the females, the male chicks are dropped into grinding machines.

Debeaking

Laying hens are routinely de-beaked when young to prevent fighting. Because beaks are sensitive, the usual practice of trimming them without anaesthesia is considered inhumane by some. De-beaked chickens will peck much less than chickens with beaks, which animal behaviourist Temple Grandin attributes to guarding against pain. The United Egg Producers says that de-beaking is not painful. It is also argued that the procedure causes life-long chronic pain and discomfort and decreased ability to eat or drink. De-beaking is described as being as painful as for a human's fingertips, rather than nails, being cut off.

Intelligence

Some groups which advocate for more humane treatment of chickens claim that they are intelligent. Dr. Chris Evans of Macquarie University claims that their range of 20 calls, problem solving skills, use of representational signalling, and the ability to recognize each other by facial features demonstrate the intelligence of chickens.

POULTRY BROILER FARMING

Poultry meat is an important source of high quality proteins, minerals and vitamins to balance the human diet. Specially developed breeds of chicken meat (broiler) are now available with the ability of quick growth and high feed conversion efficiency. Depending on the farm size, broiler farming can be a main source of family income or can provide subsidiary income and gainful employment to farmers throughout the year. Poultry manure has high fertilizer value and can be used for increasing yield of all crops.

i) The advantages of broiler farming are
ii) Initial investment is a little lower than layer farming
iii) Rearing period is 6-7 weeks only
iv) More number of flocks can be taken in the same shed

v) Broilers have high feed conversion efficiency i.e. least amount of feed is required for unit body weight gain in comparison to other livestock.
vi) Faster return from the investment
vii) Demand for poultry meat is more compared to sheep/Goat meat.

Scope for Broiler Farming and its National Importance

India has made considerable progress in broiler production in the last two decades. High quality chicks, equipments, vaccines and medicines are available. Technically and professionally competent guidance is available to the farmers. The management practices have improved and disease and mortality incidences are much reduced. Many institutions are providing training to entrepreneurs. The broiler population has increased from 4 million in 1971 to 700 million in 1998. An average annual growth rate of 20% was estimated during the eighth five year plan (1992-1997). Increasing assistance from the Central/State governments and poultry corporations is being given to create infrastructure facilities so that new entrepreneurs take up this business. Broiler farming has been given considerable importance in the national policy and has a good scope for further development in the years to come.

Financial Assistance Available from Banks/NABARD for Broiler Farming

NABARD is an apex institution for all matters relating to policy, planning and operations in the field of agricultural credit. It serves as an apex refinancing agency for the institutions providing investment and production credit. It promotes development through formulation and appraisal of projects through a well organised technical services department at the Head Office and technical cells at each of the Regional Offices.

Loan from banks with refinance facility from NABARD is available for starting broiler farming. For obtaining bank loan, the farmer should apply to the nearest branch of a commercial or cooperative or regional rural bank in their area in the prescribed application form which is available in the branches of financing bank.

The technical officers attached to or the manager of the bank can help or give guidance to the farmers in preparing the project report to obtain bank loan.

For poultry farming schemes with very large outlays detailed project reports are required to be prepared. The items of finance would include construction of broiler sheds and purchase of equipments. Cost of one day old chicks, feed, medicine and labour cost for the first 7 weeks period for the first cycle, are also considered. Facilities such as land development cost, fencing, water and electricity, essential servants quarters, godowns, transport vehicles, broiler dressing, processing and cold storage facilities can also be considered for providing loan.

Cost of land is not considered for loan. However, if land is purchased for starting a broiler farm, its cost can be treated as party's margin money upto 10% of the total cost of project.

Scheme Formulation for Bank Loan

A scheme can be prepared by the beneficiary after consulting local technical persons of State veterinary department, poultry corporation or private commercial broiler hatcheries. If possible, they should also visit the progressive broiler farmers in the area and discuss the profitability of farming.

A good practical training and experience on a broiler farm will be highly desirable, before starting a broiler farm. As broilers have to be sold after attaining 6-7 weeks of age, a regular and constant demand for broiler meat and nearness of the farm to the market should be ensured. The scheme should include information on land, water and electricity facility, marketing aspects, training facilities and expertise of entrepreneurs and the type of assistance available from State government, poultry corporations, local hatcheries. It will also include data on proposed capacity of the farm, total cost of the project, margin money to be provided by beneficiary and requirement of bank loans, estimated annual expenditure, income and profit and the repayment of loan and interest.

Requirements of Good Project

The bank officers also can assist in preparation of the scheme or filling in the prescribed application form. The scheme so formulated should be submitted to the nearest branch of bank. The bank will then examine the scheme for technical feasibility and economic viability.

Technical feasibility-this would briefly include :

(a) Suitability of climate and potentiality of the area
(b) Technical norms including schedule for replacement of flocks
(c) Facilities and infrastructure available for supply of inputs, veterinary aid, marketing, training/experience of the beneficiary.

Financial viability-this would briefly include :

(a) Unit cost and loan requirement
(b) Input costs for chicks, feed, veterinary aid, labour and other overheads
(c) Output costs i.e. sale of broiler for meat, manure and other miscellaneous items.
(d) Calculation of annual gross surplus (income-expenditure)
(e) Cash flow analysis

(f) Repayment schedule i.e. repayment of principal loan amount and interest.

Other documents such as loan application forms, security aspects, margin money requirements etc. are also examined. A field visit to scheme area is undertaken for conducting techno-economic feasibility study for appraisal of the scheme. The model economics of Broiler farming unit of 4000 birds.

Sanction of Bank Loan and its Disbursement

After ensuring technical feasibility and financial viability, the scheme is sanctioned by the bank. The loan is disbursed in kind in 2 or 3 stages, such as against the creation of specific assets, construction of sheds, purchase of equipment and machinery, recurring cost on purchase of chicks, feeds, medicines, etc. The end use of the loan is verified and constant follow up is done by the bank.

3

Chicken Behaviour and Their Social World

A hierarchal order is very important to the social lives of chickens. The head rooster protects the territory the group inhabits, as well as the chicks and hens in the group. Groups are composed of more dominant hens who remain close to the head rooster as well as more submissive hens and roosters who keep closer to the periphery. Roosters display a number of courting rituals to attract mates. Hens are attracted to roosters based on both their physical and behavioural characteristics. The pecking order, once established, maintains order and stability within the group.

Additionally, Smith identifies specific chicken behaviours that demonstrate their complex social world, including:

- Self-assessment or making comparisons between themselves and others in a group: "Chickens demonstrate an awareness of themselves as separate from others"
- Learning from others in a group: "Chicks gain information about palatable food from their mother and she in turn changes her behaviour in response to the competency of her chicks."
- Recognition of the social status of numerous individuals in a group, widely accepted as a measure of logical reasoning ability socially-dominant individuals tend to be *group leaders* from which the others learn, most likely through imitation or emulation.
- Behavioural flexibility, the ability to deviate from established routines to solve novel problems, including innovation (i.e., novel solutions to environmental or social problems), social learning (the acquisition of information from others), and tool use
- Long-term relationship-building that requires long term memory
- Ability to coordinate group activities such as foraging and group defense

Connecting the Dots: Chickens, Primates and Humans

An article in *Science Daily* called *Bird brain? Birds and humans have similar brain wiring* (July, 2013) presents the findings of a research team at the Imperial College London who found that "areas [of the brains of humans and birds] important for high-level cognition, such as long-term memory and problem solving, are wired up to other regions of the brain in a similar way." Professor Murray Shanahan, author of the study, wrote: "Birds have been evolving separately from mammals for around 300 million years, so it is hardly surprising that under a microscope the brain of a bird looks quite different from a mammal. Yet, birds have been shown to be remarkably intelligent in a similar way to mammals such as humans and monkeys."

Yet, as many animal ethicists and behavioural experts point out, there are problems with these comparisons that prevent us from a more authentic understanding of how chickens think and feel. Karen Davis, Ph.D., president of United Poultry Concerns, has presented a tremendously thought-provoking analysis of cross-species comparisons in her article entitled, Are Chickens Smarter Than Toddlers? A View of Cross-Species Comparisons. Leading avian neurologist and researcher Lesley Rogers argues that instead of ranking animals according to a simplistic, anthropocentric model of intelligence, we would be more accurate and just in our assessments if we recognized that there are many different measures and kinds of intelligence. And evolutionary biologist Marc Bekoff explains in his article, Are Pigs as Smart as Dogs and Does it Really Matter?, that such comparisons are silly and dangerous, as if to suggest *dumber* animals suffer less than smarter ones.

Moreover, we'll never be able to know for certain what forms of intelligence other animals might possess that could simply be outside of human understanding. As author Annie Potts explains, "While chickens display feelings comparable to those of humans (such as grief, fear or happiness), they no doubt also possess their own exceptional forms of emotion and consciousness that even the most rigorous scientific tests may not begin to uncover — simply because these inimitable perspectives of chickens do not register conceptually or experientially within the human domain."

BEHAVIOUR OF MATURE CHICKENS

Individual Recognition

Birds that normally form a social hierarchy, such as chickens, doves, and pigeons, usually attack a new bird of the same species or breed that is introduced into the pen or cages. In order to develop a pecking order, birds must be able to recognize individuals in a flock. This ability allows them to identify and peck only those hens lower in the pecking order. It is not clear what clues chickens are using in order to identify individual chickens within a flock.

Early research examined the effect of returning an experimentally modified bird to a flock. If the bird was pecked, researchers assumed that the others in the flock did not recognize the bird. For example, it was shown that if the loppy comb of a hen was moved to the other side of the head, she was not recognized by the others in the flock. Similarly, when individual dubbed hens were returned to a flock, they were attacked by the hens that had previously been below them in the pecking order. If, however, a larger number of dubbed hens were returned to the flock, the chickens were able to develop a new pecking order. This would suggest that the comb is not the only factor used in identifying individuals in a flock. Research showed that individual birds react to feather changes and make adjustments. Intense color changes on white individuals are more effective in producing a loss of recognition than different shades or tints. Alterations of the head and neck were shown to be more effective in producing a loss of recognition than changes to areas of the main body. Although some features are more influential than others, no single feature is the sole means of recognition.

Recent research suggests that laying hens are able to recognize around 30 individuals. The social structure developed in small groups begins to break down in flocks of 30 to 60 birds. When there are more than 60 the birds in a flock, the chickens become less aggressive and more tolerant of each other.

Preening

Grooming activity in birds is referred to as preening. Feathers are important for insulation and waterproofing (in addition to flight for those birds that can fly). Feathers are composed of a shaft with several long thin structures called barbs. These barbs are held together by smaller barbules. Sometimes the barbs are pulled apart, which makes the feather ineffective for insulation and waterproofing. A bird runs its feathers through its beak when it preens, which realigns the barbs and makes the feathers better able to perform their functions. Birds also need to keep their feathers oiled to prevent them from becoming brittle and to help with insulation and waterproofing. Birds have a single oil gland near the base of the tail, referred to as the preen gland. Birds pinch this gland with their beaks to extract a waxy oil, which they then apply as they pass their feathers through their beaks. Chickens preen on their own, but they prefer to do it as a group activity.

Fighting

Chicks start fighting when they are only a few weeks old. They are already starting to establish their rank in the flock. This fighting often continues until they reach maturity and the pecking order is well established. Sometimes fights occur among adult birds. This can occur when a member of the flock becomes tired of its position in the social hierarchy and decides to challenge a higher-ranking bird. More commonly, however, fights occur when a new bird is introduced into the flock and has to find its place in the pecking order or when a bird is reintroduced to the flock after a long absence.

Although both male and female chickens fight, fights between males tend to be more violent and are more likely to result in injury or death. When two birds are on the verge of a fight, they will eye each other and may casually circle around each other, each pretending to peck at something on the ground while watching the other. When the fight begins, the birds will raise their neck feathers and point their wings toward the ground, spreading them apart from the body. They will then stand as tall as they can and try to face each other down. If neither bird backs down, they will start pecking, scratching, and jumping at each other. They will also beat at each other with their wings.

Foraging

In the wild, jungle fowl spend 61% of their time foraging. Foraging behaviours include pecking and scratching at potential food sources, as well as looking for and sampling possible food sources. Providing chickens with a complete feed eliminates the need for foraging in order to obtain nutrients, but the hens will continue performing this behaviour. Although finding food is not the ultimate goal of the foraging behaviour in domesticated fowl, researchers have have not yet been able to determine the motivation for this behaviour. There are a number of theories, but little evidence to support them.

Nesting

Domestic hens prefer to lay in nests containing loose material that they can settle into, molding the material with their bodies and feet, and that they can manipulate with their beaks. When given a choice, the former condition is more important than the latter. It is important for pullets to have access to nesting boxes before they start to lay. If a hen will have jump up to nest, she must be trained to do so as a pullet. If she does not learn in the laying house, she could end up laying a greater number eggs on the floor. Birds are mimics, and the first layers become the teachers for the remaining pullets in a flock.

Hens can differ in their preference for nesting location. When a group of hens was given the choice between a nest box and a litter tray, the majority preferred the nest box. There were some hens, however, who preferred the litter tray. Those that selected the litter tray tended to spend more time exploring during the hour prior to laying an egg than did those that selected the nest box. Their final trip to the nest, when the egg was laid, was shorter for those that selected the litter tray.

The prelaying behaviour of domestic chickens is similar for most hens. Before laying, a hen shows restlessness and begins to look for a nest, poking her head into the nest boxes provided. Between nest examinations, she typically resumes other behaviour she had been performing—eating, preening, sleeping, and so on.

Over time, the hen puts more and more of her body into the nest boxes she is examining, eventually entering one and settling down. Hens may stay in the nest after the egg is laid. They may later cackle and leave the nest. Different breeds may exhibit some aspects of prelaying behaviour more than others. Leghorn hens, for example, typically show pronounced searching and nest-selection behaviour. As a result, these hens spend more time visiting and investigating a number of potential nest sites before choosing one. In contrast, hybrid layers of brown-shelled eggs tend to sit longer in nests and perform nest building activities.

Prelaying behaviour is triggered by hormones associated with the last ovulation and not by the presence of an egg in the shell gland. Normally, the prelaying behaviour begins an hour or two before the egg is ready to be laid. If egg laying is delayed for some reason, the period for prelaying behaviour will pass, and the hen will no longer be motivated to search for a nest. In these cases, the egg may be laid outside the nest while the hen goes about other activities. This can happen, for example, when dominant hens prevent subordinate hens from entering nests.

Dust Bathing

Dust bathing is the act of rolling or moving around in dirt to cleanse the skin and feathers of parasites, dead skin, and other skin irritants. It also helps prevent the buildup of the oil from preening. When chickens do not have access to dust baths, they will nonetheless go through the motions of dust bathing. In behavioural studies, hens have shown a willingness to work to gain access to material for dust bathing.

Perching

Chickens have a desire to roost. At about three weeks of age, chicks start to jump up to higher surfaces. The structure of a chicken's claws ensures a firm grip while the chicken is perching and will prevent the chicken from falling off a tree branch, even when the bird is asleep. Chickens go to perches about half an hour before twilight, with the actual time depending on light intensity. For example, they will perch earlier than expected on a dull, cloudy day and later than expected on a bright, clear day. They seem to perch when the light is about 1.25 foot-candles. The "flying down" time in the morning is typically 30 minutes before dawn, at around 0.003 foot-candles of light. Again, the actual timing of this activity varies depending on the weather conditions. Chickens snuggle together during the night and start spreading out about two hours before the lights come on.

Responding to High Ambient Temperatures

Chickens can tolerate with cold weather better than hot. Chickens cannot sweat—they cool themselves by dunking their beaks in cold water or flapping their wings to air out their feathers. They may also pant when they are desperate to cool down.

Drinking

Chickens must have access to a supply of clean, fresh water. Water in the crop softens feed so that digestion can occur. Without water, dry feed forms clumps in the crop. The clumped feed can press on the bird's carotid artery, decreasing blood flow to the brain. This can cause paralysis and possible death. Poultry have a split in the upper hard palate of the beak that allows air into the nasal passages. This prevents a vacuum from forming in chickens' mouths. As a result, chickens rely on gravity to draw water into the crop. This is why chickens lift their heads after dipping their beaks in water.

CHICKEN BEHAVIOUR AND EMOTIONS

Emotional intelligence is yet another measure of cognition or awareness in animal minds. Science aside, most of us can easily identify emotions in animals we are close to like dogs or cats.

And those of us who spend a lot of time around chickens see a visceral and diverse expression of emotions, yet our society still generally doesn't believe that chickens express emotional states and act on their emotions. But in the case of chicken behaviour and emotions, science is proving popular opinion wrong. A Spring, 2011 study from the University of Bristol gained important new insight into the minds of domestic hens, discovering, for the first time, that they show a clear physiological and behavioural empathic response to their chicks.

"We found that adult female birds possess at least one of the essential underpinning attributes of 'empathy'; the ability to be affected by, and share, the emotional state of another," reported Jo Edgar, PhD student involved in the Bristol study. The research team believes this finding is of great importance since chickens in modern agriculture are routinely forced to witness pain, suffering and death of other flock mates. Such witnessing of trauma and distress could exacerbate the alreadydeplorable conditions in which these animals are forced to live.

CHICKEN BEHAVIOUR AND MEMORY

Those of us who observe chickens on a daily basis see their memory and recall in action in a wide variety of everyday situations. Recent science tell us that chickens recognize over 100 individual faces even after several months of separation.

They also confirm that chickens consider the future and practice self-restraint for the benefit of some later reward, something previously believed to be exclusive to humans and other primates.

As stated earlier, chickens do not just learn through trial and error. They retain what they've learned from past experiences, then recall and apply what they've learned in future situations. Researcher Andy Lamey of Monash University in Australia released the findings of his study of chicken behaviour in May of 2012.

An important part of this study involved the observation of mother hens and their chicks, specifically, how and what the mother hens taught their young about edible food items, what and how the chicks learned (and retained what they learned), and how the mother hens then modified their teaching based on the progress of their chicks' learning.

Incredibly Precocious Chicks

One recent high profile study of chicken behaviour by 20-year veteran researcher Christine Nicol (University of Bristol) credits chickens with the ability to perform complex skills within days of hatching, such as basic arithmetic, self control and basic structural engineering — skills that don't develop in humans until their toddler years. The mass media turned these comparisons into catchy headlines, like Can chickens REALLY be cleverer than a toddler?

Ethologist Dr. Giorgio Vallortigara of the University of Trento, Italy, is widely recognized as a pioneer in chicken behaviour and cognition research, specifically with newly hatched chicks.

His work demonstrates how chicks are born with an understanding of basic arithmetic, geometry and physics, advanced problem-solving, and quick learning and retention. Italian psychologists Rosa Rugani, Lucia Regolin and Vallortigara showed chicks prefer to join groups of more objects (4) over a single object or a smaller set of objects.

The chicks in these studies were found to imprint (bond) with these "objects" as if they were their mothers or flock mates. "The most complex numerical ability is to manipulate numbers by performing simple arithmetic. We know rhesus monkeys can do this and we know that five-day-old chicks can too," explain these researchers.

In a recent interview with Uncooped, Vallortigara explains "Basically, I use the young domestic chicks to investigate the origins of knowledge; I'm interested in core knowledge abilities like number, space, time and cause, and I am trying to clarify how much of these abilities are already available at birth, before interactions with objects of the world may have shaped them through learning and experience. We found that indeed newly hatched chicks do possess surprisingly sophisticated abilities at birth, they know about basic principles of physics (such as solidity), could perform basic arithmetic (with small numerousness), they can deal with the geometry of enclosed surfaces to orient and navigate...."

"Enriched colony cages" for egg laying hens in European farm. This is the new "ethical" standard for hens. They look as miserable here as the ones stuck in the old cage system.

How Science Can Drive Ethics

While some scientific researchers appear reluctant to extrapolate the ethical implications of their work in chicken behaviour, many of them now identify how routine chicken farming practices present serious ethical problems.

From thehatching stage through the raising and slaughtering of chickens, the science presented here confirms that chickens exploited for meat and eggs endure a staggering degree of physical and psychological suffering.

Neuroscientist Lesley Rogers, author of *Development of the Brain and Behaviour in the Chicken,* argues that we are compelled to understand the cognitive abilities of chickens above all other birds because they are the most exploited and least respected avian species. Even Vallortigara, who claims to see no ethical implications from his discoveries, nonetheless makes a clear ethical judgment when he says, "I would urge people to treat chickens with respect even if they were not intelligent as they are."

Moreover, the exploitation of some 40 billion chickens every year when we have no biological requirement for animal flesh is morally indefensible. When we can easily make choices that do not harm these animals, then we should, as Karen Davis so eloquently articulates in her article, *Eliminating the Suffering of Chickens Bred for Meat.*

UNDERSTANDING CHICKEN BEHAVIOUR

We all behave in certain ways. Humans do and so do chickens. If you familiarize yourself with the way chickens behave, you can understand their basic needs and cater to them accordingly.

Pecking Order

This is where the chickens work it out amongst themselves. There's no point in trying to intervene. There's a dominant hen and she will and can peck any chicken that is below her.

The second in line can peck any hen below them but NOT the one above them! Pity the bird at the bottom of the totem pole. They can and are pecked by all of the flock! Not fair!

As strange as it appears, the system does work. Once the flock has established its pecking order, it can co-exist in peace and harmony. Introducing a new bird upsets this order and the new addition may be bullied. It's best to add more than one hen at a time because this can ease matters.

Put them in an enclosure first so they can become acquainted while looking through safety wire. Then it's good to introduce them into an area with a lot of space so the new hens can escape the bullying behaviour. Make sure you provide extra hiding places and perches around the run so the hens can get away to peace and safety. If things get out of hand, try removing the dominant bird to a new environment until the newcomers become established.

Vocalization

Yes, all chicken breeds crow but some are nosier than others. Believe it or not, the larger breeds tend to have a pleasanter-sounding crow. And if you believe roosters only crow at dawn, perish that thought. They crow throughout the day. And it's most likely they are crowing for the same reason that our songbirds sing at dawn. Not, as we like to believe, for the joy of singing, but to see if any neighboring bird didn't make it through the night and may have left prime real estate for them to move into!!!

Roosters will also crow in defiance and to let others know danger has passed. If they hear another rooster crow, they will answer with a blast of their own. You see how it can become quite noisy! If noisy roosters are driving you crazy, you can remove the offending birds to a dark box at night and return them to the run at a more suitable hour in the morning. To help dull the sound of the roosters, you can plant bamboo and conifers around their habitat. Low-toned wind chimes can help as well.

Chickens, also, have many different vocalizations. It is informative to learn to recognize the sounds. Hens have a soft, growling sound when broody. They cackle when they have just laid an egg. (so would I!) And they make a "took, took" sound to call their chicks to come and eat. Chickens will let off with a screech when alarmed. (same as I do) They make a burring sound to tell others about danger.

Courting Chickens

If a rooster finds an interesting treat, he will let the chickens know all about it. Now the hen isn't clueless. She knows he has more on his mind than those treats. There are some roosters that will be gentlemanly all year round but the majority will be using treats for one reason only!

If the hen comes near and accepts the food, the rooster will then prance around the hen with one wing dropped, before attempting to move in for action. If the hen accepts his advances, she will squat to allow mating to take place. Hens that are not ready to fall for the rooster's advances, will grab the treat and then take off like a bat out of hell so they can't be caught! LOL!

Aggression

Spring and summer is the breeding season and some males can become very aggressive. For adults, it may be amusing but for children this behaviour can be startling as the bird is batting furiously all over the place and could attack anyone within range.

Unfortunately, the aggressive birds are most in demand because they are the most virile and fertile. Unless needed for breeding, large fowl that are very aggressive are best suited to be on our dinner plates. This is because they hit too hard, jump too high and can cause injury.

To cure the habits of antisocial birds, many people throw water on them or dip them in a bucket of water. Others suggest cuddling. But these are temporary measures as the birds are soon back to their "beat up the human" game. When you need to catch that aggressive bird, hold a coat in front of you to protect yourself and as the bird approaches, throw it over them. Pin the bird to the ground inside of the coat. If you don't want the bird to breed, put it in an enclosure that you don't need to go into often.

Do not pass on an aggressive male to an innocent buyer without telling them all about the bird's temperament. Good on you!

Egg Eating

As much as this distresses me, it can be a problem. If you collect your eggs on a regular basis, which you should, you are less likely to have this problem of egg eating. This can be infuriating. No sooner has the hen laid an egg and she will peck it open and eat its contents.

Not only that, but when other hens see that behaviour, they start to copy it! You must intervene right away. If not, you will have the whole flock gobbling up their eggs. Don't let your hens find out how good the eggs taste! If you can find out which hen is doing this, remove her from the enclosure so she can't teach the other hens the bad behaviour.

To prevent egg eating, make sure the nestbox is in the darkest part of the henhouse and facing away from any window. This makes it harder for them to see the eggs. You can make these boxes darker by hanging material over the boxes. Make sure the wood shavings in the nest boxes are deep. 3-4 inches deep. Fluff up the shavings. This way the eggs will settle down and become less visible to the chickens. You can also leave a few fake eggs around the chicken run. This will discourage the hens.

Chickens are just as quirky as humans. To study and understand their behaviour can go a long way in understanding and loving our feathered friends.

ETHICAL IMPACTS OF CHICKEN BEHAVIOUR RESEARCH

Much of the research on chicken behaviour and biology is motivated by the poultry industry's objective to more efficiently exploit chickens as a resource. As author Annie Potts points out in her book *Chicken,* "It is no coincidence that the first creature to have a full genome map was the chicken: Gallus is the most studied species in the world. Every biological feature was experimented on with the aim of rendering chickens more serviceable to humans."

Free from Harm opposes animal breeding and exploitation (which includes animal testing), and we recognize that even observational studies, conducted in as natural an environment as possible to encourage natural behaviour, present their own ethical problems. Aside from these ethical challenges, observational studies of chicken behaviour that are intended to benefit the species, rather than the industry that exploits them, may have great value in changing society's attitudes toward chickens. The birds in such studies are spared lives as agricultural commodities. And some researchers work to rehome animals to sanctuaries or to private individuals who will care for them as companions.

Chicken Behaviour Beyond Science

While science provides important empirical validation to our understanding of chicken behaviour, anyone with an inquisitive mind and an interest in chickens can learn a great deal about them just by observing and interacting with them. In a short time, their individual personalities and rich life experiences are revealed.

Free from Harm has documented each of its chicken rescues, using photos, videos and stories to provide an intimate portrayal of each chicken we've had the pleasure of getting to know.

BIOLOGY AND HABITAT

Chickens are omnivores. In the wild, they often scratch at the soil to search for seeds, insects and even animals as large as lizards, small snakes or young mice.

Chickens may live for five to ten years, depending on the breed. The world's oldest chicken, a hen, died of heart failure at the age of 16 according to Guinness World Records.

Roosters can usually be differentiated from hens by their striking plumage of long flowing tails and shiny, pointed feathers on their necks (*hackles*) and backs (*saddle*), which are typically of brighter, bolder colours than those of females of the same breed. However, in some breeds, such as the Sebright chicken, the rooster has only slightly pointed neck feathers, the same colour as the hen's. The identification can be made by looking at the comb, or eventually from the development of spurs on the male's legs (in a few breeds and in certain hybrids, the male and female chicks may be differentiated by colour). Adult chickens have a fleshy crest on their heads called a comb, or cockscomb, and hanging flaps of skin either side under their beaks called wattles. Collectively, these and other fleshy protuberances on the head and throat are called caruncles. Both the adult male and female have wattles and combs, but in most breeds these are more prominent in males. A *muff* or *beard* is a mutation found in several chicken breeds which causes extra feathering under the chicken's face, giving the appearance of a beard. Domestic chickens are not capable of long distance flight, although lighter birds are generally capable of flying for short distances, such as over fences or into trees (where they would naturally roost). Chickens may occasionally fly briefly to explore their surroundings, but generally do so only to flee perceived danger.

Social behaviour

Chickens are gregarious birds and live together in flocks. They have a communal approach to the incubation of eggs and raising of young. Individual chickens in a flock will dominate others, establishing a "pecking order", with dominant individuals having priority for food access and nesting locations. Removing hens or roosters from a flock causes a temporary disruption to this social order until a new pecking order is established. Adding hens, especially younger birds, to an existing flock can lead to fighting and injury. When a rooster finds food, he may call other chickens to eat first. He does this by clucking in a high pitch as well as picking up and dropping the food. This behaviour may also be observed in mother hens to call their chicks and encourage them to eat.

A rooster's crowing is a loud and sometimes shrill call and sends a territorial signal to other roosters. However, roosters may also crow in response to sudden disturbances within their surroundings. Hens cluck loudly after laying an egg, and also to call their chicks. Chickens also give a low "warning call" when they think they see a predator approaching.

Courtship

To initiate courting, some roosters may dance in a circle around or near a hen ("a circle dance"), often lowering his wing which is closest to the hen. The dance triggers a response in the hen and when she responds to his "call", the rooster may mount the hen and proceed with the mating.

Nesting and laying behaviour

Hens will often try to lay in nests that already contain eggs and have been known to move eggs from neighbouring nests into their own. The result of this behaviour is that a flock will use only a few preferred locations, rather than having a different nest for every bird. Hens will often express a preference to lay in the same location. It is not unknown for two (or more) hens to try to share the same nest at the same time. If the nest is small, or one of the hens is particularly determined, this may result in chickens trying to lay on top of each other. There is evidence that individual hens prefer to be either solitary or gregarious nesters. Some farmers use fake eggs made from plastic or stone (or golf balls) to encourage hens to lay in a particular location.

Broodiness

Under natural conditions, most birds lay only until a clutch is complete, and they will then incubate all the eggs. Many domestic hens will also do this– and are then said to "go broody". The broody hen will stop laying and instead will focus on the incubation of the eggs (a full clutch is usually about 12 eggs). She will "sit" or "set" on the nest, protesting or pecking in defense if disturbed or removed, and she will rarely leave the nest to eat, drink, or dust-bathe. While brooding, the hen maintains the nest at a constant temperature and humidity, as well as turning the eggs regularly during the first part of the incubation. To stimulate broodiness, an owner may place many artificial eggs in the nest, or to stop it they may place the hen in an elevated cage with an open wire floor.

Modern egg-laying breeds rarely go broody, and those that do often stop part-way through the incubation. However, some "utility" (general purpose) breeds, such as the Cochin, Cornish and Silkie, do regularly go broody, and they make excellent mothers, not only for chicken eggs but also for those of other species—even those with much smaller or larger eggs and different incubation periods, such asquail, pheasants, turkeys or geese. Chicken eggs can also be hatched under a broody duck, with varied success.

Hatching and early life

At the end of the incubation period (about 21 days), the eggs, if fertile, will hatch. Development of the egg starts only when incubation begins, so they all hatch within a day or two of each other, despite perhaps being laid over a period of two weeks or so. Before hatching, the hen can hear the chicks peeping inside the eggs, and will gently cluck to stimulate them to break out of their shells. The chick begins by "pipping"; pecking a breathing hole with its egg tooth towards the blunt end of the egg, usually on the upper side. The chick will then rest for some hours, absorbing the remaining egg yolk and withdrawing the blood supply from the membrane beneath the shell (used earlier for breathing through the shell). It then enlarges the hole, gradually turning round as it goes, and eventually severing the blunt end of the shell completely to make a lid. It crawls out of the remaining shell, and its wet down dries out in the warmth of the nest.

The hen will usually stay on the nest for about two days after the first egg hatches, and during this time the newly hatched chicks live off the egg yolk they absorb just before hatching. Any eggs not fertilized by a rooster will not hatch, and the hen eventually loses interest in these and leaves the nest. After hatching, the hen fiercely guards the chicks, and will brood them when necessary to keep them warm, at first often returning to the nest at night. She leads them to food and water; she will call them to edible items, but seldom feeds them directly. She continues to care for them until they are several weeks old, when she will gradually lose interest and eventually start to lay again.

4

The Poultry Industry

FACTS ABOUT THE POULTRY INDUSTRY

The average consumer may not be aware of the suffering of billions of birds raised for meat and egg production in the United States each year. The U.S. Department of Agriculture (USDA)'s National Statistics Service reported that 7.07 billion "broiler" chickens, 67 billion "egg" chickens, and 321 million turkeys were killed in 1998 for food. In addition, millions of birds die as a result of disease, injury, and during transportation.

Egg Production

Egg-laying hens in the United States number more than 459 million. Of these millions of birds, 97% are confined to "battery" cages, tiny cages roughly 16 by 18 inches wide. Five or 6 birds are crammed into each cage, and the cages are stacked in tall tiers. As many as 50,000 to 125,000 battery hens, in sheds with minimal light, strain to produce 250 eggs per year, ten times the number of eggs they would produce in the wild.

Battery cage confinement does not allow birds to turn around or take part in any other natural behaviour, such as preening, dust bathing, and foraging for food. Prolonged forced confinement causes unnatural behaviours such as cannibalism and increases the incidence of disease and injury. Laying hens are also forced to live in a polluted environment due to toxic feed ingredients, accumulated feces, and excretory ammonia fumes. A successful battery system relies heavily on antibiotics that are routinely administered to laying hens to decrease the incidence of disease among these immune-repressed birds.

Battery hens often die in their cages as the result of disease or injury. Those who survive but stop producing adequately are considered "spent" hens and are sent to slaughter to be used for human and animal food. Male chicks are of no value to egg producers. Each year more than 200 million male chicks are killed or left to die after hatching.

Egg-producing birds that are not confined to battery cages seldom fare much better. Eggs labelled "Cage Free" or "Free Range" simply mean that the birds are not confined to battery cages, not necessarily that the hens are allowed a more natural existence. Neither guarantees that they have adequate space to move around, or that they are allowed outdoors to roam about and forage or dust bathe.

Forced Molting

Molting is the natural process of shedding old feathers and the growth of new feathers. Molting initiates a new egg-laying cycle. The natural molting process takes about four months to complete. However, on factory farms, poultry producers induce starvation to control egg production in laying hens (eggs for human consumption) and breeding hens (eggs that hatch into birds used for meat or egg production) to reduce the molting period to one to two months. Performed to increase farm profits, this "forced molting" is extremely stressful to hens. Forced molting methods include food and water deprivation, medications, and simulated light and dark cycles. A 1992 *Poultry Science* report found that forced molting in combination with a Salmonella infection created an actual disease state in tested hens. Salmonella infection can be passed on to consumers through egg consumption.

Debeaking and Toe Clipping

Debeaking is a painful procedure whereby the bird's sensitive beak is sliced off with a hot blade. Poultry meat and egg producers that use battery cages and crowded floor systems remove one-half to two-thirds of the birds' beaks to discourage cannibalistic pecking, a behaviour that occurs when birds are kept in close confinement with no regard for their natural behaviours. Behavioural studies indicate that debeaked birds are often unable to eat, drink, and preen properly. They also exhibit behaviours associated with chronic pain and depression.

Toe-clipping is the amputation of a bird's toes just behind the claw. This painful procedure is performed to reduce claw-related injuries on factory farms.

Meat Production

Genetic engineering of broiler chickens and turkeys often results in a bird too heavy to stand or walk. They suffer from pain in their legs and sores on their feet that are induced by their extreme, unnatural size. Kept in polluted dark sheds with as many as 25,000 birds per shed, these birds suffer many of the same ailments as battery hens, such as being debeaked and being forced to live in a toxic environment. Thousands of these birds never make it to slaughter — they will die while still on the farm from injuries, disease, or their inability to reach food and water.

Transport and Slaughter

Millions of birds die during the loading of trucks and while en route to slaughter. These sensitive birds, often in very poor physical condition, are grabbed by their legs and thrown into densely packed cages to be transported by truck to slaughterhouses that are sometimes hundreds of miles away. Many die from shock, injury, and suffocation in the process.

The U.S. Federal Humane Slaughter Act does not apply to poultry, meaning that there is no federal law that requires birds to be stunned prior to slaughter. This allows for diversity in commercial poultry slaughter approaches and stunning equipment. When slaughterhouses do use stunning equipment, lack of regulation often results in birds allowed to raise their heads prior to reaching the water bath stunner and therefore not adequately stunned. Problems also exist in neck-cutting equipment, which may result in prolonged and extreme pain caused by necks improperly cut during the killing process.

POULTRY INDUSTRY IN INDIA

Poultry is one of the fastest growing segments of the agricultural sector in India today. While the production of agricultural crops has been rising at a rate of 1.5 to 2 percent per annum, that of eggs and broilers has been rising at a rate of 8 to 10 percent per annum. As a result, India is now the world's fifth largest egg producer and the eighteenth largest producer of broilers. Driving this expansion are a combination of factors-growth in per capita income, a growing urban population and falling real poultry prices.

India is the fifth largest producer of eggs and ninth largest producer of poultry meat in the world, producing over 34 billion eggs and about 600,000 tons of poultry meat in 2004. In the overall market for poultry products, India was positioned 17 in World Poultry Production. And analysts estimate that the poultry sector in India has been growing at a much faster rate, along with other industries such as BPO and Securities market. Over the past decade the poultry industry in India has contributed approximately US $229 million, to the Gross National Product (GNP).

Several breakthroughs in poultry science and technology have led to the development of genetically superior breeds capable of higher production, even under adverse climatic conditions that offer opportunities for overseas entrepreneurs to expand export and import of poultry products on a large scale.

The average per capita poultry meat consumption is also estimated to increase from 0.69 to 1.28 kilograms, during the 2000-2004. Overall, analysts studies that the total egg consumption is estimated to increase from 34 billion in 2000 and to 106 billion in 2020, while poultry meat consumption is predicted to increase from 687 million kilograms to 1,674 million kilograms.

In the context of this emerging scenario, questions are being raised about the impact of the scaling up of production-through structural factors, externalities and policies-on small-scale producers. Do the transaction costs, policy distortion and environment externalities place the small-scale producer at a disadvantage? Why do some poultry farms have higher income than others? Do large farms earn more profit per unit of output than small ones? What explains the differentials in profitability? This report *, which forms part of an ongoing international comparison study on poultry, seeks to address these questions. It attempts to assess the impact of policy and environmental factors on the scale of poultry operations in India as well as the implications of that impact for small-scale production. The study aims to collect and analyse consistent data.

BROILER INDUSTRY STRUCTURE

The broiler production process is very much an industrial one. There are several distinct components of the broiler supply chain.

PRIMARY BREEDING SECTOR

The "primary breeding sector" consists of companies that breed pedigree stock. Pedigree stock ("pure line") is kept on high level biosecure farms. Their eggs are hatched in a special pedigree hatchery and their progeny then goes on to the great grandparent (GGP) and grandparent (GP) generations. These eggs would then go to a special GP hatchery to produce Parent Stock (PS) which passes to the production sector. In 2006, out of an estimated world population of 18 billion poultry, about 3% are breeding stock. The US supplied about 1/4 of world GP stock. Worldwide, the primary sector produced 417 million parent stock (PS) per year. A single pedigree-level hen might have 25000 parent stock bird descendents, which in turn might produce 3 million broilers.

Numerous techniques are used to assess the pedigree stock. For example, birds might be examined with ultrasound or x-rays to study the shape of muscles and bones. The blood oxygen level is measured to determine cardiovascular health. The walking ability of pedigree candidates is observed and scored.

The need for high levels of R&D spending prompted consolidation within the primary breeder industry. By the late 2000s only three sizable breeding groups remained:

- Aviagen (with the Ross, Arbor Acres, Indian River and Peterson brands)
- Cobb-Vantress (with the Cobb, Avian, Sasso and Hybro brands), and
- Groupe Grimaud (with the Hubbard and Grimaud Frere brands).

In the UK, 2 international firms supply about 90% of the parent stock. Due to the high levels of variation in the chicken genome, the industry has not yet reached biological limits to improved performance.

The full chicken genome was published in Nature, in December 2004. Today, all primary breeding groups are investing heavily in genomics research. This research mostly focuses on understanding the function and effect of genes already present in the breeding population. Research into transgenics – removing genes or artificially moving genes from one individual or species to another – has fewer prospects of gaining favor among consumers.

BROILER BREEDER (PARENT STOCK) FARMS

Broiler breeder farms raise parent stock which produce fertilized eggs. A broiler hatching egg is never sold at stores and is not meant for human consumption. The males and females are separate genetic lines or breeds. The chicks they produce will therefore be hybrids or 'crosses'. Since the birds are bred mainly for efficient meat production, producing eggs can be a challenge. In Canada, the average producer houses 15,000 birds that begin laying hatching eggs at 26 weeks of age. Each bird will lay about 150 hatching eggs for the next 34 to 36 weeks. This cycle is then repeated when the producer puts another flock of 26 week-old birds into his barns to begin the process again. As a general rule, each farmer produces enough broiler hatching eggs to supply chicks for 8 chicken producers. (Other sources indicate a parent hen will lay about 180 eggs in 40 week production period.)

Generally, parent flocks are either owned by integrated broiler companies or hatcheries or are contracted to them on a long-term basis. Broiler breeder growing is typically a two-stage process. Parent stock purchased from a primary breeder is delivered as day old. Most are first placed with on specialist *rearing houses* or starter farms until approximately 18 weeks of age. The starter farm has the specialized brooding equipment to raise the chicks.

Rearing house

A typical rearing house (also called a shed or barn) design for Alabama-like climate (100 °F (38 °C) in summer and 20 °F ("7 °C) in winter):

- 40 by 400 feet (12 m × 122 m) size, single storey.
- 11,000 bird capacity (about 1.4 sq ft (0.13 m) per bird)
- Ceiling is insulated
- Exterior curtain side walls.

- A "minimum ventilation" system is required for the heating period to provide a certain amount of fresh air.
- A separate "tunnel ventilation" system with evaporative pad cooling is desired (minimum wind speed is 400 fpm) for hot weather in the later stage of the bird's growth.
- Air inlets may be automatically adjusted.
- A negative ventilation system helps keep dirt and dust out of egg storage areas.
- The entire house may be heated, or individual "brooders" may be used.
- The floor is flat. There are no "slats" or "pits" for manure. There are no cages, and no nests. "Litter" (shavings or straw) covers the floor. When the chicks are introduced temporary barriers are used to keep them close to the heated areas.
- "Black-out" design to keep out external light, so the day-night cycle can be controlled.
- An automatic timer-controlled lighting system. Dimmers allow light intensity to be adjusted.
- Automatic feeders to distribute feed. Typically this consists of an endless chain in a trough or with individual pans. A silo or bin outside provides storage.
- Automatic drinkers provide water. There are several different designs, with "nipples" or "round" drinkers being popular.
- Feeders and drinkers are height adjusted as the birds grow, and can be raised on chains or wires to allow cleanout of the barn.

Chicks require warm air temperatures, which is reduced as the birds mature:

Age	Brooder Temperature	Whole-House Heating Temperature
0 days	34–35 °C	31–32 °C
14 days	31–32 °C	24–25 °C

Chicks might be debeaked at 7–10 days age. During rearing, bird weight is carefully monitored, as an over-weight bird will be a poor egg producer. The feed mix will be adjusted to meet nutritional needs at each stage. Feed might be restricted to control body weight, for example with "skip a day" feeding, or feeding 5 days out of 7.

A vaccination programme is carried out, which ensures the longevity of the parent stock, and the immunity may be passed to the broiler progeny. Males (cockerels) and females (pullets), are usually raised separately.

Laying house

The birds are then moved to broiler breeder *laying houses* or production barns. The birds are typically placed into crates, and transported by truck to a separate facility. Males and females are raised together at this point. Outwardly the laying house will resemble the rearing house. Inside, about one-half of the floor might consist of raised 'slats.'During the production run, manure will drop through the slats and accumulate in the pit underneath the slats. The birds are not generally caged, especially since the roostersmust mate with the hens to fertilize the eggs. Nests are provided for laying hens. Both automatic and manual (example) nesting systems exist. Manual nests are usually stuffed with straw or shavings and eggs are hand-collected. Automatic systems usually have a plastic carpet lining, with an belt for egg collection. Careful layout and attention to bird behaviour is required to avoid 'floor eggs'.

Depending on breed, egg production starts at 24–26 weeks of age. Production percentage (daily eggs per hen) climbs rapidly to a peak of 80–85% at 29–32 weeks, and then gradually declines with age. Hatchability tends to peak (at perhaps 90%) somewhat later than production at 34–36 weeks. Overall flock production will decline as mortality reduces the size of the flock.

When the rooster mates with the hen, sperm enter the hen's oviduct and are stored within sperm storage glands. These glands can store more than half a million sperm, and sperm can remain viable for up to 3 weeks. However, a hen will have maximum fertility for only about 3 to 4 days after one mating. Therefore, the male-to-female ratio in a flock must be enough to ensure mating of every hen every 3 days or so. To maintain fertility, younger roosters may be introduced as the flock ages. Eggs are collected a minimum of twice a day, and usually more frequently. Cracked or dirty eggs are separated, as they are not suitable for hatching. Undersized, oversized or double-yolk eggs are also unsuitable. The eggs might be disinfected by fumigation, are packed in 'flats' or trays, placed in wheeled trolleys, and stored in a cool (15-18C) climate-controlled area. The egg packing room and storage rooms are kept segrated to reduce contamination. The trolleys are delivered by truck to a hatchery perhaps twice a week.

At the end of the production cycle, the birds are called "spent fowl". Disposal of spent fowl may be a problem as consumer demand for them is poor.

Hatcheries

Hatcheries take the fertilized eggs, incubate them, and produce day old broiler chicks. Incubation takes about 21 days, and is often a two-step process. Initial incubation is done in machines known as *setters*. A modern setter is the size of a large room, with a central corridor and racks on either side. Eggs are held relatively tightly (large end up) in trays, which are stored in the racks. Inside the setter, temperature and humidity are closely maintained.

Blowers or fans circulate air to ensure uniform temperature, and heating or cooling is applied as needed by automated controls. The racks pivot or tilt from side to side, usually on an hourly basis. As an example, one commercial machine can hold up to 124,416 eggs and measures about 4.7 metres wide by 7.2 metres deep. Setters often hold more than one hatch, on a staggered hatch-day basis, and operate continuously. The setter phase lasts about 18 days.

On or about day 18, the eggs are removed from the setters and transferred to *hatchers*. These machines are similar to setters, but have larger flat-bottom trays, so the eggs can rest on their sides, and newly hatched chicks can walk.

Having a separate machine helps keep hatching debris out of the setter. The environmental conditions in the hatcher are optimized to help the chicks hatch. As a commercial example, a large hatcher has capacity for 15,840 eggs, and measures about 3.3 metres by 1.8 metres.

Some incubators are single-stage (combining setter and hatcher funcations), and entire trolleys of eggs can be rolled in at one time. One advantage of single-stage machines is that they are thoroughly cleaned after each hatch, whereas a setter is rarely shutdown for cleaning.

The single-stage environment can be adjusted for eggs from different producing flocks, and for each step of the hatch cycle. The setter environment is often a compromise as different egg batches are in the machine at one time.

On hatch day (day 21), the trays are removed ("pulled") from the hatchers, and then the chicks are removed from the trays. Chicks are inspected, with the sickly ones being disposed of.

Chicks may be by vaccinated, sorted by sex, counted, and placed in chick boxes.(Example1) (Example2) Stacks of chick boxes are loaded into trucks for transport, and arrive at the broiler farm on the same day. Specialized climate-controlled trucks are typically used, depending on climate and transport distance.

Chick sexing is optionally done to improve uniformity – since males grow faster, the weights are more uniform if males and females are raised separately. The birds are bred so that males and females have unique feather patterns or color differences. Unlike egg-laying poultry, males are not culled.

Typical hatchability rate in Canada in 2011 was 82.2%. (i.e. 82.2% of eggs set for incubation produced a saleable chick). A UK source estimates 90% hatchability.

SAFETY MANAGEMENT STRATEGIES IN THE POULTRY MEAT INDUSTRY

The safety of poultry meat and poultry meat products in Australia is controlled through a variety of regulatory and non-regulatory food safety management strategies which are described briefly in Attachment 2.

Current regulation of the poultry meat industry at the farm level of the primary production phase or poultry farm level is predominately concerned with animal disease control, animal welfare and environmental issues (air, water, soil, noise pollution). In addition to existing government regulations, the poultry meat industry has self-regulatory schemes in place that rely on voluntary compliance with codes of practice and industry preferred standards.

Strategies that exist at the poultry farm level which could impact on food safety include:

- Regulations for the importation of fertilised eggs and for the registration, sale and use of pesticides and veterinary medicines; and
- Regulations and non-regulatory codes of practice and guidelines for poultry feed (general stock feed requirements), poultry farming practices (including the layout and construction of farms), biosecurity, animal health and welfare and the transportation of live poultry.

The implementation of, and extent of compliance with these strategies varies depending of whether it is a legislative requirement or voluntary scheme and depending on the State or Territory.

Current State and Territory poultry meat regulation specific to food safety covers the slaughter, further processing, transport, and retail (including food service) of poultry meat products.

Objective

Poultry Meat is to cost effectively address the risk to public health and safety associated with the consumption of poultry meat and poultry meat products, in accordance with FSANZ's statutory obligations.

Of the FSANZ Act:

- The protection of public health and safety;
- The provision of adequate information relating to food to enable consumers to make informed choices; and
- The prevention of misleading or deceptive conduct.

In developing and varying standards, FSANZ must also have regard to:

- The need for standards to be based on risk analysis using the best available scientific evidence;
- The promotion of consistency between domestic and international food standards;
- The desirability of an efficient and internationally competitive food industry;
- The promotion of fair trading in food; and
- Any written policy guidelines formulated by the Ministerial Council.

In addition, the Standard for Poultry Meat will aim to:

- Complement existing food safety management strategies to ensure complete coverage of the poultry meat supply chain;
- Be based on a comprehensive scientific risk analysis, using the best available scientific evidence;
- Be outcome-based and minimal effective regulation;
- Be nationally consistent thereby facilitating fair-trading in poultry meat and poultry meat products between States and Territories;
- Promote consumer confidence in an industry that is already highly regarded;
- Have the overall system costs commensurate with the assessed level of risk associated with the poultry meat industry and commensurate with the benefit to the poultry meat industry;
- Be consistent with internationally recognised poultry meat standards and internationally recognised principles of food safety;
- Encourage collaborative action among enforcement agencies to optimise the use of resources and to optimise the effectiveness of food safety standards in the poultry meat industry; and

- To have regard to the relevant policy guidelines formulated by the Ministerial Council and notified to FSANZ, regarding primary production and processing Standards.

Scientific assessment

As part of the FSANZ standard development framework, an assessment, *Scientific Assessment of the Public Health and Safety of Poultry Meat in Australia,* was undertaken in the context of the current regulatory and non-regulatory environment in the poultry meat industry and using international risk assessment protocols. The outputs of the scientific risk assessment were used to inform the development of risk management measures.

In particular, the assessment work identified:

- The food safety risks in the poultry supply chain; and
- Where these risks could best be managed in this chain.

The conclusions from the assessment were used to determine the gaps with the current management strategies in place, that is, where there are no or insufficient controls measures for an identified risk. Such gaps may be referred to as residual risk.

Scope of the Assessment

The risk assessment determined:

- The extent of food safety risk associated with the consumption of poultry meat and poultry meat products in Australia; and
- The factors along the poultry meat supply chain that have the greatest impact on public health and safety.

The risk assessment examined food safety hazards across the entire poultry meat supply chain– from importation of fertilized eggs through to consumption of poultry meat products. The microbiological hazards considered included *Salmonella* and *Campylobacter* species, pathogenic *Escherichia coli, Staphylococcus aureus, Clostridium perfringens,* and *Listeria monocytogenes*. Chemical hazards considered were agricultural and veterinary chemicals, contaminants, food additives and processing aids.

The assessment considered the major avian species consumed in Australia– including chickens, ducks, turkeys, geese, pigeons, quail, pheasants and guinea fowls. Wild caught birds (*e.g.* magpie geese and mutton birds) where processed in a registered establishment were also considered. However, ratites (emus and ostriches) were not included in this assessment as, they are processed using different methods to those used for the other avian species considered and the vast majority are processed in export-registered premises which are heavily regulated. Ratites will be considered in a subsequent primary production and processing standard.

As chicken meat represents the majority of poultry consumed, the risk assessment was largely informed by chicken meat data. The majority of the Australian data used was obtained from members of the poultry standard development committee. The hazards associated with chicken meat and chicken meat products were assumed to be similar to those associated with products from other poultry species, unless contrary data was available. This assumption was supported by the poultry standard development committee.

Main findings of the assessment

Salmonella and Campylobacter

Salmonella and *Campylobacter* are two of the most commonly reported causes of food-borne illness in Australia. Symptoms generally consist of self-limiting gastroenteritis, sometimes requiring hospitalisation. In a small proportion of cases, infection can lead to more severe, long-term illness such as septicaemia, reactive arthritis or Guillain Barré syndrome.

Based on epidemiological data, results from raw carcase microbiological surveys and outputs from the probabilistic model, there is reasonable evidence to indicate poultry is the vehicle for a proportion of salmonellosis and campylobacteriosis cases in Australia, however, due to a lack of quantitative data it is not possible to estimate the extent to which this is the case.

The following is a description of factors along the primary production, primary processing and food service/consumer handling and preparation stages that impact on the likelihood of contamination.

TYPICAL STRUCTURE OF CHICKEN MEAT FLOCKS

Great Grand Parent (GGP) and Grand Parent (GP) Flocks

In 2008, there were an estimated 6.5 to 7 million adult breeder birds (Meat GGPs, GPs and Parents) in Australia.

Since 2005, the importance of these elite flocks as repositories for overseas breeding stock has increased. The number of GP's and parent breeders exported out of Australia is expected to increase significantly over the next few years. This is particularly so with the recent acquisition of a PAQ facility and GGP and GP facilities by a large international company. The increase is also likely now that two of the three Australian producers of broiler breeder stock are independent of the chicken meat producers. There are currently no specific health issues affecting Australian breeding stock, unlike the health issues associated with J-Leucosis in the early 1990s. All strains of breeders, however, have experienced increased difficulties with male fertility and hatchability under increased husbandry requirements.

After importation through either Torrens Island or private quarantine facilities, the small GGP flocks are maintained in facilities under a high level of husbandry and biosecurity. Typically, in the GGP import there will be one male line and two female lines.

Within each of these lines there are both male and female lines. Genetic selection for growth and meat yield in the broiler has put significant pressure for reproductive performance on the meat breeder. Hence, while the male line is essentially selected for broiler traits, the female lines still maintain some selection pressures for egg production and hatchability.

Despite this, there is still the need for specialised husbandry practices with chicken meat lines in order to achieve reasonable reproductive performance. Because of the high value of individual birds, facility quality and husbandry inputs are optimal. Vaccinations are usually typical of what all levels of breeder stock obtain but in some cases certain vaccines like those for Mycoplasma may be excluded to assist avian disease serological monitoring programmes where vaccination could make differential from wild type infection difficult.

Where limited exports occur with breeding stock, this may also restrict the ability to use certain vaccines. While vaccination for Newcastle disease (NDV) is obligatory in most states in Australia, some companies are seeking to implement strict biosecurity practices at their GGP facilities. This stock is also usually maintained under tight physical security to avoid theft of valuable genetic material and when flocks are depopulated they are invariably slaughtered under strict agreements.

Where imports are not regular, GGP birds must be generated from existing GGP stock. The disease status of these GGP birds is critical as the multiplier effect from GGP to GP to Parent Breeder to progeny is substantial. Similarly, undesirable genetic traits in individual birds can have a major impact.

GP flocks are usually located in the same locality as the GGP and they are maintained under similar husbandry conditions. There are two GGP facilities in New South Wales, one in South Australia and one in Victoria.

A designated hatchery is used for the hatching of parent breeders (PBs). These PBs are the source of broiler progeny and are transported as day olds to the various PB rearer farms that are located in most states in Australia. This may be to company farms or those of other integrated chicken meat companies.

While all feed supplied to the mainstream chicken meat companies is heat treated pellet feed, there is some interest in using vegetable based protein ration for GGP and GP flocks based on concerns about salmonella in meat and bone meal; however, sterility may be affected more by the milling process than the source of the protein.

Parent Breeders (PBs)

Physical treatment of birds may include trimming of the back toe of males at one day of age and beak tipping of male and females at around five days of age. Females are less commonly beak-tipped as the incidence of cannibalism and egg picking has been reduced by improved facilitation and management. Males are still commonly beak-trimmed to reduce the amount of neck scruffing damage done to females during mating. Back toe removal in the male is to similarly avoid damage to the female during mating.

The vaccination programme in PBs is quite extensive. The value of stock justifies this investment against disease and to boost maternally transferred antibody levels to protect the young broiler chick against immunosuppressive disease such as Infectious Bursal Disease (IBD). More recently, to avoid loss of uniformity during rearing due to challenges with coccidiosis, most breeder rearing is done using a coccidial vaccination programme. Killed NDV vaccination is not mandatory in broiler breeders but live NDV (V4) with monitoring serology must be undertaken. A new imported coccidial vaccine has been introduced onto the market and now industry may choose between using the imported or locally produced product. Salmonella vaccination is undertaken by some operators using autogenous killed products.

PBs can be reared either in "day old to death" facilities or in designated rearing facilities where birds are moved to designated breeder facilities at around 20 weeks of age, referred to as "rear and move". Since 2005, the latter is becoming more common due to changes in production shed design. New designs use slats and automated nest box systems rather than the older style deep litter sheds with manual collect nest boxes. Each approach has its advantages and the choice is influenced by available company facilities, time requirements, disease control programmes and available staffing. Shed designs are varied but include the three major types which include natural ventilation, fan-assisted and controlled environment (CE). All housing is based on floor rearing referred to as the barn or deep litter system.

This is distinct from the trend in commercial layers for colony cage rearing. Preferably young birds are reared in light controlled sheds which can be blacked out in the newer controlled environment type sheds or dimmed in the case of the older style fan-assisted sheds. All new shedding has automatic nest box collection systems with partially slatted floors in the sheds. While these systems benefit from a lower labour cost and greater hatching egg recovery, there are some losses in hatching egg fertility.

Ambient light control is required to reduce the birds' activity while being reared on significantly controlled feed intakes. PBs have the genetic growth potential of broilers and if allowed to eat ad lib, the males will approach weights of 3.0 kilograms at 7 weeks of age and the females 2.3 kilograms. For successful reproductive performance these weights need to be reached at closer to 20 weeks of age.

Such strict weight control necessitates ambient light control of around 10 to 12 hours per day, low density feeds and automated feeder systems that allow rapid distribution of prescribed quantities of feed to all birds almost simultaneously. Compared to ad lib feeding times with broilers and commercial layers, feed times for rearer breeders are between 30 and 120 minutes. Under these specific husbandry conditions, the manager must also ensure that the young breeders maintain the correct body weight to age profiles, correct conformation and, most importantly, flock uniformity. The weekly weighing of a sample population of birds is required to allow quantitative feed adjustments and the grading of birds into various pens containing particular weight profiles is common.

From around 20 weeks of age the light intensity and period for PBs are increased in order to stimulate laying. In a rear and move system, the PBs are moved across to the production (laying) farm at around 21 weeks of age. Light hours are further increased as are the feed quantities (up to around 16 to 17 hours light at 27 weeks of age or around 70 per cent production). Peak production of around 85 per cent hen day production is achieved at around 30 weeks and on a peak feed intake of around 155 to 175 grams (this compares to commercial layers which peak around 95 per cent on 110 grams of feed).

The male to female ratio is around eight to ten per cent males and a female breeder hen will produce around 150 fertile hatching eggs by 64 weeks of age. At this age the flocks are usually depopulated. As in rearing, the monitoring of body weights and maintaining the correct body weight profile against net nutrient intake is critical if a producer is to achieve optimal breeder performance and hatchability.

Sheds of breeder farms usually contain between 7000 to 10 000 birds and each single age farm unit has between 20 000 to 40 000 PBs. The actual farm size is dependent on the company's weekly hatching egg requirement. As the hatchability of fertile eggs declines rapidly after eggs have been stored in a cool room for ten days, it is critical that production outputs match hatching egg requirements. This again emphasises the importance of planning in the chicken meat industry where shortages or over production can be economically damaging.

Breeder farms are generally located away from broiler grow outs and other types of poultry. Since 2006, a number of new broiler breeder facilities have been built in South Australia, Queensland and Victoria. Some operations, as a consequence of historical growth, still have breeder facilities located regionally near broiler farms or hatcheries. New expansions are generally undertaken on breeder farm complexes where there may be several rearing and breeding farms located within eyesight of each other but usually at least 500 metres distance. These complexes are multi-age.

The majority of breeder farms are maintained under biosecure conditions which include perimeter fences, shower on facilities and mechanisms by which hatching eggs and (in some cases) feed and other services can interact with the farm without entering the farm proper. Water supplies are not uncommonly derived from non-main water supplies because of the isolation of some of these farms. Underground or surface water is used as an alternative, the later sanitised using chlorine or chlorine dioxide. Feed is always processed pelleted feed and delivered in sealed transport vehicles. Inside sheds, feed delivery systems are both trough or pan feeders and the majority of farms have nipple drinkers.

Egg collection systems are progressively moving away from the traditional single or double tiered manual collect nest box to automated egg collection systems. While the cost of labour and its availability is the driving force here, aspects related to occupational health and safety (OH&S) are also considerations. Such systems consist of a percentage of the floor being slatted with the rest consisting of deep litter. Nest boxes are either of the single hole or colony nest type with an automated egg belt running back into the centralised collection point in a partitioned area at the end of the shed. Variations on this include the inter connection of a number of sheds with anacondas (egg conveyors) as seen in commercial egg laying farms.

Egg collection costs range from around four to six cents per egg for manual collection systems, to two cents for automated systems. Manual floor collections are still generally required for the small number of eggs that are laid on the floor and/ or slats and this is undertaken between eight to four times a day depending on the production time cycle. Nest box or egg belt collection occurs three to four times a day. Recovery of useable settable eggs is around 95 per cent with the remaining rejects and double-yolkers being utilised in a number of ways, including egg pulp, through the commercial laying company grading and processing plants.

There are also new style broiler breeder facilities which are certified to European standards with colony cages. These are the most modern type of PB facilities developed in Europe.

Breeder hens are depopulated around 64 weeks of age and are taken to either company processing plants or to specific poultry processing plants that specialise in processing spent breeder and layer hens. Recently, the trend has been for the owners of spent broiler breeder hens to slaughter birds, rather than independent processors. The meat from these birds is used in further processed products such as chicken loaf and soups.

Transport contractors involved in spent hens movements pose a potential biosecurity risk.

PLAIN MEAT PROCESSING UNDER BASIC CONDITIONS

Meat processing can be carried out even under basic conditions at a very small-scale level such as a village or rural setting.

Such small-scale meat products manufacture can be recommended from the nutritional point of view, as it enables communities to fully utilise animal food materials derived from small-scale slaughtering and allows for extension of meat products with locally available suitable plant food. This type of meat processing also provides the option to manufacture products with increased shelf life, *e.g.*, through drying or other preserving measures, *e.g.*, salting, smoking, fermentation or heat treatment enabling communities to cater for periods meat might not be available.

Basic processing equipment can be manually operated for the smallest units with little throughput. The availability of single-phase electrical power allows for larger quantities to be processed using basic electrically powered equipment. In least-developed and developing countries the high capital investment required to construct a purpose-built facility may not be feasible. In these cases the conversion of a suitable building of good standard can be acceptable as long as basic hygienic measures are introduced and followed.

Facilities

A purpose built area is highly recommended for commercial small-scale meat processing. As a guide, facilities should have the following minimum characteristics:

- The floor must be of hard, smooth and waterproof material in anti-slip finishing. Materials such as high-grade concrete, terrazzo (= concrete mixed with small stones and smoothened on the surface after hardening), floor tiles or plastic coating are recommended. Floors must be sloped to drain off surface water.
- To avoid difficult-to-clean spots, rounded junctions of walls and floors are strongly recommended.
- The surface of interior walls must be waterproof and smooth and should be covered by wall tiles or coated with washable paint up to a height of 2.0 m.
- The surface of the ceiling should be smooth, flat, sufficiently high and preferably also painted with washable paint.
- To avoid high humidity in the facility, sufficient ventilation must be guaranteed.
- All windows, doors and other ventilation openings need to be insect proof.
- A drainage system should be built-in to allow rapid disposal of effluents. The openings inside and outside must be covered with a removable netting to allow collection of solid particles and prevent rodents and other small animals from entering the system. If facilities are not in use, all inlets and outlets need to be closed hermetically.
- Areas of clean operations (meat cutting and processing) and dirty operations (cleaning of intestines) must be divided by a wall or carried

out in separate rooms. In warmer climates the dirty area can be semi-open, in colder regions a small room is needed.
- Potable water must be available for cooking of raw materials and processed products and cleaning of facilities and equipment.
- Wastage such as solid particles from the drainage system and the content of the gastro-intestinal tract could be collected and converted into biogas to be used for heating and light.

Equipment and Tools

Without electrical power the meat processor is limited to manually operated equipment. A meat grinder is needed to cut meat and non-meat ingredients to the desired size. A manual sausage stuffer allows for easy filling of sausage mixes into the casings. Other tools like knives, hand bone saw, sharpening steel, buckets, one big and several small containers (plastic) and meat hooks are also needed. For grating of peeled roots, stainless steel grating plates are very helpful tools as they are unbreakable.

Cleaning and Hygiene

Even when processing is done under such simple and basic conditions, due attention needs to be paid to hygiene. Cleanliness of facilities, installations and personnel is an essential pre-condition in all food processing. A sufficient amount of potable water, boiling facilities (charcoal cookers, gas stoves) and detergents and disinfectants must be available. Raw materials brought to the processing area must be fresh, clean and disease-free. It is essential that the facilities, machinery and tools are properly cleaned before and immediately after processing.

A high level of personal hygiene is required and therefore essential that staff involved in processing must be in good health and undergoes regular medical check ups. Staff members should never enter the food processing area in street clothes and shoes, but wear clean protective clothing, and also carefully attend to personal hygiene.

Product Range

The range of products depends on the climatic conditions under which the processing is done, when manually operated equipment is used and refrigeration facilities are lacking.

In tropical and subtropical countries with temperatures of above +25°C during the day and no significant decrease in temperature during the night the production is limited to products which are immediately consumed or products which are dried, salted and smoked in simple smoking units.

Fresh coarse sausages, burgers and meat-mixes (meats/vegetables) are typical products for immediate consumption. Dried and/or fermented sausages of small diameter for rapid drying and dried meat sticks can also be produced. In moderate climates, smaller raw-fermented hams and larger calibre dried-fermented sausages can be produced during colder seasons. Some of the precooked-cooked products, such as coarse liver sausage, stuffed in natural casings of smaller calibre can be produced for immediate consumption.

PACKAGING FORMS AND MATERIALS

Packaging constitutes both flexible and rigid materials, alone or in combination with other preservation methods, to offer the necessary barrier, inactivation, and containment properties required for successful food packaging. Examples of typical flexible packaging materials include polyester, polypropylene, polyethylene, polyvinyl, polyolefins, vinylidene, vinyl chloride, surlyn, or nylon, which provide the needed characteristics such as strength, permeability, and saleability in the food industry.

Additionally, flexible packaging materials can be combined with gaseous environments to extend the shelf life of many foods, including meat and poultry. Besides synthetically derived packaging materials, flexible packaging can encompass the use of edible films, gels, or coatings made from polysaccharides, proteins, lipids, or composites of any or all three. The benefits of using edible films as packaging materials are threefold: these films may resist the migration of outer moisture into the food during storage; films may serve as gas and solute barriers; and films compliment other types of packaging by improving the quality and shelf life of foods. And finally, the combination of rigid packaging materials made from metal, glass, or plastic and combined with heat, provides the most effective and widely used method of food preservation. The various traits of materials used in packaging of meat. Nearly all-available films for meat packaging are of thermoplastic materials, and therefore heat seal able, resulting in hermetically sealed plastic pouches, bags, etc. A high oxygen barrier is important in the application of films for packaging meat and meat products. Films made of polyvinylchloride (PVC), polyethylene (PE) or polypropylene (PP) have a relatively high oxygen permeability, whereas polyvinylidene chloride (PVDC), polyester (PETP), polyamide (PA) and cellulose film (ZG) are less or almost non-permeable to oxygen. The latter materials are therefore better suited for packaging meat and meat products. However, the materials of the first group are frequently used as laminates with materials of the second group in order to achieve special effects regarding mechanical strength, heat sealing properties or making the package practically impermeable to both oxygen and water vapour.

Packaging Techniques

Choice of packaging systems and the use depend on many factors including cost, the volume of product being handled, and presentation. Some of the recent methods used in meat industry are:

Vacuum Packaging

Vacuum packaging refers to packaging in containers (rigid or flexible), from which substantially all air has been removed prior to final sealing of container. This method of packaging is actually a form of "modified atmosphere" since normal air is removed from the package. The various advantages of vacuum packaging are that these extend shelf life by controlling oxidative rancidity and by preventing the growth of normal spoilage bacteria (aerobic organisms such as pseudomonas are suppressed and lactic acid bacteria are favoured which can grow to high numbers without causing spoilage), reduce freezer burn and loss of moisture at product surface, require minimum storage space and Leakers are easily detected (small puncture or pin hole in a vacuum pack is easily detected by looking for loose packages).

Today vacuum packaging is the most widely used method employed to extend the storage life of fresh meat. The air within the package must be evacuated to normal anoxic levels, *i.e.*, less than 500ppm to prevent browning due to residual oxygen. The exclusion of oxygen from meat surface immediately after carcass is broken into primals preserves the meat's potential to re-oxygenate soon after retail pack display. The preservative effect of vacuum packaging is by inhibition of potent spoilage bacteria at normal meat pH under optimum vacuum packaged conditions. The microenvironment within the pack will determine the type of micro-flora, which develops. When meat is first vacuum packaged any residual oxygen remaining in the pack is consumed by meat and muscle pigments and CO_2 is produced as an end product of tissue and microbial respiration. Under a good vacuum the package head space consists of <1 per cent O_2 and 10-20 per cent CO_2 which restricts the growth of aerobic microorganisms such as pseudomonas and favours desirable facultative anaerobic organisms such as lactobacillus but also undesirable Bronchothrix thermosphacta. These slow growing bacteria cause less offensive types of spoilage even at higher bacterial numbers than other aerobic organisms and will eventually cause spoilage but only after many weeks of storage. If vacuum packaging procedures are followed correctly, the storage life of meat can be extended.

Care must be taken to keep initial bacterial load as low as possible by following strict hygienic procedures. The temperature must be maintained at or near 0-degree Celsius. High pH and DFD meat must be avoided as early spoilage may occur. High vacuum levels result in the most desirable muscle colour and fat appearance. Vacuum packaged meat of normal pH (<5.8) can be stored for 12 to 14 weeks at 0°C. However, vacuum packaging is considered unsuitable for red meats for retail display purposes since the oxygen-depleted atmosphere causes the meat in these packages to appear purplish in colour and therefore not acceptable to consumers. Vacuum packaging is ineffective for whole carcasses or cuts which prevent the packaging film being closely applied to all surfaces.

There are four basic ways; the first one involves the use of heat shrinking flexible packaging material around the primal cuts. When exposed to heat it shrinks and increases film thickness, improves mechanical resistance and reduces the drip loss.

The second type involves the use of preformed plastic bags/pouches made up of polyamide (PA) as the outer layer, while the inner core is polyethylene (PE). Polyamide provides barrier properties and physical strength while polyethylene provides sealing properties. The third type provides the use of thermoforming trays in line from a base web. Here the product is placed into the tray and then a film web is allowed to cover the tray from a second reel of film followed by pack evaluation and vacuum sealing. The fourth type is vacuum skin packaging, in which the meat is placed in a rigid preformed tray or on the flat surface of a flexible base material followed by heat softening, evacuation and vacuum shrink sealing.

Gas Packaging

Gas packaging can be defined as the alteration of the proportional volumes of the gases, which comprise a normal atmosphere. This type of packaging generally falls into two categories:

1. *Modified Atmosphere Packaging (MAP):* Refers to enclosing a product in some type of barrier and modifying the atmosphere either by drawing a vacuum or filling with a gas mix. During storage the level of these gases will change due to respiration of the product and permeability of the film.
2. *Controlled Atmosphere Packaging:* A system where gases are added or removed to maintain a desired balance is called controlled atmosphere packaging. In this case the bulk bin or the storage vessel is virtually impermeable.

Advantages of Gas Packaging

Advantages of gas packaging are that it allows meat to bloom (if the oxygenated red colour is desired, blend incorporated oxygen can be used to control colour), extends shelf life by controlling oxidation by displacing the oxygen with CO_2 and N_2 inhibits growth of normal aerobic spoilage organisms besides surface molds, prevents crushing of soft products as gas mixtures of CO_2 and N_2 equalise the pressure in the package and prevent package collapse and retains moisture but water can move from centre of product to surface resulting in staling.

In MAP systems each gas has a specific role to play in extending the shelf life and maintaining the appearance of packaged meat. The most commonly used gases for the packaging of meat is CO_2, N_2 and O_2 although other gases including CO, N_2O, Argon, SO_2 and Ozone have been tried to a limited extent. The most commonly used gas mixture for fresh red meat is high O_2, which has a minimum 60-70 per cent O_2 and 30-40 per cent CO_2. Packaging in high oxygen extends the time for occurrence of microbiological spoilage and discolouration of meat. Most chilled poultry products are sold in prewrapped O_2 permeable film, which prevents moisture loss and the spread of contaminating microorganisms. However, where O_2 impermeable films are used, mainly for duck and turkey, the benefits are in extended shelf life.

There are also reports that high CO_2 atmosphere packaging of poultry extends the storage life up to three times that of storage in air. The modified atmosphere packaging for cured meat products has generated certain problems viz colour stability of cured meat products stored under illumination during retail display. Light exposure including intensity of light or illuminance, oxygen transmission rate of packaging material and residual level of O_2 have been found to effect the colour stability of cured meats.

Discolouration in controlled atmosphere packaging can be prevented only by exclusion of all O_2 from the package, which requires special evacuation equipment and totally gas impermeable packaging materials. If CO_2 is a major or sole component of the input atmosphere, then the quantity of added gas must be adjusted to assure that the intended atmosphere persists after dissolution of the gas into the product. For chilled meat, the most effective technology to date is the high CO_2 controlled atmosphere packaging system. This regime limits microbial deterioration through optimal storage temperatures (-1.5°C), high levels of CO_2, low residual O_2 (=0.05 per cent), and use of a gas impermeable films.

Active and Intelligent Packaging

An active or intelligent packaging is a packaging, which has an additional desired role that improves the quality of the food product as a supplement to pure packaging properties. These properties can either be integrated in the packaging material or separated from it. Intelligent packaging contains an external or internal indicator for the active product history and quality. It has an inherent ability to gather information on its operating environment or history, to process that information in order to draw intelligent inferences from it and to act on those inferences by changing its characteristics in an advantageous manner. Active packaging has an extra function in addition to that of providing a protective barrier against external influence. It can control, and even react to, phenomena taking place inside the package. It actively and constantly changes either package permeation properties or the concentration of various volatiles and gases in the package headspace during storage, or actively adds microbial, antioxidative or other quality improving agents, *e.g.*, flavour enhancing substances, via packaging material into food in small amounts during storage.

Examples of active packaging are those that exhibit preferential permeability; temperature compensating attributes; oxygen, carbon dioxide, alcohol, or ethylene scavenging systems; moisture absorbers; antimicrobials incorporated directly into the packaging matrix; controlled release of colourants, flavours, spices, minerals, antimicrobials, ethanol, or antioxidants; or the ability to absorb odors. Based on their way of functioning, active packaging are categorised into four groups viz scavengers, emitters, indicators and others.

The first three types can be evaluated as groups, because of the similarities in the intended function of the product but for other types (*e.g.* Susceptor materials) of active packaging, an individual evaluation will have to be done from case to case.

Active Packaging Scavengers

Active packaging scavengers consist of ingredients, which are intended to absorb, remove and then eliminate substances, such as oxygen, ethylene, moisture, or taint from the interior of a food package. The constituents of active packaging material and articles have an effect on the shelf life or the organoleptic properties of the food. The examples are the oxygen scavengers and ethylene scavengers, which are used for eliminating oxygen and ethylene respectively from the package resulting in an extended shelf life of the food. Commercial oxygen scavengers are in most cases based on iron powder, which, in the presence of oxygen, forms iron oxide. Non-metallic and organo-metallic compounds have also been developed.

Active Packaging Indicators

Various indicators, *viz* indicators for temperature, microbial spoilage, package integrity, physical shock, and product authenticity etc can give information on the quality of the food product directly, besides the package and its headspace gases, as well as on the storage conditions of the package. Some indicators do not need to interact with the product or the headspace, while others do. These indicators are often called intelligent packaging and certain concepts are already commercially available, and their uses seem to be increasing. New concepts of leak indicators and freshness indicators are patented, and it can be expected that new commercially available products will be available in the near future.

Antimicrobial Agents

Quite recently, the idea of incorporating antimicrobial agents directly into packaging films has been developed. Thus, the packaging material can serve as a source of releasing preservatives or antimicrobial agents, or even prevent the growth of microorganisms. Flores and others (1997) reviewed the products and patents in the area of active packaging and identified antimicrobial packaging as one of the most promising versions of an Active Packaging system. Of the active packaging applications, the incorporation and/or slow release of antimicrobials is receiving considerable attention as a means of extending the bacterial lag phase, slowing the growth rate of microorganisms, prolonging shelf life, and maintaining food safety. The general premise of antimicrobial packaging is a controlled migration of the compound to the food through diffusion or partitioning (Han, 2000), which not only allows for initial inhibition of undesirable microorganisms, but also retains residual activity over time.

Active Packaging Emitters

This group of active packaging contains, or produces, substances, which are meant to migrate into the food packaging headspace or into the food in order to obtain a technological effect in the atmosphere in the packaging or in the food itself as, *e.g.*, food additives, flavourings or biocides. In these cases, the consumer together with the food ingests the components.

Edible Films

Considerable research has been conducted to develop and apply bio-based polymers mainly from a variety of agricultural commodities and/or waste of food products to reduce the amount of synthetic polymer waste. Edible coatings and films offer a variety of advantages such as biodegradability, edibility, biocompatibility, aesthetic appearance, and barrier properties. The benefits of using edible films as packaging materials are threefold. Since the water activity (aw) is critical for microbial, chemical, and enzymatic activities, edible films may resist the migration of outer moisture into the food during storage.

They may serve as gas and solute barriers and compliment other types of packaging by improving the quality and shelf life of foods. With the incorporation of antimicrobials into the matrix, edible gels, films, or coatings can exhibit active packaging characteristics, which are attributes necessary for controlling undesirable microbes in muscle foods. Antimicrobial compounds such as organic acids (acetic, propionic, benzoic, sorbic, lactic, lauric), potassium sorbate, bacteriocins (nisin, lacticin), grape seed extracts, spice extracts (thymol, p-cymene, cinnamaldehyde), thiosulfinates (allicin), enzymes (peroxidase, lysozyme), proteins (conalbumin), isothiocyanates (allylisothicyanate), antibiotics (imazalil), fungicides (benomyl), chelating agents (EDTA), metals (silver), or parabens (heptylparaben) can be added to edible films to reduce bacteria in solution, on culture media, or on a variety of muscle foods. The incorporated antimicrobial agents must be edible food grade compounds since they have to be consumed along with the edible gels, films, or coatings.

Biopolymers

Research efforts since 1940s have been devoted to develop bio-based polymer films derived from natural sources such as plant and animal materials. The use of plant material to form films is an active research topic. The advantages of using biopolymers for food packaging include: reduced dependence on petroleum-based packaging, use of a renewable agricultural resource, the biopolymers can act as carriers to deliver shelf-life extenders such as antimicrobials or antioxidants, and biodegradability. Since the forming of a film requires cross-linking of molecular units to impart strength and flexibility, proteins and carbohydrates are often the best candidates for biopolymer films. Proteins investigated include wheat gluten, corn zein, whey, pea protein, meat proteins, egg proteins, and soy. Starches studied in the literature include alginate, polysaccharides, cellulose, carrageenans, and microbial polysaccharides. Pearce and Lavers reported using carrageenan to protect frozen poultry and Klose *et al.* incorporated an antioxidant into a gelatin coating to slow the development of oxidative rancidity in cut poultry meat prior to freezing. Edible film packaging of meat act as a moisture barrier, oxygen barrier, texture modifier, breading adhesion aid, mold suppressor, bacterial inhibitor, physical protectant, oil barrier, antimicrobial carrier and antioxidant carrier. The colour stability of freshly cut beef surfaces has been reported to improve by exposing the meat surface to antioxidant-impregnated corn zein films.

MODERN MEAT CHICKEN INDUSTRY

The modern broiler industry has developed a hybrid that is unlike any other breed. The initial breeds used in modern broiler hybrids were Cornish and Plymouth Rocks. Today's broiler can achieve a 5-pound market weight in five weeks. Forty years ago, it took 10 weeks to achieve a 4-pound market weight. These advances are the result of scientific progress in genetic, nutritional, and environmental research.

Primary Breeders

The primary breeder flocks are owned by an international breeder company. These flocks produce highly efficient breeding lines (parent lines) that are sold to the integrated broiler companies. Chicks are hatched at the breeder's hatchery and then sold and delivered to the integrated companies' parent breeding farms.

Parent Stock Breeders

Once the chicks arrive at the integrated company's breeder growing farm, the birds are raised to 20 weeks of age under environmentally controlled conditions. Controlling the length of daylight is extremely important. Breeders do not receive more than 10 hours of light daily as they are growing so they are not prematurely stimulated to lay eggs. During the 20 weeks of the grow-out, each bird will eat 30-35 pounds of feed and will grow to 6-8 lbs. Once they reach 20 weeks of age, they are transported to the breeder farm.

The parent breeders are the birds that produce the fertile eggs that will become the broiler chickens that are harvested for meat. Breeders are raised in open floor houses with automatic watering, feeding, and egg collection systems. Males and females are allowed to mate naturally. Females begin producing eggs around 24 weeks of age and will lay efficiently for 40 weeks per cycle. An average broiler breeder female will lay 150-180 eggs in a year.

Hatching Eggs

When the broiler breeder female reaches 24 weeks of age, she will be laying. It takes a female between 24 and 32 hours to produce a fertile egg.

The eggs are automatically collected daily, transported to the hatchery, and stored at 55-65° F and 70 per cent humidity until they are set in the incubator. The eggs are held here for about three to 10 days prior to being placed in an incubator. One fertile hatching egg is worth $.28 each and weighs around 65g.

Incubation

Most Integrated companies own their own hatchery to produce the chicks. Incubators will hold thousands of eggs in a very controlled environment. They are then transferred into hatching baskets. On the 21st day the chicks hatch.

Hatching

After the chicks hatch, they are removed from the hatchers and processed before being taken to the grow-out farm. Processing of broiler chickens include sexing (separating the males and females if the company raised the two sexes separately) and vaccination. They are then counted and placed in baskets for delivery to the farm within 12 hours of hatch. A broiler chick is worth about $.36 and weights around 44g.

Grow-out

The chicks are then placed in floor rearing houses where they are raised under environmentally controlled conditions. Ventilation of the broiler house is criti.cal for controlling temperature and humidity in the grow-out house. Birds are grown to different sizes depending on the market they are meant to fill. On average a broiler consumes about 9 pounds of feed (current cost of about $1.50 or $.30/pound) and reaches 5 pounds (live weight) in 5 weeks.

When the birds reach the desired weight, a company catching crew will catch and load the birds onto trucks to be transported to the processing plant. The catching crew takes a great deal of care in carefully handling the birds to prevent bruises or injury.

Harvesting

At the processing plant, birds are humanely slaughtered as quickly as possible. After slaughter, the feathers, offal , head, legs, and other items are removed so that they have a whole dressed carcass ready for sale or to send onto further processing.

The cost of processing a broiler is about $.18 per pound. The wholesale price for a whole broiler is about $.53 per pound.

Further Processed Products

This is where we make the product more convenient as well as add value to the product. In the meat industry, further processing means something is done to the whole carcass such as cut-up, deboning, and fabricating poultry meat into value-added products. The cut-up operation is often done at the processing plant. However, some companies ship the whole carcasses to the further processing plant for specialized cut-up. Cut-up is where machines cut the whole carcass into individual parts. Deboning is where the bones are removed from specific parts to produce items like breast filets or other boneless products.

Value added refers to fabricating the carcass into consumer-ready products that requires additional time or labour. These products usually involve seasoning, breading, sauces, and marinating, as well as special packaging to meet market demands for convenient products. The added value result in higher margins and profits while providing a large product choice for the consumer.

5

Chicken Breeding

Modern varieties of chicken such as the Cornish Cross, are bred specifically for meat production, with an emphasis placed on the ratio of feed to meat produced by the animal. The most common breeds of chicken consumed in the US are Cornish and White Rock.

Chickens raised specifically for food are called broilers. In the United States, broilers are typically butchered at a young age. Modern Cornish Cross hybrids, for example, are butchered as early as 8 weeks for fryers and 12 weeks for roasting birds. Capons (castrated cocks) produce more and fattier meat. For this reason, they are considered a delicacy and were particularly popular in the Middle Ages.

The modem fowl is much superior with regard to its productive capacity, in terms of number and size of eggs and quality and quantity of meat, as compared to its ancestors. This has been made possible through the environment and the improved breeding methods. Poultry breeding is, thus, a scientific practice which aims at genetic improvement of the birds through successive generations by virtue of planned reproduction. A successful breeder should have adequate knowledge of the various qualities and capabilities of different breeds of poultry in order to select the right type of birds and to combine all the desirable qualities to a fairly high degree. Highly scientific breeding of poultry may not be possible in our villages. But an average farmer may follow the fundamental principles of scientific breeding that are practicable in the villages where they are properly instructed and guided. An effort is made here to discuss the various aspects of poultry breeding relevant to the village conditions, in a simple and systematic way.

BREEDING

Origins

The domestic chicken is descended primarily from the Red Junglefowl (*Gallus gallus*) and is scientifically classified as the same species. As such it can and does freely interbreed with populations of red jungle fowl. Recent genetic analysis has revealed that at least the gene for yellow skin was incorporated into domestic birds through hybridization with the Grey Junglefowl (*G. sonneratii*).

Researchers have found chickens' bones in unusual amounts and out of natural jungle range, thus denoting a breeding place. Bones of domestic chickens have been found about 6000-4000 BC in Yangshao and Peiligan, China, while the Holocene climate was not naturally suitable for the *Gallus* species. Archaeological data is lacking for Thailand and southeast Asia. Later traces are found about 3000-2000 BC in Harappa and Mohenjo-Daro, Pakistan, and-according to linguistic researchers-in Austronesian populations travelling across southeast Asia and Oceania. A northern road spread chicken to the Tarim basin of central Asia, modern day Iran. The chicken reached Europe (Romania, Turkey, Greece, Urkraine) about 3000BC, and the Indus Valley about 2500 BC. Introduction into Western Europe came far later, about the 1st millennium BC. Phoenicians spread chickens along the Mediterranean coasts, to Iberia. Breeding increased under the Roman Empire, and was reduced in the Middle Ages. Middle East traces of chicken go back to a little earlier than 2000 BC, in Syria; chicken went southward only in the 1st millennium BC. The chicken reached Egypt for purposes of cock fighting about 1400BC, and became widely bred only in Ptolemaic Egypt (about 300 BC). Little is known about the chicken's introduction into Africa. Three possible ways of introduction in about the early first millennium AD could have been through the Egyptian Nile Valley, the East Africa Roman-Greek or Indian trade, or from Carthage and the Berbers, across the Sahara. The earliest known remains are from Mali, Nubia, East Coast, and South Africa and date back to the middle of the first millennium AD. Domestic chicken in the Americas before Western conquest is still an ongoing discussion, but blue-egged chicken, found only in the Americas and Asia, suggest an Asian origin for early American chickens.

A lack of data from Thailand, Russia, the Indian subcontinent, Southeast Asia and Sub-Saharan Africa makes it difficult to lay out a clear map of the spread of chickens in these areas; better description and genetic analysis of local breeds threatened by extinction may also help with research into this area.

Poultry Farming

More than 50 billion chickens are reared annually as a source of food, for both their meat and their eggs. Chickens farmed for meat are called broiler chickens, whilst those farmed for eggs are called egg-laying hens. In total, the UK alone consumes over 29 million eggs per day. Some hens can produce over 300 eggs a year. Chickens will naturally live for 6 or more years, but broiler chickens typically take less than six weeks to reach slaughter size. For laying hens, they are slaughtered after about 12 months, when the hens' productivity starts to decline.

The vast majority of poultry are raised using intensive farming techniques. According to the Worldwatch Institute, 74 percent of the world's poultry meat, and 68 percent of eggs are produced this way. One alternative to intensive poultry farming is free range farming.

Friction between these two main methods has led to long term issues of ethical consumerism. Opponents of intensive farming argue that it harms the environment, creates human health risks and is inhumane. Advocates of intensive farming say that their highly efficient systems save land and food resources due to increased productivity, stating that the animals are looked after in state-of-the-art environmentally controlled facilities.

Artificial Incubation

Chicken egg incubation can successfully occur artificially as well. Nearly all fertilized chicken eggs will hatch after 21 days of good conditions-99.5 °F (37.5 °C) and around 55% relative humidity (increase to 70% in the last three days of incubation to help soften egg shell). Eggs must be turned regularly (usually three to eight times each week) during the first part of the incubation. If the eggs aren't turned, the embryo inside will stick to the shell and may hatch with physical defects. Some incubators turn the eggs automatically. This turning mimics the natural process. An incubating hen will stand up several times a day and shift the eggs around with her beak. However, if the egg is turned during the last week of incubation the chick may have difficulty settling in the correct hatching position. Many commercial incubators are industrial-sized with shelves holding tens of thousands of eggs at a time, with rotation of the eggs a fully automated process. Home incubators are boxes holding from half a dozen to 75 eggs; they are usually electrically powered, but in the past some were heated with an oil or paraffin lamp.

Chickens as Food

The meat of the chicken, also called "chicken", is a type of poultry meat. Because of its relatively low cost, chicken is one of the most used meats in the world. Nearly all parts of the bird can be used for food, and the meat can be cooked in many different ways. Popular chicken dishes include roasted chicken, fried chicken, chicken soup, Buffalo wings, tandoori chicken, butter chicken, and chicken rice. Chicken is also a staple of fast food restaurants.

Chickens as Pets

Chickens are sometimes kept as pets and can be tamed by hand feeding, but roosters can sometimes become aggressive and noisy. Some have advised against keeping them around very young children. Certain breeds, however, such as silkies and many bantam varieties are generally docile and are often recommended as good pets around children. Some people find chickens' behaviour entertaining and educational.

While some cities in the United States allow chickens as pets, the practice is not approved in all localities. Some communities ban only roosters, allowing the quieter hens. The so called "urban hen movement" harks back to the days when chicken keeping was much more common, and involves the keeping of small groups of hens in areas where they may not be expected, such as closely populated cities and suburban areas. City ordinances, zoning regulations or health boards may determine whether chickens may be kept. A general requirement is that the birds be confined to the owner's property, not allowed to roam freely. There may be strictures on the size of the property or how far from human dwellings a coop may be located, etc.

In Asia, chickens with striking plumage have long been kept for ornamental purposes, including feather-footed varieties such as the Cochin from Vietnam, the Silkie from China, and the extremely long-tailed Phoenix from Japan. Asian ornamental varieties were imported into the United States and Great Britain in the late 1800s. Distinctive American varieties of chickens have been developed from these Asian breeds. Poultry fanciers began keeping these ornamental birds for exhibition, a practice that continues today. Individuals in rural communities commonly keep chickens for both ornamental and practical value.

PRINCIPLES OF BREEDING

The fundamental principles of scientific breeding are as follows:

1. Breeding should be purposive and the breeder should know the purpose of the breeding and the standard to which the birds are to be bred. It may be for size, weight, egg production, meat quality or combination of these factors. For example, poorly bred or desi hens are often voracious feeders, but because they are not bred for egg production, they do not lay correspondingly large number of eggs. The efficiency of conversion of feed into the eggs is an inherited trait and can only be reproduced in the succeeding generations by careful selection and breeding.
2. Breeding should be done from parents which conform as closely as possible to the required standard.
3. In selection and mating, all the birds which fail to possess the desired standards should be discarded.
4. The parents selected for breeding should also be pure breeds.
5. For a successful breeding, selection must be practiced continuously and carefully, from the hatching to maturity.
6. Environment plays an important part in breeding. So a favourable condition should be created in respect of housing, feeding, sanitation and general care.
7. Pedigree breeding is an important practice wherein efficiency of matings can be measured and the selection and mating operations modified to ensure improvement But this is possible only in well-established farms, requiring lot of technical expertise, and accurate mating and breeding rewards.

Types of Mating

Mating is an act of joining cock with hen so that the hens may produce fertile eggs for hatching and multiplication. The number of female birds allowed to be served by a male bird depends upon the factors like breed, body weight, virility, season, age and physical condition of the male. For example, more females may be allowed for each male in the Leghorns (light breeds) than in the heavier breeds such as the Rhode Island Reds.

Similarly a young cockerel (young male} can be given more pullets than an old cock. More females can be allowed in the mating pen during spring than during winter (where the winters are very cold). In summer, mating should be suspended as fertility will be very poor and the birds get exhausted.

Matings are of several kinds viz. (1) pen mating, (2) flock mating, (3) stud mating, (4) alternating males, (5) artificial insemination. Artificial insemination may not be a feasible proposal for the village level poultry, as the villagers may not have the necessary infrastructure or expertise in this field.

Pen Mating

In this type of mating, ten hens are kept in a breeding pen and one cock is permitted to mate and live with them freely. Eggs collected, a week after letting in the cock, will normally be fertile.

Flock Mating

Here a large flock of hens is kept with a num ber of cocks in the proportion of one cock for every ten hens. But under confined conditions, the males develop a tendency to fight each other and generally one male becomes the aggressor preventing the others from mating. This may affect the fertility seriously. The eggs also cannot be traced to the cock concerned and so pedigree breeding is not possible. On the other hand, on a free range, there will not be much scope for fighting and the birds are free to run about. Flock mating is preferred where ordinary farm conditions are prevalent and no pedigree breeding is undertaken. It also permits housing for a large number of fowls as one unit and thereby reduces the overhead costs.

Stud Mating

Stud mating consists of keeping the cocks and hen in separate pens or confining the males in separate coops in the pen of the females. The hens are let into the male's pen one by one at intervals, and after mating they are removed to their own pen.

Alternate Males

In this method two males are used for mating, but only one is allowed to serve the hens at a time for one full day, while the other is confined to the coop. The following day the male that had been employed is removed to the coop, and the second one is let in with the flock. In this method, too, the paternity of the off-spring cannot be determined.

POULTRY BREEDS

Ameraucana: the American Easter Egg Bird

The Ameraucana is an American made bird that lays blue eggs of various shades. It was developed from the Chilean Araucana breed with the intent to get rid of the lethal allele combination.

Class: Standard: All Other Standard Breeds Bantam: All other Combs, Clean Legged

Size: Standard Male: 6.5 Ibs. / Standard Female: 5.5 Ibs. Bantam Male: 30 oz. / Bantam Female: 26 oz.

Comb, Wattles & Earlobes: Pea comb with small or absent wattles and small round earlobes. All are red.

Colour: Eyes are reddish brown and the beak is horn to dark horn unless otherwise noted. Shanks are slate coloured and bottoms of feet and toes are white, unless noted otherwise.

Black: Standard black plumage, including beard and muffs, black beak, with shanks being dark slate to black. Bottoms of feet and toes are still white.

Blue: Standard blue plumage.

Blue Wheaten: Male: Plumage is predominately blue (ranging from dark blue to bluish gray) highlighted with striking orange contrasts, including light orange on head and back of neck, bright reddish orange on back, golden orange on saddle, and orange stripe on bow of wings. Female: Plumage is highlighted by wheaten shades (tans to golden yellows) with hints of light blue on tail and wings and very light grayish blue beard and muffs.

Brown Red: Standard brown-red plumage.

Buff: Standard buff plumage.

Silver: Standard silver plumage. Male: black beard and muffs. Female: Light gray beard and muffs, salmon at lower extremity of beard.

Wheaten: Standard wheaten plumage.

White: Standard white plumage. Light horn beak.

Place of Origin: United States

Conservation Status: Not applicable

Special Qualities: Lays blue eggs that vary in shades of blue.

The modern breed of the Ameraucana was developed in the United States in the 1970's. Breeders began developing this bird to gain a bird that layed coloured eggs that did not have the lethal allele combination trait that the Araucana birds have.

The breed has good looking birds that have a medium length tail, muffs, and a relatively small pea comb. They do have a somewhat stocky build and large eyes. These birds are good egg layers and can usually have an impressively long laying season without the need to use artificial light to keep the birds laying year round. They are also a quite hardy and active breed with a good temperment.

They were first admitted into the APA in 1984.

Ancona Chickens: A Good Egg Layer

Ancona chickens are closely related to the Leghorn breed. They tend to lay longer into the winter without supplemental light than most breeds.

Class: Standard: Mediterranean / Bantam: Single Comb, Clean Legged and Rose Combed, Clean Legged

Size: Standard Male: 6 Ibs. / Standard Female: 4.5 Ibs. / Bantam Male: 26 oz. / Bantam Female: 22 oz.

Comb, Wattles & Earlobes: There are two varieties based on comb.

Single Comb: Bright red, medium size red combhas five distinct points. *Male:* All five points stand upright. *Female:* First point stands upright; other four droop to one side.

Rose Comb: Bright red, medium size red rose sits square in front.

Their wattles are bright red and their earlobes are white. *Male:* Long, well-rounded wattles and smal almond shaped earlobes, close to head. *Female:* Medium well-rounded wattles and oval earlobes close to the head.

Colour: They have a yellow beak, though some have black or horn shading at the centre. They have reddish brown eyes and their shanks and toes are yellow, though yellow mottled with black is acceptable. The plumage is shiny greenish black with white speckling on the tips for the feathers. These are distributed evenly and fequently across the body.

Place of Origin: Italy

Conservation Status: Threatened

Special Qualities: Lays long into the winter without artificial light.

This breed originated along the Italian coast and made their way to Britain in the mid-nineteenth century and soon thereafter to the United States. Ancona Chickens are closely related to the Leghorns. When they first arrived in the U.S. some even referred to them as "Mottled Leghorns."

Much like the Leghorns, they are excellent layers of large white eggs. The hens are not known to be broody. The breed is considered to be very hardy and the birds are very active. They are excellent foragers as well and could be excellent free range birds. Their alert activity and their black colouring also make them excellent birds where there are chances of birds of prey, such as hawks and owls. These alert birds can hold their own.

The APA admitted the single comb variety in 1898 and the rose comb variety in 1914.

Andalusian Chickens: The Graceful Bird

Andalusian Chickens have an ornamental layer. When you mate blue parents they have a hybrid Characteristic that can yield black, splash, and blue chicks.

Andalusian Chickens The Facts:

Class: Standard: Mediterranean / Bantam: Single Comb, Clean Legged.

Size: Standard Male: 7 Ibs. / Standard Female: 5.5 Ibs. / Bantam Male: 28 oz. / Bantam Female: 24 oz.

Comb, Wattles & Earlobes: The comb is single with five distinct points. It is medium-sized. *Male:* All five points stand upright. *Female:* The first point stands upright and the other four droop to the side. The wattles are moderately long, thin, smooth, bright red and medium sized. The earlobes are almond-shaped and bright white.

Colour: They have a horn beak with dark slate shanks and toes. They have standard blue plumage.

Place of Origin: Spain

Conservation Status: Critical

Special Qualities: Hybrid characteristics.

These birds originate from Andalusia, Spain and took this name on after being called the Blue Minorca for a time.

The breeders that began this old breed (some trace it back to ancient Rome) began by crossing black with whites.

This produced a bird that had a blue colour and feathers that were laced with a darker blue colour. When they then bred these birds together the hybrid trait began and their offspring would range from black, blue, and splash in colour.

The blacks and splashes are not eligible to be shown, but they can be used for breeding stock. Keeping a good line of these birds going can be quite a challenge at times.

This reality is part of the reason that the breed is at the critical conservation level. It takes work to keep a good blue flock going.

Modern Andalusian Chickens are beautiful birds who have graceful movements and carries itself with their chest upright. The hens produce large chalky white eggs and rarely go broody.

The birds are large, rather active, and often very talkative. They are also rugged and healthy. This breed is not meant for confinement, but they excel in free range conditions.

The breed was first admitted into the APA in 1874.

The American Game Bantam: The Showy Bird

The American Game Bantam is a sprightly bird that is showy, yet easy for beginners to handle.

American Game Bantam Facts

Size: Male: 30 oz. / Female: 27 oz.

Comb, Wattles & Earlobes: They have a small single comb with five points that stand upright. They have small, thin, and smooth wattles and earlobes. They are all bright red unless otherwise noted. The comb, wattles, and earlobes are dubbed (removed) in cocks for show.

Colour:

Birchen: The comb, wattles, and earlobes are mulberry and the beak is black. The eyes are dark brown and the shanks and toes are black. They have standard birchen plumage.

Black: The comb, wattles, and earlobes are mulberry and the beak is black. The eyes are dark brown and the shanks and toes are black. They have standard black plumage.

Black-Breasted Red: The beak is dark horn streaked with black and the eyes are red. The shanks and toes are a bluishslate. They have standard black-breasted red plumage.

Blue: The beak is dark horn streaked with black and the eyes are red. The shanks and toes are a bluish slate colour. They have standard blue plumage.

Blue Red: The beak is dark horn streaked with black and the eyes are red. The shanks and toes are a bluish slate colour. They have standard blue red plumage.

Brassy Back: The beak is a dark horn streaked with black and the eyes are red. The shanks and toes are bluish slate. *Male:* The head, hackle, and saddle are brassy (lustrous yellow) with a black stripe down the centre of each feather. The back is lustrous brass and the front of the neck, breast, body, wings, tail, and legs are black to lustrous black. *Female:* Primarily chocolate to chocolaty black, with some brassiness on the hackle and back.

Brown Red: The beak is black and the eyes are dark brown. The shanks and toes are black. They have standard brown red plumage.

Golden Duckwing: The beak is dusky horn and the eyes are red. The shanks and toes are a bluish slate. They have standard golden duckwing plumage.

Red Pyle: The beak is horn and the eyes are red. The shanks and toes are pinkish slate. They have standard red pyle plumage.

Silver Duckwing: The beak is dusky horn and the eyes are red. The shanks and toes are a bluish slate colour. They have standard silver duckwing plumage.

Wheaten: The beak is dusky horn and the eyes are red. The shanks and toes are bluish slate. They have standard wheaten plumage.

White: The beak is horn and the eyes are red. The shanks and toes are pinkish slate. They have standard white plumage.

Place of Origin: New Jersey

Conservation Status: N/A

Special Qualities: A sprightly, showy bird that is easy for beginners to handle.

Frank Gary, a new Jersey Breeder, is credited with coming up with this breed of chicken. Gary began trying to craft this show bird in the 1940's by breeding a common "pit game" bantam (a small fighting bird) with Red Jungle Fowl. Some were showing these Pit Game Bantams at the time, but they were not recognised by any organisation.

Gary's goal was to develop a standard breed that would be recognised and he accomplished this. The APA still does not recognise the American Game Bantam, but they are recognised by the ABA. He accomplished standardizing the traits such as the colour of the legs and earlobes and extra length on the plumage of the hackle.

The American Game Bantams are hardy and vigorous birds. The females are good layers that go broody and are exceptional mothers. These birds can tolerate confinement better than most game birds, but the males should not be confined together as they will fight.

Appenzeller Chickens: The Showy Swiss Breed

Appenzeller Chickens are an ornamental breed that comes from Switzerland. There are two types that are known as the Spitzhauben and the Barthuhner.

Size: Standard Male: 4.5 Ibs. / Standard Female: 3.5 Ibs. / Bantam Male: 24 oz. / Bantam Female: 20 oz. Comb, Wattles & Earlobes: They have a red V-shaped comb that is moderately large and oblong red wattles. The earlobes are moderately large and white. *Colour:* The beak is dark horn and the eyes are dark brown. The shanks and toes are blue.

Black: They have standard black plumage.

Golden Spangled: Standard golden spangled plumage.

Silver Spangled: Standard silver spangled plumage.

Place of Origin: Switzerland

Conservation Status: N/A

Special Qualities: An ornamental layer with an interesting top hat.

There are two types of this breed. The first is the Spitzhauben which has a rather funky looking top hat that sticks straight up and doesn't cover the eyes as much as the Polish breeds. The Barthuhner is the other. Neither of these are recognised by the APA or ABA. In North America, you can find the Spitzhauben from some breeders, but the Barhuhner is almost non-existent.

These are very active birds that are good fliers. They can take care of themselves and are great free range birds and foragers.They often roost in trees if allowed to do so. Considering these traits, they do not do well in confinement.

The hens lay a fair amount of medium-size white eggs and will occassionally go broody.

The Unique Araucana Chickens

Araucana Chickens most unique quality is the colour of it's eggs. They can range from an aqua blue colour togreen hues and even pink or yellow.

Class: Standard All other standard breeds. Bantam All other combs, Clean legged.

Size: Standard Male: 5 Ibs. / Standard Female: 4 Ibs. Bantam Male: 26 oz. / Bantam Female: 24 oz.

Comb, Wattles & Earlobes: Small pea comb; wattles are very small or absent; earlobes are very small and smooth and covered by an ear tuft. All are bright red. Another destinction of this breed is the absence of a tail. Saddle feathers flow over the rump.

Colour:

Black: Black beak, shanks and toes; brown eyes; standard black plumage.

Black-Breasted Red: Horn beak with reddish bay eyes and grayish yellow shanks and toes. Male: Head, hackle, and saddle are reddish changing to gold at lower extremities. Front of neck and breast are lustrous black. Tail and wings are black with reddish bay highlights. Undercolour is slate. Female: Head and hackle are reddish chestnut against a light brown body. Tails and wings have some black. Undercolour is slate to light brown. *Blue:* Standard blue plumage.

Buff: Standard buff plumage.

Golden Duckwing: Horn beak with red eyes and willow shanks and toes. Standard duckwing plumage.

Silver: Standard silver plumage.

Silver Duckwing: Horn beak with red eyes and willow shanks and toes. Standard silver duckwing plumage.

White: Yellow beak, shanks, and toes with red eyes. Standard white plumage.

Place of Origin: Chile

Conservation Status: Study

Special Qualities: Lays multi-coloured eggs, sometimes referred to as Easter eggs because of their varying colours.

Araucana Chickens were developed in Chile in the early 1900's. They are a very unique breed. They were developed bya professor of animal science. He took ancient birds kept by a native Chilean tribe and bred them into the breed.

Besides the colour of their eggs, some other interesting attributes of the breed are their lack of a tail and the factthat their earlobes are partially hidden by tuft feathers. These traits can be traced back to these birds being crossed withthe Collonca, who had no tail and the Quetero, which had tufts at their ears. The colour of their eggs also come from the Collonca breed that laid blue eggs.

When crossed with any other breed of chicken the Araucana Chickens offspring will produce a variety of coloured eggs from greenishblue to green, pink, and yellow. This is how the breed really took off in the 1970's as hatcheries advertised the Easter eggbirds that laid multi-coloured eggs.

The breed was first introduced into the APA in 1976.

Aseel: The Ancient Breed

The Aseel chicken Breed is an almost prehistoric looking bird. The breed probably is over two-thousand years old and it is probably the gameiest of all game birds. They will fight at the drop of a hat.

Class: All Other Standard Breeds

Size: Male: 5.5 Ibs. Female: 4 Ibs.

Comb, Wattles & Earlobes: They have a small bright red pea comb and earlobes with no wattles.

Colour: The beak is yellow to horn and the eyes are pearl. The shanks and toes are yellow.

Black-Breasted Red: They have standard black-breasted red plumage.

Dark: They have standard dark plumage.

Spangled: They have standard spangled plumage.

Wheaten: They have standard wheaten plumage.

White: They have standard white plumage.

Place of Origin: India

Conservation Status: Critical

Special Qualities: They are the parent to the Cornish breed we know today. They are very aggressive.

Game birds were originally developed for fighting and the Aseel may be the top of the class. It is definitely one of the oldest game breeds and has been bred in India and surrounding countries for over two-thousand years. The breed was bred to fight with it's natural strength and sharp spurs.

The breeds fighting traits are so strong that it is said that chicks will fight almost immediately after hatching. Cocks must be seperated from all other males as they will fight to the death. Although the hens are also quite aggressive for hens, they seem to be calmer when they are kept with less aggressive breeds. The hens are excelent mothers and do go broody.

The breed is absolutely not suited for an inexperienced poultry person or a mixed flock situation. There is a real need for enthusiasts to keep the breed alive in North American though. Although we do not fight birds, this bird was the root of the Cornish breed, and is very important to the preservation of many other breeds. They are important to keep around. This breed stands very tall with high shoulders and a tail that sits below horizontal. They are remarkably athletic and have tight feathering.

They were first admitted into the APA in 1981.

Australorps: The Australian Bird

Australorps are a very good all purpose breed of chicken. They have a relatively meaty body and are very good layers as well.

Australorp Facts:

Class: Standard English

Size: Standard Male: 8.5 Ibs. / Standard Female: 6.5 Ibs.

Bantam Male: 30 oz. / Bantam Female: 26 oz.

Comb, Wattles and Earlobes: Moderately large single comb with five evenly spaced, perfectly straight points. Front point is smallest. Oblong, smooth earlobes. Male: Medium size, smooth round wattles. Female: Small, well rounded wattles.All bright red.

Colour: Black beak; dark brown eyes; shanks are black to dark slate; bottoms of feet and toes are pinkish white. Standard black plumage.

Place of Origin: Australia

Conservation Status: Recovering

Special Qualities: Good dual purpose bird that has a relatively meaty body for a layer.

The Australops were originated from Black Orphintons that were imported to Australia from England in the late 1890's and early 1900's.

These Black Orphingtons were crossed with a variety of Minorca, White Leghorn, Plymouth Rock, and Langshan breeds to come up with the final mix. It is now Australia's unofficial national breed of chicken.

The breeders that came up with the Australorp focused on utility. Today, that is still what the breed is known for. It is a great dual purpose bird that has a meaty body, but can also lay two hundred plus eggs a year as well. Sometimes called Black Australorps as well, the breed matures early and is considered to be docile, quiet birds. Theyhave loose and fluffy feathers that make them weather hardy as well. They were first admitted into the APA in 1929.

Barnevelder: The Layer Of Copper Eggs

The Barnevelder chicken breed has a lovely shiny colour to their plumage and lays coppery brown eggs.

Barnevelder Facts:

Class: Standard: Continental / Bantam: Not Recognised

Size: Male: 7 Ibs. / Female: 6 Ibs.

Comb, Wattles & Earlobes: They have a single comb with straight, upright, well-defined points. They have a medium size wattle and earlobes. They are all bright red in colour.

Colour: They have a horn coloured beak, reddish bay eyes, and yellow shanks and toes. *Male:* The head, neck, and back have black feathers laced with bronze. The saddle and breast have bronze feathers laced with a lustrous greenish black.Their tail is greenish black and the wings are black and bronze. The overall affect by the colouring is dark, but glistening. Female: The head and hackle are greenish black. The front of the neck, back, breast, and wings are primarily bronze with lacing of greenish black. The tail is black. The female seems to shimmer in the sunlight.

Place of Origin: Holland

Conservation Status: N/A

Special Qualities: They have a lovely colouring and lay coppery brown eggs.

This breed comes from the region of the Netherlands with the same name. This region has long been the poultry area of Holland. They developed the breed by crossing Asiatic breeds such as Brahma, Cochin, Langshan, and Maleier. The breeders were seeking to increase egg production of brown eggs, and to give the brown eggs a coppery tinge.

There are four different varieties of this bird in the Netherlands, but only one of those is recognised by the APA. The one described here is rather showy with a unique iridescent sheen to it.

The breed was first recognised by the APA in 1991.

Bearded D'Anvers Bantam: The True Bantam

The Bearded D'Anvers Bantam chicken breed is only available as a bantam with no standard sized counterpart. They are a good layer of small white eggs.

Bearded D'Anvers Bantam Facts:

Class: Rose Comb, Clean Legged

Size: Male: 26 oz. Female: 22 oz.

Comb, Wattles & Earlobes: The rose comb is small and covered with rounded points. Breeders prefer birds with small or absent wattles. The earlobes are flat and almond shaped but generally hidden by the muffs. All of these are bright red.

Colour: The beak is various shades of horn and the eyes are reddish bay, unless otherwise noted. The beards and muffs are the same colour as the plumage, unless otherwise noted.

Black: The eyes are black and the shanks and toes are bluish black to slate. They have standard black plumage.

Black-Breasted Red: The beards and muffs are black and the shanks and toes light slaty blue. They have standard black-breasted red plumage.

Blue: The eyes are dark brown and the shanks and toes are bluish to black slate. They have standard blue plumage.

Blue Quail: The eyes are dark brown and the beard and muffs are brownish yellow. The shanks and toes are slaty blue. *Male:* The head, hackle, back, and saddle are brilliant bluish black laced with golden bay. The breast, body, and leg feathers are brownish yellow laced with a more intense shade of brownish yellow and straw shaft. The tail and wings are blue to black with some lacing. *Female:* The head is bluish black tinged with yellow. The hackle and back are blue to bluish black laced with golden bay. The breast, body, and leg feathers are brownish yellow laced with a lighter shade of brownish yellow and straw shaft. The tail and wings are blue to black with some lacing.

Buff: The shanks and toes are slaty white. They have standard buff plumage.

Buff Columbian: The shanks and toes are slaty blue and they have standard buff Columbian plumage.

Columbian: The beard and muffs are buff and the shanks and toes are slaty blue. They have standard Columbian plumage.

Cuckoo: They have bright red eyes and bluish white shanks and toes. They have standard cuckoo plumage.

Mille Fleur: The shanks and toes are slaty blue and they; have standard mille fleur plumage.

Mottled: The shanks and toes are slate and they have standard mottled plumage.

Porcelain: The shanks and toes are light slaty blue and they have standard porcelain plumage.

Quail: They have dark brown eyes and slate blue shanks and toes. The beard and muffs are brownish yellow. *Male:* The head, hackle, back, saddle, and wings are brilliant black laced with golden bay. The front of theneck, breast, body, and legs are brownish yellow. The tail is black. *Female:* The head is chocolaty black tinged with yellow. The neck is lustrous chocolaty black laced with golden bay. The front of the neck, breast, and body are brownish yellow laced with a lighter shade of the same colour. The tail and wings are chocolaty black laced with light brownish yellow.

Self Blue: The eyes are brown and the shanks and toes are slate. They have standard self blue plumage.

White: The shanks and toes are slaty blue to pinkish gray. They have standard white plumage.

Place of Origin: Belgium

Conservation Status: N/A

Special Qualities: They are only available as a bantam.

The Bearded D'Anvers Bantam are a true bantam that were once known as the Begium Antwerp. They are an old breed. Their ancestory is unclear, but evidence does indicate that their ancestors were present in the Netherlands and Belgium since the middle of the 1600's. By the mid-1800's, the selection was well underway for several of the varieties that are present today. Their popularity continued to increase through the first half of the twentieth century as many fanciers took to the breed.

As the name implies, the Bearded D'Anvers Bantam is bearded with thick muffs that cover the earlobes. It is an active breed, but can do alright in small areas and does tame down rather easily. The hens lay small white eggs and will go broody. The beard is unique in its asymmetric body. It stands tall and carries it's weight forward.

The Bearded D'Anvers Bantam was first admitteed to the APA in 1949.

Bearded d'Uccle: The Belgium Bird

The Bearded d'Uccle is only available as a bantam chicken and is a good layer of small eggs.

EMBRYOLOGY

In 2006, scientists researching the ancestry of birds "turned on" a chicken recessive gene, *talpid2*, and found that the embryo jaws initiated formation of teeth, like those found in ancient bird fossils. John Fallon, the overseer of the project, stated that chickens have "...retained the ability to make teeth, under certain conditions...."

BREEDING ORIGINS

The domestic chicken is descended primarily from the red junglefowl (*Gallus gallus*) and is scientifically classified as the same species.As such it can and does freely interbreed with populations of red jungle fowl. Recent genetic analysis has revealed that at least the gene for yellow skin was incorporated into domestic birds through hybridization with the grey junglefowl (*G. sonneratii*). The traditional poultry farming view is that chickens were first domesticated for cockfighting in Asia, Africa, and Europe, rather than for egg or meat production. In the last decade there have been a number of genetic studies to clarify the origins. According to one study, a single domestication event occurring in the region of modern Thailand created the modern chicken with minor transitions separating the modern breeds. However, that study was later found to be based on incomplete data, and recent studies point to multiple maternal origins, with the clade found in the Americas, Europe, Middle East, and Africa, originating from the Indian subcontinent, where a large number of unique haplotypes occur. It is postulated that the jungle fowl, known as the bamboo fowl in many Southeast Asian languages, is a special pheasant well adapted to take advantage of the large amounts of fruits that are produced during the end of the 50-year bamboo seeding cycle to boost its own reproduction. In domesticating the chicken, humans took advantage of this prolific reproduction of the jungle fowl when exposed to large amounts of food.

It has been claimed (based on paleoclimatic assumptions) that chickens were domesticated in Southern China in 6000 BC.However, according to a recent study, it is unclear whether those birds were the ancestors of chickens today. Instead, the origin could be the Harappan culture of the Indus Valley. Eventually, the chicken moved to the Tarim basin of central Asia. The chicken reached Europe (Romania, Turkey, Greece, Ukraine) about 3000 BC. Introduction into Western Europe came far later, about the 1st millennium BC. Phoenicians spread chickens along the Mediterranean coasts, to Iberia. Breeding increased under the Roman Empire, and was reduced in the Middle Ages. Middle East traces of chicken go back to a little earlier than 2000 BC, in Syria; chicken went southward only in the 1st millennium BC. The chicken reached Egypt for purposes of cock fighting about 1400 BC, and became widely bred only in Ptolemaic Egypt (about 300 BC). Little is known about the chicken's introduction into Africa. Three possible routes of introduction in about the early first millennium AD could have been through the Egyptian Nile Valley, the East Africa Roman-Greek or Indian trade, or from Carthage and the Berbers, across the Sahara. The earliest known remains are from Mali, Nubia, East Coast, and South Africa and date back to the middle of the first millennium AD. Domestic chicken in the Americas before Western conquest is still an ongoing discussion, but blue-egged chickens, found only in the Americas and Asia, suggest an Asian origin for early American chickens.

A lack of data from Thailand, Russia, the Indian subcontinent, Southeast Asia and Sub-Saharan Africa makes it difficult to lay out a clear map of the spread of chickens in these areas; better description and genetic analysis of local breeds threatened by extinction may also help with research into this area.

South America

An unusual variety of chicken that has its origins in South America is the araucana, bred in southern Chile by the Mapuche people. Araucanas, some of which are tailless and some of which have tufts of feathers around their ears, lay blue-green eggs. It has long been suggested that they pre-date the arrival of European chickens brought by theSpanish and are evidence of pre-Columbian trans-Pacific contacts between Asian or Pacific Oceanic peoples, particularly the Polynesians, and South America.

In 2007, an international team of researchers reported the results of analysis of chicken bones found on the Arauco Peninsula in south-central Chile. Radiocarbon dating suggested that the chickens were Pre-Columbian, and DNA analysis showed that they were related to prehistoric populations of chickens in Polynesia. These results appeared to confirm that the chickens came from Polynesia and that there were transpacific contacts between Polynesia and South America before Columbus's arrival in the Americas.

However, a later report looking at the same specimens concluded:

A published, apparently pre-Columbian, Chilean specimen and six pre-European Polynesian specimens also cluster with the same European/Indian subcontinental/Southeast Asian sequences, providing no support for a Polynesian introduction of chickens to South America. In contrast, sequences from two archaeological sites on Easter Island group with an uncommon haplogroup from Indonesia, Japan, and China and may represent a genetic signature of an early Polynesian dispersal. Modeling of the potential marine carbon contribution to the Chilean archaeological specimen casts further doubt on claims for pre-Columbian chickens, and definitive proof will require further analyses of ancient DNA sequences and radiocarbon and stable isotope data from archaeological excavations within both Chile and Polynesia.

FEEDING BREEDERS TO OPTIMISE CHICK QUALITY

Integration concentrates the majority of their energy and technical resources on broiler production. Breeders generally do not receive the attention they deserve. Integrators are looking to maximise egg and chick production at the lowest cost with insufficient attention being given to the quality of the chick.

There is an abundance of evidence that confirms that breeder nutrition directly impacts the progeny. However, these impacts are generally difficult to measure under commercial conditions and even under controlled trial conditions they may be obscured.

The obsession with lowering feed cost has, I believe, led us to a point where some nutrients, like vitamins and trace minerals are marginal in modern breeders. While, others like crude protein are generally fed in considerable excess and this profoundly affects breeder performance and health.

Due to fierce competition and the subsequent low profit margins, vitamin producers are reluctant to invest resources in research, so little breeder vitamin and trace mineral research has been conducted over the past 15 to 20 years. In addition, the current benchmarking practices have pressured the industry in lowering cost wherever possible.

Fifteen years ago, breeders were generally peak fed 165 to 170 grams per bird per day with peak egg production at 65 to 70 per cent. Today, the majority of breeders receive 145 to 150 grams of feed at peak with peak production at 80 to 90 per cent – this on reduced vitamin and trace mineral levels.

Measuring breeder nutrition impact on progeny is difficult due to a number of factors. Firstly, the assumption is that all birds receive the allocated feed amount; this certainly is not the case with 30- to 40-gram differences between birds being common. The birds that will be nutrient-limiting are those that are the most severely restricted. This may only be five per cent of the flock, so when assessing the commercial performance between two nutritional regimens it is difficult to have a large enough sample to be able to measure the impact. Secondly, some of the effects may only be apparent under stress conditions. Small or no differences may be seen under trial or ideal commercial conditions, but under a stress (disease, low broiler nutrient levels, chilling), the responses will be more apparent.

The Nutritionist's Role in Breeder Nutrition

Since breeders are restrict fed, it is the nutritionists responsibility to design a feed that meets the nutrient requirements of the bird under their particular set of conditions of; egg production, environmental temperature, etc. and then to ensure that that the highest quality ingredients are used in these feeds and that the feeds remain constant over time. Since the birds are restrict fed, the breeder manager needs to 'learn' how to feed the birds. With constantly changing feeds this makes every flock a new experiment, which makes it difficult to manage body weights and uniformity.

Birds do not understand percentages. Producers focus on the nutrient composition of the feed. The most common question I hear is, "What crude protein and energy level should I be feeding?" We need to understand the daily nutrient needs of the bird for a particular environment, given amount of activity and egg production. We then need to know what feeding system is being used and how well feed is distributed to the birds. Once we have this information we know daily need for: kcals of ME, mg of amino acid, grams of calcium etc that the bird requires and how many grams we need to feed it. Then we can formulate the feed to meet these requirements.

Energy and Fat

Energy is a fuel for maintaining basic metabolism, mobility and egg production. Energy is not a nutrient as such but is the result of metabolic oxidation of energy yielding nutrients – carbohydrates, fats and proteins. Having reviewed a large number of breeder formulations, energy appears to be the fist limiting 'nutrient'. This is true under both hot and temperate environments. Under hot conditions fat is helpful as a source of readily available energy, to help with the increased energy demand for increased rate of respiration – panting. Under more temperate conditions, carbohydrates are the preferred source of energy as they are not as readily metabolised and do generate additional heat during metabolism (heat increment). Fat composition and quality is important for the breeder and progeny. Essential free fatty acids are required for cell membrane integrity, immune competence, fertility and embryonic development.

It is well documented that maternal feed fat composition directly influences the fat composition of the egg. This includes fatty acid profile and fat soluble vitamins. Wang et al. (2002) were able to show that maternal dietary polyunsaturated fatty acids (PUFAs) affected the PUFA levels in the spleen of progeny. They also demonstrated feeding Omega 3 fatty acids to the breeder resulted in higher Omega 3 fatty acid levels and immune responses in progeny. The immune response was measured by reduced wing swelling in birds injected with bovine serum albumin. Some other effects of vitamin supplementation will be addressed under the vitamin section.

Crude Protein and Amino Acids

Crude protein is a measurement of the nitrogen content of a feed or an ingredient, assuming that amino acids are the source of measured nitrogen.

Crude protein does not give us any information about the amino acid composition and or availability. Modern nutritionists should only formulate feeds on digestible amino acid levels, using crude protein solely as means of easily analysing blended feeds to ensure correct blending.

Commercial feeds are generally still formulated to minimum crude protein levels, which results in feeds that, with the exception of TSAA (total sulphur amino acids), have amino acids significantly higher than required. The critical amino acids in breeder nutrition are methionine (TSAA), tryptophan, lysine and isoleucine. Methionine and tryptophan directly impact egg size and egg production. A corn/soy diet has excess lysine and isoleucine. When formulating to minimum crude protein levels, the lysine levels are often up to 40 per cent above requirement. Work by Lopez and Leeson (1995) clearly illustrated the negative effect of excess crude protein on fertility and DeBeer and Coon (2006) identified lysine and isoleucine as two amino acids directly affecting the fertility of breeders.

Minerals

All nutritionists are aware of the critical importance of the macro minerals; calcium, available phosphorus, etc. on bone and egg shell integrity. However, there is very good evidence that maternal levels of trace minerals especially zinc, manganese, copper and selenium impact levels in the egg and influence progeny. This is not new research; hen feeds deficient in zinc were shown by Edwards et al, (1959) to cause slow growth of chicks; Turk et al. (1959) to cause weak chicks, poor feathering and high mortality; and Kidd et al. (1992) showed supplementing with inorganic and/ or organic Zn increased levels of Zn in the bones and increased bone weight.

In addition to Zn's role in DNA and enzymes, Zn is particularly important in the young bird in the synthesis of two key proteins: collagen and keratin (Underwood and Suttle, 2001). Keratin is a structural protein in skin and feathers. Collagen is the major structural protein of internal tissues, including cartilage and bone. The cost of ensuring a sufficient and an available Zn source in breeder and early broiler feeds is minimal considering the impact of poor skeletal development and compromised immunity on the profitability of broiler production. As with Zn, Mn, Cu and Se levels can be affected in the egg by maternal supplementation. Manganese is vital in embryonic and post-natal bone development. Cu is essential for reproduction and development. Se has a sparing effect on vitamin E as an antioxidant.

Vitamins

Although severe vitamin deficiencies will cause a wide variety of deformities and severely affect hatch, grossly underfeeding vitamins is not commonly seen in practice. It is the marginal deficiencies caused either by low supplementation, sources of questionable quality/ availability and less dominant breeders consuming less than calculated feed quantities. The progeny will not exhibit classical deficiency syndromes, but they will not perform to their potential. Aviagen conducted a study to asses the impact on progeny where Vitamins E, K and B vitamins were supplemented at 20 per cent above Aviagen breeder recommendation. Although broiler body weights were only 20 grams heavier at term, mortality of the supplemented group was 2.2 per cent lower than the control birds, with a yield advantage of 0.2 per cent at 2kg body weight.

Egg yolk vitamin E levels were measured and a 50 per cent increase in α-tocopherol seen. In addition, candling clears at 60 and 64 weeks of age were 12.2 vs. 17.3 and 17.9 vs. 26.9 per cent per cent for the higher supplementation group.

Adequate vitamin and trace mineral supplementation with quality vitamins and available minerals is an inexpensive way to ensure that the young chick is prepared for optimal skeletal growth and a healthy immune system, to help deal with challenges during brooding.

Amino Acids and Enteritis in Broiler Chickens

An intact healthy gut is vital to the health and welfare of young chickens. The gut as a multi-cellular organ; has absorptive enterocytes, goblet cells for mucin production; immune cells and an intrinsic neural system. The gut is the first line of defence against, dietary toxins and enteric pathogen invasion. According to Reed (2001) more than 65 per cent of dietary threonine is used in gut function; the threonine content of mucin is excess of 30 per cent. Enteritis results in considerable loss of mucin, studies have shown that threonine will be partitioned away from protein deposition to support the gut and mucin production.

To demonstrate the importance of threonine under enteric stress, a threonine dose response study was conducted to evaluate the impact of L-threonine on enteritis in broiler chickens. Birds were reared to 14 days on a coccidiostat-free, corn/soy feed with increasing levels of added L-threonine (at lysine to threonine ratios from 64 to 72). At 14 days, the birds were challenged with *Clostridium perfringens* and grown to 42 days of age. Body weights of the challenged birds at the higher threonine levels showed a positive response at 31 days and were similar at 42 days. Breast meat yield on the high treatment was similar between the challenged and control groups at 42 days. This study supports the theory that animals will partition threonine away from muscle protein to support gut health and mucin production (Ajinomoto Heartland 2003).

Breeder nutrition directly affects the health, egg production and fertility of the birds. There is considerable evidence that breeder nutrition affects the progeny. Although we seldom see the gross deformities of severe nutrient deficiencies, it would appear that current nutrient levels, particularly trace mineral and certain vitamins are marginal particularly for those less aggressive birds that are unable to consume their expected feed allotment. It is these subtle deficiencies that could benefit from proper supplementation of these nutrients.

Overfeeding of crude protein:

1. Costs money; a recent evaluation indicated around $3.00 per ton.
2. Results in additional heat increment, which contributes to the heat load under heat stress conditions. New high yield breeds are particular sensitive to heat stress and nutritionists need to help minimise this stress.
3. Negatively affects fertility
4. Excess protein is excreted, and elevates the nitrogen in the faeces. High nitrogen in the litter results in foot pad lesions and excess ammonia, which can irritate mucus membranes of the eyes a respiratory tract.

Breeder hens are producing the broiler chicks that are the basis of our business. Feeding them correctly will result in healthy, virile chicks, which will have the immune system and skeletal framework required to deal with challenges and achieve their growth potential. The increase in cost of feeding a breeder hen properly compared to the total cost of producing a mature broiler chicken is marginal.

6

Chicken Feeding

Precocial birds retain internal yolk sacs after hatching, which help to sustain them while they are learning how and what to eat. Altricial birds normally use up their yolk before hatching and are fed by their parents, so most species will require food within 4 h. Parent birds have a variety of strategies for feeding chicks and it is vital to be aware of the feeding behaviour of a species when hand-rearing birds. Many precocial species such as ducks and shore birds are self-feeding and learn by trial and error; others such as quail lead their young to individual items; and others uncover food for their chicks by scratching the ground (e.g. fowl) or by cutting vegetation (e.g. swans). Altricial birds and some precocial or semi-precocial species such as auks (Alcidae) and gulls (Laridae) are fed by the parents directly placing food into their mouths or regurgitating food in front of them (O'Connor 1984).

When hand-rearing birds, the literature must be consulted to see how naturally reared chicks of that species are fed, and the hatchlings must be provided with food accordingly, teaching them how to feed if necessary. Another important consideration is that chicks may be fed different sized food items at different stages of development: for example, young bull finches (*Pyrrh ula pyrrh ula)* are fed crushed seeds and young blackbirds (*Turd us m erula)* are given segments of earthworms, but they are given whole items when they are older. The time of day at which food is presented or made available should also be considered when rearing species that feed their chicks at certain times in the wild.

Young wild birds are generally fed on protein-rich diets, even if this differs from the adult diet (O'Connor 1984), and so commercial chick crumbs can be suitable for a range of species. However, care must be taken when feeding birds on commercial chick feeds as these are formulated specifically to support the very rapid growth of broilers or for the growth of 'layer' strains of poultry.

These formulations are certainly not appropriate for all precocial species. The most common nutritional problem during the rearing of wild birds in captivity is nutritional bone disease due to absolute dietary calcium deficiency or, less commonly, vitamin D deficiency or inappropriate levels of dietary phosphorus. Due to the very rapid growth rates of altricial species, severe skeletal abnormalities can develop within days, and so great care must be taken to ensure there is an adequate calcium intake (Kirkwood 1996).

Some precocial species fed *a d lib itum* on diets containing unsuitably high protein or energy concentrations are prone to twisting and bending deformities of the limb bones.

Recommendations: Teach hand-reared birds to forage or to feed soon after hatching if necessary. Research the feeding strategies of each species and provide appropriate food at each life stage, giving consideration to feeding times. Formulate diets careful ly for growing birds to ensure appropriate dietary concentrations of nutrients, especially of calcium, phosphorus, vitamin D and protein.

Diets for Juvenile and Adult Birds

Juvenile birds should be gradually introduced to their adult diet after the period of rapid growth is completed. Adult birds should be fed on the food that they would eat in the wild, as far as possible, although supplements may be necessary, for example thiamin supplements for sea birds. However, mineral and vitamin supplements should not be used without careful consideration of the balance of the diet. Some minerals and vitamins are harmful if provided in excess, and the aim should be to correct specific dietary deficiencies with specific quantities of specific supplements (Kirkwood 1996). Many laboratory animal diet manufacturers produce pelleted food that can maintain birds but this may not be suitable for all species and can be bland.

CHALLENGE FEEDING

High and sustained peak egg production can only be achieved with uniform breeder flocks fed to meet their nutritional requirements. With 85-88% peaks now possible in the industry, it is obvious that we have to carefully plan and execute a feeding programme tailored to meet the breeders' nutrient needs. Underfeeding results in very short duration peaks, of only 3-4 weeks, and those are usually associated with the classical sign of loss or stall-out in body weight for 1-2 weeks. On the other hand overfeeding, especially with energy, will result in excessive weight gain, and while peak production may be little affected, there will be precipitous loss in egg production through 34-64 weeks of age. The basis of feed allocation at this critical time is obviously to allow genetic potential for increases in both egg numbers and egg size, and also to allow for modest weekly gains in body weight. Managers should consider "challenge feeding" as part of their feed management system at this critical time. Challenge feeding involves giving the hens extra feed on 2 or 3 days each week, based on need, without changing the base feed quantity scheduled for the flock. For example, a flock may receive 168 g/bird/day at peak, with an additional "challenge" of 7 g/bird/day given three days each week. The challenge feed is, therefore, equivalent to 3 x 7g / 7d = 3 g/bird/day. In reality birds receive the equivalent of 168 g + 3g = 171 g/bird/day. The immediate question is why bother with this more complicated system, and just give the flock a base feed allowance of 171 g/bird/day?

The advantages of challenge feeding, rather than simply increasing the base allocation are:

1. On days of challenge feeding, feeding time will increase, and this helps to improve uniformity.
2. It is easier to make adjustments to nutrient intake based on day-to-day change in needs as may occur with changes in environmental temperature.
3. Birds become accustomed to change in feed allocation, which will be important once feed withdrawal is practised after peak.
4. Ease of tailoring nutrient needs to individual flocks. For example, a base feed allocation of 165-175 g/bird/day may be standardised across all flocks, with individual flock needs at peak being tailored with the quantity and/or frequency of challenge, depending upon actual production, environmental temperature, etc.

The actual quantity and timing of challenge feeds must be flexible if they are to be used efficiently. In practice the challenge should not represent more than 5% of total feed intake, and most often the quantity will be 2-4%. On the other hand, the quantity of the challenge should be large enough to meaningfully contribute to the factors listed previously. For this reason there needs to be a balance between the quantity of feed given, and the frequency of this feeding. For example, a daily challenge of 3 g/bird/day given daily will be much less effective than 7 g/bird/day given 3 times each week. In both instances birds are receiving 21 g/week as a challenge, but in the later example the challenge quantity is more meaningful and we are more likely to see a bird response in terms of egg output.

Challenge feeding should start when birds are at 60-70% production, and should be discontinued when egg production falls below 80%. For most flocks, therefore, we can expect to practice challenge feeding from about 29 through 40 weeks of age. The idea of challenge feeding is to more closely tailor feed allocation to breeder hen needs, and so there should be no standardised system. Managers must be given flexibility to alter challenge feeding based on fluctuating needs. In most instances the challenge will be used to lead bids into a sustained peak. Because the concept of challenge feeding is to more closely tailor feed allocation to needs, then it is usual practice to alter the quantity and/or duration of challenge as birds progress through peak egg production. Maximum challenge feeding should coincide with peak egg output, with lesser quantities given prior to, and after actual peak. On this basis we recommend challenge feeding to be reduced (but not discontinued) once birds are 2% below peak egg production. Following are three examples of challenge feeding tailored to three different flock situations.

Challenge feeding can also be used post-peak if there are precipitous declines in egg production related to minor disease challenge or management or environmental stress. Under these conditions, challenges of 10 g/bird/day for two consecutive days are recommended. If no immediate response is seen in egg production, then challenge should be discontinued. If egg production returns to normal, then the challenge should gradually be reduced over the next 2-3 days.

Challenge feeding allows tailoring of feed allocation to suit individual flock needs. Managers should be flexible in actual allocations, although maximum challenge feed allocation needs to coincide with peak egg production. Breeders will respond to a good challenge programme, with sustained peak production and better post-peak persistency. On the other hand, the challenge should not usually represent more than 5% of total feed intake, because excessive challenge will invariably result in obesity and related loss in post-peak performance.

In general, when birds are subjected to such stresses as variable feed quality, mycotoxin challenge and/or fluctuating or extreme environmental temperature, then a high base feed allowance, coupled with aggressive feed challenge, is recommended. On the other hand, lower feed inputs are possible where consistent quality high-energy feeds are used, and where there is good environmental control.

FEED AND WATER

Feed

Circular or linear troughs can be used to supply feed. Feed troughs can be located either inside or outside the area where the birds are housed. If feed troughs are located outside the area where the birds are housed, then only one side of the trough is available to the birds. Unless the feeder is mounted on a wall, feeders located in the area where the birds are housed generally provide bird access to both sides of the trough.

Depending on species, specifications are for birds housed in multiple-bird pens and cages, individual cages, or aviaries. Feeder space allocation is presented as linear trough space per bird when both sides of the trough are available. If only one side of the trough is available, then the amount of feeder space per bird must be doubled. Because meat-type chickens, ducks, and turkeys have been bred for rapid growth to market age, excessive *body weight* (BW) gain of broiler breeders, duck breeders, and male turkey breeder stocks is a problem unless energy intake is controlled beginning early in life.

Because breeders are allocated limited feed to allow for a gradual increase in BW each week, birds are hungry as indicated by motivational test, stereotypic pecking on non-nutritive objects, and excessive drinking of water. Stress is also apparent in feedrestricted broiler breeders between 8 and 16 wk of age. Feed restriction of breeders allows for controlled BW gain, reduces skeletal problems, increases activity, and improves livability, fertility, immune function, egg production, and disease resistance. Evidence to date indicates that the welfare of breeders is better if they are feed restricted.

Feed should be allocated and BW routinely monitored to maintain the recommended BW for the particular stock and age. Rations may be either a fixed amount of feed allotted daily or under various alternate-day feeding schemes. Alternate-day feed restriction as opposed to limited feed each day allows more-timid birds access to feed, resulting in better flock uniformity. Inhibition of feeding by subordinate birds is likely if feeder space is limited.

Therefore, procedures that require restricted feeding should have enough feeder space so that all birds can eat concurrently. It may also be helpful to use low-density diets and to provide birds with environmental enrichment such as devices that they can manipulate to obtain small amounts of food to fulfill their feeding behaviour. Although adult broiler breeders are housed together for mating, they are fed separately to control BW gains.

If both sexes have access to the same feeder, the more aggressive males will consume more than their share of feed. The female feeder is fitted with a 4.3-cm grill sufficiently wide to allow feeding, whereas the male trough is fitted with a 5.1-cm grill. In this manner, the installation of narrow grills over the female feeder may prevent males with larger heads from consuming the hen's feed. However, some genetic lines of male breeders have smaller heads allowing them access to the female feeder, which not only deprives the hens of proper nutrient intake, but may lead to excessive BW gains for those males eating the hen's feed. University research uses a multitude of genetic lines in their studies; therefore, a one-size restriction grill does not exist to meet the head size of all breeds of meat-type chickens. To rectify this situation, small plastic pegs that are 6.3 cm in length are inserted through the nares of genetic lines of male broiler breeders known to have small heads at 20 to 21 wk of age to minimize male access to female feeders.

The behaviour of males with Noz-Bonz inserted did not appear to be affected, with resumption of foraging activities immediately post-insertion. Use of breeds or genetic lines that do not require Noz-Bonz is highly encouraged. Ducks experience difficulty consuming mash because the mash, as it becomes moist, may cake on their mouth parts. Therefore, it is recommended that all feeds for ducks be provided in pelleted form. Pellets no larger than 0.40 cm in diameter and approximately 0.80 cm in length should be fed to ducklings less than 2 wk of age. Pellets 0.48 cm in diameter are suitable for ducks over 2 wk of age.

Water

Recommendations for watering space vary widely, depending on species, type of bird, bird density, and whether water intake is restricted. Depending on type of poultry, specifications are for multiple-bird pens and cages, individual cages, or aviaries.

These recommendations assume moderate ambient temperatures. Newly hatched birds may have difficulty initially obtaining water unless they can find the waterers easily. Similar difficulties may occur when older birds are moved to a new environment, especially if the type of watering device differs from that used previously by the birds.

Watering cups that require birds to press a lever or other releasing mechanism involve operant conditioning. Because individuals may fail to operate the releasing mechanism by spontaneous trial and error, shaping of the behaviour may be required. Thus, it may be necessary to press the individual bird's beak or bill to the trigger to facilitate finding the water source.

Watering cups may need to be filled manually for several days until the birds have learned the process. Water pressure must be regulated carefully with some automatic devices and watering cups. In such cases, pressure regulators and pressure meters should be located close to the levels at which water is being delivered. Manufacturer recommendations should be used initially and adjusted if necessary to obtain optimal results.

Automatic watering devices require frequent inspection to avoid malfunctions that can result in flooding or stoppage. Waterers should be examined at least once per day to ensure they are in good working condition. The height of drinkers should be adjusted to meet bird size. Birds accessing nipple drinkers should raise their heads up while standing to activate the trigger pins. As a general guide, the bottom of the water trough should be approximately even with the back of the bird. Poultry ordinarily should have continuous access to clean drinking water. However, with some restricted feeding programmes, overconsumption of water may occur, leading to overly wet droppings that can hamper health and performance of poultry due to poor litter quality.

This situation can be controlled by restricting excessive water intake, usually by limiting water availability to certain times of the day, in accordance with accepted management programmes that consider the amount of time that feed is available and also environmental temperature conditions. There is little effect on welfare indicators of breeders with limited access to water compared with breeders consuming water ad libitum.

Water should be provided each day and also made available during the time that feed is being consumed. Adequate drinker space is needed to prevent undue competition at the drinkers when the water is turned back on. Water may also be shut off temporarily in preparation for the administration of vaccines or medications in the water. Most conventional poultry drinkers may be used for ducks, except for cup drinkers that are smaller in diameter than the width of the duck's bill. Nipple drinkers support slightly poorer duck performance during hot weather than do trough waterers. Ducks can grow, feather, and reproduce normally without access to water for swimming or wading, but weight gain may be improved slightly during summer months if such water is provided. If ducks are provided water for swimming or some other wet environment, they should also have access to a clean and dry place; otherwise, they are unable to pre-en their feathers and down properly, and the protection normally provided by this waterproof, insulated layer may be lost.

SPRAY SANITIZING HATCHING EGGS

Shell surface contamination of the hatching egg is inevitable in the breeder house environment. Normally, hatching eggs are not immediately set in the incubators upon lay but are one to ten days old before being set. During hatching egg storage there will be multiplication of any bacteria already on the shell surface. The greater the number of bacteria on the eggs, the greater the chance of those bacteria invading the interior of the egg.

The goal of the breeder house manager is to use good management strategies to minimise shell contamination. These strategies include such practices as:

- Keeping nests clean.
- Keeping storage facilities clean.
- Collecting eggs frequently.
- Maintaining proper temperature and humidity in the egg room.

In addition to good management practices, procedures for sanitizing shell surfaces can prevent microbial invasion if used properly. One method used extensively in the past was fumigating hatching eggs with formaldehyde gas after collection. This procedure proved very effective but caused the Occupational Safety and Health Agency (OSHA) to express concerns for safety. An alternative to fumigation is spraying the shell surface with an egg shell sanitizer. Numerous sanitizers on the market have proven useful, but, to be effective, the sanitizer must be used correctly.

Proper Selection and Dilution

The use of an effective sanitizer is essential to minimise contamination of the shell surface. Different classes of sanitizers (Quaternary Ammonium, Phenolics, Peroxides, etc.) kill microbes in different ways. Therefore, to assure effective control, the specific procedures for each sanitizer must be followed meticulously. Some classes of sanitizers are more effective than others when used in adverse environmental conditions like poor water quality. A sanitizer used on the egg must be effective at controlling microbial populations yet not toxic to the developing embryo. The entire sanitizer formulation should be examined to assure that none of the other compounds in the formulation can have an negative effect. Even compounds which are normally used as a hatching egg spray can be toxic if they are used at a concentration greater than the manufacturer recommendation. Sanitizers have been evaluated for optimal dilution, and using a concentration above the recommendation could potentially harm the embryo. Care must also be exercised not to use a compound which can deter the movement of oxygen to the embryo through the shell.

Implications of Improper Sanitizing

Proper selection and use of a sanitizer is essential to good spray sanitation management and can prevent additional problems in the hatchery. Since most incubators have greater than a 40,000 egg capacity, thousands of eggs and chicks could become contaminated if an infected egg explodes, breaks or becomes cracked inside the incubator. The proper practice of good management strategies will prevent microbial outbreaks and aid in the production of quality chicks.

FEEDING MANAGEMENT OF GROWING PULLETS

General Considerations

It is generally agreed that most Leghorn and brown egg strains have changed over the last five to 10 years, and because of this, nutritional management is becoming more critical. In essence, these changes relate to age at maturity, although it is questionable that this has changed suddenly in just a few years. In fact, what has been happening is that age of maturity has slowly been decreasing by about one day per year. Unfortunately, many producers are just now becoming aware of earlier maturity because their conventional programmes are no longer working, and this is especially true for many strains of brown egg pullets.

Moving birds to laying cages at 21-22 weeks is no longer feasible, and this now invariably results in management problems. Similarly, first egg appearing at 16-18 weeks means that we must critically review our rearing programmes. The key to successful nutritional management today is through maximising body weight of the pullet. Pullets that are on target or slightly above target weight at maturity will inevitably be the best producing birds for the shell-egg market.

The traditional concern with early maturity has been that it results in small egg size. Results from our early studies indicate the somewhat classical effect of early maturity in Leghorns without regard to body weight. There seems little doubt that body weight and/or body composition are the major factors influencing egg size both at maturity and throughout the remainder of the laying period. Summers and Leeson (1983) concluded that body weight is the main factor controlling early egg size.

We concluded that although there is evidence to indicate that nutrients such as protein, methionine and linoleic acid can influence egg size throughout the laying cycle, these nutrients have little effect on early egg size. This is probably related to the pullet producing at maximum capacity at least up to the time of peak egg mass.

Although it is fairly well established that body weight is an important criterion for adequate early production, there is still insufficient evidence regarding optimum body structure and composition. Frame size is being discussed, and is now most frequently included in breeder management guides as a form of monitoring. It is known that most (90%) of the frame size is developed early, and so by 12-16 weeks of age, the so-called "size" of the pullet is fixed. While this parameter is useful as another monitoring tool and its measurement should be encouraged, we have had little success in affecting frame size without also affecting body weight. It therefore seems very difficult to produce, by nutritional modification, pullets that are below target weight yet above average frame size and vice versa. The relationship between body weight and shank size is further complicated by the fact that environmental temperature also affects bone length independent of nutrition.

It would appear that early maturing chickens reach sexual maturity at significantly younger ages, but at similar body weights compared to later maturing birds. It seems as though early maturing birds achieve a threshold level of body mass and commence production when the minimum physiological age is reached, while late maturing birds at the same age do not have the body mass required for production. Recent reports have indicated the requirement of a certain lean body mass prior to onset of maturity. With most mammals, attainment of minimum fat reserves are essential for puberty, and so it seems likely that body composition is as important as total body mass in influencing the onset of egg production. In studies involving a relatively small number of birds, we have seen no correlation between age at first egg and either percentage or absolute levels of body fat. While no clear picture has yet emerged with respect to body composition and maturity, it seems likely that birds having some energy reserve as they approach peak egg production are less prone to subsequent problems.

Our experience suggests that if this type of production loss is not due to an identifiable disease and/or management problem, then it most likely relates to birds being deficient in energy. It is perhaps not too surprising that birds are in such a precarious situation with respect to energy balance. Most mammals such as cows and sows must lose body weight during peak lactation in order to meet energy requirements. Perhaps the most classical case of energy deficiency at this time is seen with the turkey breeder. Due to a decline in feed intake from time of first lighting through to peak egg production, the turkey breeder necessarily loses considerable body mass in an attempt to maintain energy balance. It is likely that the same situation applies to both the Leghorn and modern brown egg type pullet. Obviously, the effect is most pronounced for underweight flocks with small appetites where energy intake is minimal.

The key to solving many of our present industry problems would therefore seem to be attainment of "heavy" pullets at desired age of maturity. In this instance, "heavy" refers to the weight and condition which will allow the bird to progress through maturity with optimum energy balance. It is likely that such conditions will be a factor of the flock in question, being influenced by stocking density, environmental temperature, feather cover, etc. Unfortunately, attainment of desired weight for age has not always proven easy, especially where earlier maturity is desired or when adverse environmental conditions prevail. Leeson and Summers (1981) suggested that energy intake of the pullet is the limiting factor to growth rate, since regardless of diet specifications; pullets seem to consume similar quantities of energy.

All of these birds were of comparable weight even though diet specifications were dramatically variable. These data suggest that if adequate protein intake is achieved, additional diet protein does little to stimulate growth rate.

In more recent studies, we have reared Leghorn pullets on diets varying in protein or energy, and again, energy intake seems to be the major factor influencing body weight.

These studies indicate the growth rate is more highly correlated with energy intake than with protein intake. This does not mean to say that protein (amino acid) intake is not important to the growing pullet. Protein intake is very important, but there does not seem to be any measurable return from feeding more than 800g of protein to the pullet through 18 weeks of age. On the other hand, it seems as though the more energy consumed by the pullet, the larger the body weight at maturity. Obviously, there must be a fine line between maximising energy intake and creating an obese pullet.

Maximising Nutrient Intake

If one calculates expected energy output in terms of egg mass and increase in body weight, and relates this to feed intake, then it becomes readily apparent that the Leghorn must consume at least 90g/bird/day and the brown egg bird close to 100g/bird/day at peak production. With egg-type stock, feeding is related to appetite and so our management programmes must be geared to stimulating appetite. The practical long-term solution is to rear birds with optimum body weight and body reserves as they begin production. This situation has been aggravated in recent years, with the industry trend of attempting to rear pullets on minimal quantities of feed. Unfortunately, this move has coincided with genetically smaller body weights and hence smaller appetites, together with earlier sexual maturity.

In order to maximise nutrient intake, one must consider relatively high nutrient dense diets, although these alone do not always ensure optimum growth. Relatively high protein (16-18% CP) with adequate methionine (2% CP) and lysine (5% CP) levels together with high energy levels (2800-3000 kcal/kg) are usually given to Leghorn pullets, especially in hot weather situations. However, there is some evidence to suggest that high energy diets are not always helpful under such warm conditions. This situation may relate to stimulation of nutrient intake when lower energy diets are fed at high temperatures. In this recent study, Leghorn pullets were heavier at 126 days when fed the high energy diet in the cool environment, but diet had no effect at 30°C. As expected, pullets ate less of the high energy diet, and because all other nutrient levels were fixed, this results in reduced intake of all nutrients except energy. Pullets therefore ate less protein and amino acids when fed 3000 vs 2500 kcal ME/kg, and this can be critical where intake per se is less at 30°C. The pullets fed 3000 kcal/kg are borderline in intake of balanced protein at 870g versus our requirement for 800 g to this age. High energy diets may therefore not always be beneficial under heat stress conditions, and intake of other nutrients such as protein and amino acids must be given priority during formulation.

The Leghorn pullet eats for energy requirement, albeit with some imprecision, and so energy:protein balance is critical. All too often, we see inadequate amino acid intake when high energy corn-based diets are used, the result of which is pullets that are both small and fat at maturity.

One of the most important concepts today in pullet feeding, is to offer diets according to body weight and condition of the flock, rather than according to age. For example, traditional systems involve feeding starter diets for about six weeks followed by grower and then perhaps developer diets. This approach does not take into account individual flock variation, and today this can be most damaging to underweight flocks. It is becoming more difficult to attain early weight for age. This means that flocks are often underweight at four to six weeks of age. This can be for a variety of reasons such as sub-optimal nutrition, heat stress, disease, etc. The worse thing that can happen to these flocks is an arbitrary introduction of a grower diet, merely because the flock has reached some set age.

To change this flock to a grower at six weeks of age will cause problems because the flock will likely stay small until maturity, then be late maturing and produce a sub-optimal number of eggs that will also be small. This type of flock can most effectively be "corrected" by prolonged feeding of the starter diet. In this situation, the birds reach the low end of the guide weight at almost 10 weeks of age. At this time, a grower diet could be introduced. Since the flock is showing a growth spurt, then feeding to almost 12 weeks could be economical – we now have a flock that is "heavy". We have therefore converted the flock from being underweight and a potential problem, to one that is slightly over weight and so ideally suited to realising maximum genetic potential during peak production. Some producers, and especially contract pullet growers, are sometimes reluctant to accept this type of programme, since they correctly argue that feeding a high protein diet for 10-12 weeks will be more expensive. Depending upon local economic conditions, feeding an

18% protein starter diet for 12 versus six weeks of age, will cost the equivalent of two eggs. A bird in ideal condition at maturity will produce far in excess of these two eggs relative to a small underweight bird at maturity.

Suggested Feeding Programme

The following schedule is recommended for growing pullets to maturity:

Starter 18-19%CP; 2750-2900 kcal ME/kg

Day old ____________Target body weight

Grower 15-16%CP; 2750-2900 kcal ME/kg

Target wt ___________Mature body size

Pre-lay or layer 16-18%CP; 2750-2900 kcal ME/kg

Mature body size _________1st egg

As previously indicated, we are not making recommendations regarding age or even dictating the body weight at which diet changes should occur. Rather, the recommendations dictate the need for flexibility and the treatment of each flock as an individual case. For example, the starter diet is to be used until target weight for age is achieved. Hopefully, this will be at around 450g when the Leghorn bird is six to eight weeks of age. However, each flock will be subjected to varying environmental conditions, and so this may vary. The time of change to a lower-nutrient dense diet is when a desired weight-for-age is achieved, which we suggest is a weight that will be towards the top side of the breeder's growth curve. Changing at a specific weight, or a specific age in isolation can lead to disastrously underweight flocks.

In our recommendations, we suggest the lower-nutrient dense grower diets to be fed from this target weight-for-age up until the desired mature body size is achieved. Again, we are not dictating a specific mature body weight, since this may be varied at the desire of the pullet grower. Pre-lay diets should only be used in an attempt at conditioning the calcium metabolism of the bird and not as a means of initiating catch-up growth. Such growth spurts rarely occur at this age, and as such, pre-lay diets are being used as a "crutch" for poor rearing management.

An argument that is often heard about the role of body weight at maturity is that it is not, in fact, too important, because the pullet will show catch up growth prior to first egg ie: if the pullet is small, it will take a few days longer to mature, and start production at the "same weight". This does not seem to happen, as small birds at 18 weeks are smaller at first egg.

These data suggest that the smaller pullet does show some compensatory growth to the time of the first egg, although this is insufficient to allow for total "catch-up" growth. It is also interesting to note the relationship between body weight and age at first egg, and also between body weight and size of first egg. In other studies, we have followed up on the growth of the pullet through a production cycle in relation to 18-week (immature) body weight. Again, there is a remarkably similar pattern of growth for all weight groups indicating that immature weight seems to "set" the weight of the bird throughout lay.

When the lightest weight birds were fed diets of very high nutrient density (20% CP, 3000 kcal ME/kg) they failed to match egg production and egg size of the largest weight pullets that were fed very low nutrient dense diets (14% CP, 2600 kcal ME/kg). These results emphasize the importance of body weight in attaining maximum egg mass output. The actual body weights to be achieved during rearing will obviously vary with breed and strain. Most Leghorn strains should weigh around 400g, 900g and 1300g at six, 12 and 18 weeks respectively. Similarly, the brown egg birds should weigh around 500g, 1000g and 1500g at these ages. As a rule of thumb, these weights for age can be used as guidelines for anticipated diet change.

Discussion to date has focused on the role of body weight and appetite of the growing pullet. While rearing programmes such as reverse-protein (Leeson and Summers, 1979) have application where delay in maturity is required (usually due to inadequate light control) nutritional management programmes today must allow for maximum early growth so as to attain breeder's recommended weight goals as soon as possible. This type of nutritional management obviously entails accurate monitoring of body weight, a task that has too often been neglected with Leghorn pullets.

Manipulation of Mature Body Size

In the preceding discussion, we have outlined the importance of maximising body weight at sexual maturity, and the reasons for this have been explained. Under certain conditions, it is realised that some tempering of mature body size may be economically advantageous. Because body size has a dramatic effect on egg side, large birds at maturity can be expected to produce large eggs throughout their laying cycle. Depending upon the pricing of various egg grades, a very large egg may be uneconomical to produce, and in most instances, tempering of egg size of birds at 40-65 weeks of age is often difficult to do without some accompanying loss in egg numbers. Because body weight controls feed intake and egg size, an easier way of manipulating life-cycle egg size is through the manipulation of mature body size.

If the maximum possible egg size is desired, then efforts must be made to realise the largest possible mature weight. However, where a smaller overall egg size is economical, then a smaller pullet is desirable. Such light weight pullets can be achieved by growing birds slower through the growth cycle, or more economically by light-stimulating pullets at an earlier age.

Pre-lay Nutrition

Pre-lay diets are often used to try and manipulate body size or to bring about a transitional change in the birds calcium metabolism prior to maturity.

***Pre-lay Calcium*:** There is still considerable confusion and variation practised in the levels of calcium given to birds prior to egg production. During the laying cycle, the bird utilises its medullary bone reserves, in the long bones of the leg, to augment its diet supply when a shell is being formed. Because egg production is an "all or none" event, the production of the first egg obviously places a major strain on the bird's metabolism, when it has to contend with a sudden 2g loss of calcium from the body. Some of this calcium will come from the medullary bone, and so the concept has arisen of building up this bone reserve prior to first egg. This obviously means higher levels of calcium in pre-lay diets. There are basically three options for calcium feeding around the time of maturity.

As previously mentioned, the largest weight pullets in a flock will likely mature earlier, and so it is these birds that may be disadvantaged with inadequate levels of calcium at this time. If such birds receive a 1% calcium grower diet at the time they are producing their first few eggs, they will only have a sufficient calcium reserve to produce two to three eggs. At this time, they will likely stop laying, or less frequently continue to lay and exhibit cage layer fatigue. If these earlier maturing birds stop laying, they do so for four to five days, and then try to start the process again. The bird goes through very short clutches, when at this time she is capable of a very prolonged 30-40 egg first clutch. Advocates of prolonged feeding of grower diets suggest that it makes the bird more efficient in the utilisation or absorption of calcium, such that when she is eventually changed to a layer diet, improved efficiency continues for some time, and so the bird has large quantities of calcium available for shell synthesis.

If 1% calcium grower diets are used as pullets mature, these diets should not be used after appearance of first egg, and to 0.5% production at the very latest. It must be remembered that under commercial conditions, it is very difficult to precisely schedule diet changes, and so decisions for diet change need to precede actual time of diet change, such that production does not reach 5-10% before birds physically receive the calcium enriched diets.

Use of 2% Calcium Pre-lay Diets: Specialised pre-lay diets are a compromise, in that they provide more calcium than do most grower diets, but still not enough for sustained production. The concept of using so-called pre-lay diets is to build up the medullary reserves without adversely influencing general mineral metabolism. However, as previously discussed with grower diets, 2% calcium pre-lay diets are inadequate for sustained egg production, and should not be fed past 1% egg production. The main disadvantage of pre-lay diets is that they are used for a short period of time, and many producers do not want the bother of handling an extra diet at the layer farm. There is also reluctance by some producers with multiage flocks at one site to use pre-lay diets, where delivery of diets with 2% calcium to the wrong flock on site can have disastrous effects on production.

Early Introduction of 3.5 - 4.0% Calcium Layer Diets: In terms of calcium metabolism, the most effective programme is early introduction of the layer diet. Such high calcium diets allow sustained production of even the earliest maturing birds. As previously mentioned, higher calcium diets fed to immature birds, lead to reduced percentage retention, although absolute retention is slightly increased.

Feeding layer diets containing 3.5% calcium prior to first egg, therefore results in a slight increase in calcium retention of about 0.16 g/day relative to birds fed 0.9% calcium grower diets at this time. Over a 10-day period, however, this increased accumulation is equivalent to the output in one egg.

Early introduction of layer diets is therefore beneficial in terms of optimising the calcium balance of the bird. However, there has been some criticism levelled at this practice. There is the argument that feeding excess calcium prior to lay imposes undue stress on the bird's kidneys, since this calcium is in excess of the immediate requirement and must be excreted. Recent evidence suggests that pullets must be fed a layer diet from as early as six to eight weeks of age before any adverse effect on kidney structure is seen This is perhaps too simplistic a view, since there is other evidence to suggest that excess calcium may be absorbed by the immature bird at this time. Such evidence is seen in the increased water intake and excreta water content of birds fed layer diets prior to maturity.

Early introduction of a layer diet seems to result in increased water intake, and a resultant increase in excreta moisture. Unfortunately, this increased water intake and wetter manure seems to persist throughout the laying cycle of the bird.

These data suggest that birds fed high calcium layer diets during the pre-lay period will produce manure that contains 4-5% more moisture than birds fed 1% calcium grower or 2% calcium pre-lay diets. There are reports of this problem being most pronounced under heat stress conditions. A 4 to 5% increase in manure moisture may not be problematic under some conditions, although for those farms with a chronic history of wet layer manure, this effect may be enough to tip the balance and produce a problem.

In summary, the calcium metabolism of the earliest maturing birds in a flock should be the criterion for selection of calcium levels during the pre-lay period. Prolonged feeding of low-calcium diets is not recommended. Early introduction of layer diets is ideal, although where wet manure may be a problem, a 2% calcium prelay diet is recommended. There seems to be no problem with the use of 2% calcium prelay diets, as long as birds are consuming a high calcium layer diet not later than 1% egg production.

***Pre-lay Body Weight and Composition*:** Pre-lay diets are often formulated, and used, on the assumption that they will improve body weight and/or composition, and so correct problems arising with the previous growing programme. Body weight and body condition should not really be considered in isolation, although at this time we do not have a good method of readily assessing body condition in the live pullet. For this reason, our main emphasis at this time is directed towards body weight.

The most important criterion used during rearing is pullet body weight as described previously. Each strain of bird has a characteristic mature body weight that must be reached or surpassed for adequate egg production and egg mass output. In general, pre-lay diets should not be used in an attempt to manipulate mature body size. The reason for this is that for most flocks, it is too late at this stage of rearing to meaningfully influence body weight - all too often, pre-lay diets are used as a crutch for poor rearing management.

However, if underweight birds are necessarily moved to a layer house, then there is perhaps a need to manipulate body weight prior to maturity. With black-out housing, this can sometimes be achieved by delaying photostimulation - this option is becoming less useful in that Leghorns and brown egg strains seem now to be maturing early without any light stimulation. If pre-lay diets are then necessarily used in an attempt to correct rearing mismanagement, then it seems as though the bird is most responsive to energy. This fact likely fits in with the effect of estrogen on fat metabolism, and the significance of fat used for liver and ovary development at this time. While such high nutrient density pre-lay diets may be useful in manipulating body weight, it must be remembered that this late growth spurt (if it occurs) will not be accompanied by any meaningful change in skeletal growth. This means that in extreme cases, where birds are very small in weight and stature at approximately 16 -18 weeks of age, then the end result of using high-nutrient dense pre-lay diets may well be pullets of correct body weight, but of small stature. These short shank length pullets seem more prone to prolapse/pickout, and so this is another example of the limitations in use of classical pre-lay diets.

While body composition at maturity may well be as important as body weight at this age, it is obviously a parameter that is difficult to quantitate. There is no doubt that energy is likely the limiting nutrient for egg production for all strains of bird, and around peak production, feed may not be the sole source of energy. Labile fat reserves at this time are therefore, essential to augment feed sources that are inherently limited by low feed intake. These labile fat reserves become critical during situations of heat stress or general hot weather conditions. Once the bird starts to produce eggs, then its ability to deposit fat reserves is greatly limited. Obviously if labile fat reserves are to be of significance, then they must be deposited prior to maturity. As with most classes of bird, the fat content of the pullet can best be manipulated through changing the energy:protein balance of the diet. If labile fat reserves are thought necessary, then high energy, high fat pre-lay diets should be considered. As previously stated, this scenario could well be beneficial if peak production is to coincide with periods of high environmental temperature.

The requirements for a specific body composition at the onset of maturity have not been adequately established. With mammals, onset and function of normal estrus activity is dependent on the attainment of a certain body fat content. In humans for example, onset of puberty will not occur if body fat content is less than around 14%. No such clear cut relationship has emerged with egg layers. Work conducted with broiler breeders, in fact indicate a more definite relationship between lean body mass and maturity, rather than fat content and maturity.

***Subsequent Egg Weight and Egg Composition*:** It seems as though egg size is ultimately controlled by the size of the yolk that enters the oviduct. In large part this is influenced by body weight of the bird, and so factors described previously for body weight can also be applied to concerns with egg size. There is a general need for as large an early egg size as is possible, especially with breeder hens. Most attempts at manipulating early egg size have met with limited success. Increased levels of linoleic acid in prelay diets may be of some use, although levels in excess of the usual 1% found in most diets produce only marginal effects on early egg size. From a nutritional standpoint, egg size can best be manipulated with diet protein, and especially methionine concentration. It is logical, therefore to consider increasing the methionine levels in pre-lay diets.

For breeder hens, one also has to consider egg composition in relation to successful embryo development. It is well known that hatchability of eggs from young breeders is lower. The reasoning for this suboptimal hatch seems to relate to "maturity" of embryonic membranes, and movement of nutrients from the yolk and albumen to the embryo. However, part of this problem may also relate to inadequate passage of certain nutrients from the breeder hen into the egg. For example, it is known that young breeders do not deposit normal quantities of biotin into the egg - normal biotin concentration in the egg is apparently not achieved until production of the 8 - 10th egg. If this is a general effect with a number of key nutrients, then it would seem worthwhile to study the effect of pre-lay nutrient intake on egg composition in relation to embryonic needs.

Pre-pause: In recent years, there has been interest in some countries of so-called pre-pause feeding programmes. The idea behind these programmes is to withdraw feed, or feed a very low nutrient dense diet at time of sexual maturity. This somewhat unorthodox programme is designed to "pause" the normal maturation procedure, and at the same time to stimulate greater egg size when production resumes after about 10-14 days. This type of pre-lay programme is therefore most beneficial where early small egg size is undesirable.

Pre-pause can be induced by simply withdrawing feed, usually at around 1% egg production. Under these conditions, pullets immediately lose weight, and fail to realise normal weight-for-age when refed. Egg production and feed intake normalise after about 22 weeks, although there is 1-1.5g increase in egg size.

The most noticeable effects of a pre-pause diet such as wheat-bran, are very rapid attainment of peak egg production and an increase in egg size once re-feeding commences. These effects are undoubtedly due to increased feed intake. This management system could therefore be used to better synchronise onset of production (due to variance in body weight), to improve early egg size or to delay production for various management related decisions. The use of such pre-pause management will undoubtedly be affected by local economic considerations.

Urolithiasis: Kidney dysfunction often leads to problems such as urolithiasis, and this most commonly occurs during the late growing or early egg production phase of the pullet. While infectious bronchitis can be a confounding factor, urolithiasis is most often induced by diet mineral imbalance in the late growing period. At post-mortem, often one kidney is found to be enlarged and contain mineral deposits known as uroliths. Some outbreaks are correlated with a large increase in diet calcium and protein in layer versus grower diets, coupled with the stress of physically moving pullets at this time, and being subjected to a change in the watering system (usually onto nipples in the laying cages). The uroliths are most often composed of calcium-sodium-urate.

The occurrence is always more severe when growing pullets are fed high calcium diets for an extended period prior to maturity. For example, urolithiasis causing 0.5% weekly mortality, often occurs under experimental conditions when pullets are fed layer diets after 10-20 weeks of age (relative to maturity at 18-19 weeks). However there is no indication that early introduction of a layer diet for just two to three weeks prior to maturity is a causative factor.

Because diet electrolytes can influence water balance and renal function, it is often assumed that an electrolyte excess or deficiency may be predisposing factors in urolithiasis or gout. Because salts of uric acid are very insoluble, then the excretion of precipitated urate salts could serve as a water conversation mechanism, especially when cations are excreted during salt loading or when water is in short supply. When roosters are given saline water (1% NaC1) and fed high-protein diets, uric acid excretion rates are doubled relative to birds offered the high protein diet along with non-saline drinking water. Because uric acid colloids are negative charges, they attract cations such as Na, and so when these are in excess, there is an increased excretion via urates, presumably at the expense of conventional NH_4 compounds. There is some evidence of an imbalance of Na+K-C1 levels influencing kidney function. When excess Na+K relative to C1 is fed, a small percentage of the birds develop urolithiasis. It is likely that such birds are excreting a more alkaline urine, a condition which encourages mineral precipitation and urate formation.

Urolithiasis therefore seems to be most problematic in laying hens fed high levels of calcium well in advance of sexual maturity. Although the situation is often confounded with IBV infection, it seems obvious that no more than 1% calcium should be fed to Leghorn birds prior to maturity.

Feeding prelay (2% Ca) or layer diets containing 3% calcium for two to three weeks prior to first egg is not problematic, and surprisingly, uroliths rarely form in adult male breeders fed high calcium diets. High levels of crude protein will increase plasma uric acid levels, and potentially provide conditions conducive to urate formation. Certainly numerous mycotoxins influence kidney function, and so general mill management regarding quality control and/or use of feed additives to suppress their harmful effects would likely be beneficial.

In humans at least, urolith formation can be controlled by adding urine acidifiers to the diet. Studies with pullets show similar advantages. Adding 1% NH4C1 to the diet results in a more acidified urine, and uroliths rarely form under these conditions. Unfortunately, this treatment results in increased water intake and associated wet manure. One of the potential problems in using NH4C1 in laying hens, is that it induces a metabolic acidosis and this is detrimental to egg shell quality especially under conditions of heat stress.

Such treatment also assumes the kidney can clear the increased load of H+, and for a damaged kidney, this may not always occur. As a potential urine acidifier without such undesirable side effects, several researchers have studied the role of Alimet® a methionine analogue. From five to17 weeks of age, pullets were fed diets containing 1 or 3% calcium in combination with 0, 0.3 or 0.6% Alimet®. Birds fed the untreated high calcium diet excreted alkaline urine containing elevated calcium concentrations together with urolith formation and some kidney damage. Feeding 0.6% Alimet® acidified the urine, but did not cause a general metabolic acidosis. Alimet® therefore reduced kidney damage and urolith formation without causing acidosis or increased water consumption.

It is concluded that urine acidification can be used as a prevention or treatment of urolithiasis, and that this can be accommodated without necessarily inducing a generalised metabolic acidosis. From a nutritional viewpoint, kidney dysfunction can be minimised by not oversupplying nutrients such as calcium, crude protein and electrolytes for too long a period prior to maturity.

Brown-egg Pullets: There is very little information available on specific nutrient needs of brown egg pullets, and whether or not they need diets any different to those used for white egg birds. It is generally assumed that white and brown egg pullets are similar in their nutrient needs relative to body weight. Brown egg pullets are usually heavier than white egg birds, although this difference seems to be decreasing over the last few years. For example, in the past it has been fairly common practice to start physical feed restriction after 10-12 weeks of age, in order to control growth rate. Today, with many strains of pullet, this feed restriction is unnecessary, and in fact may be detrimental in hot weather conditions. The principle of feeding management of brown egg pullets is essentially the same as described for the slightly smaller white egg bird as outlined in the previous sections. Achieving target weight-for-age must be the major criterion of the growing programme, because this ensures the best chance of realising the bird's genetic potential as a layer.

If physical feed restriction is necessary, due to birds becoming overweight, then bird uniformity becomes a major concern. With a mild restriction programme, birds can be allowed to "run-out" of feed one day per week and, usually this will do little harm to uniformity. If it is necessary to impose a greater degree of feed restriction, on a daily basis, then it is important to ensure rapid and even feed distribution, much as subsequently discussed for broiler breeders. Feed restriction should be relaxed if birds are subjected to any stresses such as beaktrimming, vaccination, general disease challenge or substantial reduction in environmental temperature. An alternative management procedure for overweight birds, is to schedule an earlier light stimulation and move to layer cages. There is an indication that young brown egg pullets may not adjust feed intake too precisely in response to adjusting diet energy level.

As energy level is increased at a fixed protein level, a reduction in growth rate is sometimes seen because protein and amino acid intake are limited. Brown egg pullets seems to change their feed intake very little under these conditions, and consequently there is improvement in growth rate. In another study, pullets were fed diets at 2750 or 3000 kcal ME/kg. Over the 126 days growing period, brown egg pullets consumed 6% more energy when fed the high energy diet (20.6 versus 19.4 Mcal). Contrary to this increased energy intake, white-egg pullets consumed about 18 Mcal ME regardless of energy level in the diet.

An alternative scenario in explaining these results is that the heavier brown-egg pullet has reduced amino acid needs, and so when fed high energy diets there is less effect on amino acid intake relative to needs. In a series of studies, we have shown the brown egg pullet to grow quite well on very low levels of lysine relative to that recommended by most breeders.

Up to 42 days of age, the lysine requirement of the pullet seems to be 0.58 - 0.68% of the diet, which is substantially less than values of 0.9-1.0% as recommended by most breeders. From 84- 126 days during the later phases of growth, there was no response to growth rate with more than 0.46% diet lysine. These experimental results suggest that under moderate environmental temperatures, it may be inadvisable to use high energy diets for growing brown egg pullets. On the other hand, assuming their response to diet energy is independent of temperature, then it may be easier to stimulate growth of these pullets under heat stress conditions, simply by increasing the nutrient density of the diet.

7

Chicken Production

USE OF ROXARSONE IN CHICKEN PRODUCTION

In many factory farms, chickens are routinely administered with the feed additive Roxarsone, an organoarsenic compound which partially decomposes into inorganic arseniccompounded in the flesh of chickens, and in their feces, which are often used as a fertilizer. The compound is used to control stomach pathogens and promote growth. In a 2013 sample conducted by the Johns Hopkins School of Public Health of chicken meat from poultry producers that did not prohibit roxarsone, 70% of the samples in the US had levels which exceeded the safety limits as set by the FDA. The FDA has since revised its stance on safe limits to inorganic arsenic in animal feed by stating that "any new animal drug that contributes to the overall inorganic arsenic burden is of potential concern."

Antibiotic resistance

Information obtained by the Canadian Integrated Programme for Antimicrobial Resistance (CIPARS) "strongly indicates that cephalosporin resistance in humans is moving in lockstep with the use of the drug in poultry production." According to the Canadian Medical Association Journal, the unapproved antibiotic ceftiofur is routinely injected into eggsin Quebec and Ontario to discourage infection of hatchlings. Although the data are contested by the industry, antibiotic resistance in humans appears to be directly related to the antibiotic's use in eggs.

A recent study by the Translational Genomics Research Institute showed that nearly half (47%) of the meat and poultry in US grocery stores was contaminated with *S. aureus,* with more than half (52%) of those bacteria resistant to antibiotics. Furthermore, as per the FDA, more than 25% of retail chicken is resistant to 5 or more different classes of antibiotic treatment drugs in the United States. An estimated 90-100% of conventional chicken contains, at least, one form of antibiotic resistance microorganism. While organic chicken has been found to have a lower incidence at 84%.

Fecal matter contamination

In random surveys of chicken products across the United States in 2012, the Physicians Committee for Responsible Medicine found 48% of samples to contain fecal matter.

On most commercial chicken farms (Concentrated Animal Feeding Operations) CAFO, the chickens spend their entire life standing in, laying on, and living in their own manure, which is somewhat mixed in with the bedding material (e.g. sawdust, wood shavings, chopped straw, etc.).

During shipping from the CAFO farm to the abattoir, the chickens are usually placed inside shipping crates that usually have slatted floors. Those crates are then piled 5 to 10 rows high on the transport truck to the abattoir. During shipment, the chickens tend to defecate, and that chicken manure tends to sit inside the crowded cages, contaminating the feathers and skin of the chickens, or rains down upon the chickens and crates on the lower levels of the transport truck. By the time the truck gets to the abattoir, most chickens have had their skin and feathers contaminated with feces.

There is also fecal matter in the intestines. While the slaughter process removes the feathers and intestines, only visible fecal matter is removed. The high speed automated processes at the abattoir are not designed to remove this fecal contamination on the feather and skin. The high speed processing equipment tend to spray the contamination around to the birds going down the processing line, and the equipment on the line itself. At one or more points on most abattoirs, chemical sprays and baths (e.g. bleach, acids, peroxides, etc.) are used to partially rinse off or kill this bacterial contamination. Unfortunately, the fecal contamination, once it has occurred, especially in the various membranes between the skin and muscle, is impossible to completely remove.

With slaughter lines processing up to 140 birds/minute, safety inspectors do not have adequate time to properly examine visible fecal matter. The USDA is currently allowing some abattoirs to process at unlimited line speeds (i.e. in excess of 140 birds/minute), further exasperating the fecal contamination issue.

CHICKENS AS PETS

Keeping chickens as pets became increasingly popular in the 2000s. among urban and suburban residents. Most chickens are kept on farms for the agricultural production of meat and eggs but some chickens are kept as pets, along with homegrown eggs and sometimes meat. With the growing interest in all-natural pest control alternatives, people also began to keep chickens to rid their property of unwanted insects and larvae.

Background

Chickens can be tamed by hand feeding and by being handled. Some people are afraid that roosters will become aggressive, but this problem can easily be avoided if the rooster is handled properly. Breeds such as Silkies and many bantams are generally docile, making them ideal pets for owners with small children. Some cities in the United States allow chickens as pets but others ban them. Some may only ban roosters due to the crowing. City ordinances, zoning regulations or health boards may determine whether chickens may be kept. A general requirement is that the birds be confined to the owner's property, not allowed to roam freely. There may be restrictions on the size of the property or how far from human dwellings a coop may be located, etc. Hens continue to lay eggs in the absence of a rooster, but like most supermarket eggs, they are unfertilized.

The so-called "urban hen movement" harks back to the days when chicken keeping was much more common, and involves the keeping of small groups of hens in areas where they may not be expected, such as closely populated cities and suburban areas. In the UK a charity, the British Hen Welfare Trust, rescues commercial hens who would otherwise be sent to slaughter when they become no longer commercially viable. Supporters of the charity adopt the birds as family pets, with the intention of providing them a "retirement". In Asia, chickens with striking plumage have long been kept for ornamental purposes, including feather-footed varieties such as the Cochin and the Silkie from China, and the extremely long-tailed Phoenix from Japan. Asian ornamental varieties were imported into the United Statesand Great Britain in the late 1800s. Distinctive American varieties of chickens have been developed from these Asian breeds. Poultry fanciers began keeping these ornamental birds for exhibition, a practice that continues today. Individuals in rural communities commonly keep chickens for both ornamental and practical value. The rarest breed in Britain is the famous Scots Dumpy.

In Hong Kong, keeping chickens and other poultry without a licence has been banned since 2006 because of the threat of avian flu, whether as pets or for consumption. Only licensed farms are legally allowed to keep chickens and other poultry.

Housing

A chicken coop is a housing where chickens are kept. Inside there will often be nest boxes for egg laying along with perches on which the birds can sleep. Backyard coops are small and fenced, often with chicken wire, allowing chickens an area to roam, peck and hunt insects.Chicken tractors are floorless coops which can be dragged about a yard. Some backyard chickens are allowed to free range, and sleep in coops.

Urban chicken keeping has led to manufactured chicken coops such as the Eglu, which are designed for tight spaces and have a tidy look. Chicken waterers and feeders are an important part of keeping chickens as pets. There are hanging waterers/feeders, nipple waterers and waterer cups. When creating a home for their flocks, owners should plan on a specific amount of coop space and roosting space, nest boxes, food and water for the number of birds in their flock and also select breeds with an eye towards how many eggs they wish to harvest.

Show chickens

Chicken shows may be found both at county fairs and sanctioned shows hosted by regional poultry clubs. 4,000 or more birds may be entered in some shows. The Poultry Club of Great Britain sanctions poultry shows in Britain while the American Poultry Association and the American Bantam Association do likewise in America. Such organizations also work with poultry breed clubs of people who have interests in specific breeds of chickens.

PROCESSED POULTRY PRODUCTS

Poultry may be further processed into other products. The number of processed poultry products has increased dramatically since the 1970s because of the low cost of poultry and its versatile, bland flavour.

Battering And Breading

Some poultry products are battered (*e.g.*, with beer batter) or battered and breaded (*e.g.*, with cracker meal, bread crumbs, or cornmeal) for frying. The meat may be either cooked or raw prior to coating. For battered and breaded poultry, the pieces are passed through a flour-based batter containing leavening and then through the breading ingredients. Many types of baked breadings have been developed to meet different tastes (*e.g.*, Cajun or Japanese). To hold the breading to the poultry, the product is deep-fried for a short time. If the poultry is fully cooked in this process, the consumer will only have to heat the product before eating it. Chicken nuggets are a battered and breaded product that is marinated before coating.

Tumbling and Massaging

In the manufacturing of many poultry products, the meat is mixed with a variety of non-meat ingredients, including flavourings, spices, and salt. Tumbling and massaging are gentle methods that produce a uniform meat mixture. A tumbler is a slowly rotating drum that works the meat into a smooth mixture. A massager is a large mixing chamber that contains a number of internal paddles. Cured turkey products (*i.e.*, treated with sodium nitrite), such as turkey ham and turkey pastrami, are often tumbled or massaged during processing.

Smoking

Poultry may be smoked. Prior to smoking, the birds must be brined (soaked in a salt solution containing certain flavourings) and then allowed to dry. Smoking can be done using real wood shavings or a smoke flavouring. In the last case this must be labeled in the United States as "natural smoke flavour added."

Deboning and Grinding

Further processed poultry products leave the backs, necks, and bones available for their own processing. These materials are run through a machine called a mechanical deboner or a meat-bone separator. In general, the crushed meat and bones are continuously pressed against a screen and the edible, soft materials pushed through the screen. The resulting minced product is similar in texture to ground beef and has been used for many poultry products such as frankfurters (hot dogs) and bologna. Poultry frankfurters and bologna are made using a process similar to that for beef and pork.

The meat is combined with water or ice, salt, and seasonings and chopped to emulsify the materials. The mixture is stuffed into plastic casings and cooked in a smokehouse. The meat is then quickly chilled, peeled, and vacuum-packaged. Bologna is stuffed into a larger casing and is not necessarily peeled.

Processed Chicken

As consumers' lives become more hectic and time poor, they are searching for services that save them time and offer high levels of convenience. Processed food is an ideal solution for providing quick meals. In response to this development, the supply of processed-food categories is expanding, both in terms of the number of companies and as well products. However, the health factor will impact on the future demand for processed foods, with sectors such as sandwiches, chicken and pizza likely to be the fastest-growing areas of the market.

Chicken

If there is one word that could describe chicken, it would be versatility. Roasted, broiled, grilled or poached, and combined with a wide range of herbs and spices, chicken makes a delicious, flavourful and nutritious meal. No wonder chicken is the world's primary source of animal protein and a healthy alternative to red meat. It is available to enjoy throughout the year.

History

The practice of raising chickens for food is ancient, with the first domestication of poultry thought to have occurred in southern Asia over 4,000 years ago. Initially, chickens were raised by individual families for their own consumption, as the Neo-lithic villages expanded and population size increased, surplus chickens were sold or bartered for groceries.

With the introduction of modern refrigeration methods and with the development of faster transportation systems in the late 19th century there was a further increase in poultry production. However, it was not until after World War II that scientific developments in poultry industry, made commercial production of chickens viable.

Definition of Processed Chicken

At the present, there does not exist a clear-cut definition of what "processed chicken" is, and major players in the poultry industry apply the term to refer to different products. Despite differing terminological interpretations we have identified ready-to-cook chicken meat as well as frozen chicken under processed chicken category. The ready-to-cook chicken meat would generally comprise of added value products like Nuggets, Chicken Burgers, Grills and Steaks, Coated Fillets, etc.

Health Benefits of Chicken

Protein is an essential dietary requirement of human beings. We derive our amino acids from animal and plant sources of protein, then rearrange the nitrogen to make the pattern of amino acids we require. Chicken is a very good source of protein. It can provide for almost 68 per cent of the daily need for protein in 4 ounces. People who are non-vegiterians, but are looking for ways to reduce the amount of fat in their meals, should try eating more chicken. The leanest part of the chicken is the chicken breast.

Chicken is also a good source of the cancer-protective B vitamin, niacin. Components of DNA require niacin, and a deficiency of niacin has been directly linked to genetic damage. A four-ounce serving of chicken provides 72.0 per cent of the daily value for niacin. Chicken is also a good source of the trace mineral, selenium. Selenium is of fundamental importance to human health. It is an essential component of several major metabolic pathways, including thyroid hormone metabolism, antioxidant defence systems, and immune function.

Market Potential

Chicken is sold in three forms: Live chicken, frozen chicken and processed chicken. Till date the local market selling live chicken has the lion's share of the country's wallet. While frozen chicken has proved to be an important foreign exchange earner for the country. Factories, processing plants, feed mills and slaughterhouses have developed their operations to the required international standards, and frozen chicken has been exported to countless foreign markets, all over the world.

However, it has been difficult for the companies dealing in Processed Chicken. But the processed chicken market is poised for a big leap. The bird flu epidemic in South East Asian nations could be a blessing in disguise for the Indian poultry industry with demands surging from overseas buyers for processed chicken from India. With processed chicken prices rising in the global market from about $1,200 per tonne to $1,450 per tonne in the wake of the bird flu, this is the opportune moment to venture into processed chicken segment.

In the domestic front, quality broiler chickens are processed and packed in a scientific hand-free process, instantly chilled at 2 degrees Celsius and supplied to the customer the same day. The instant chilling procedures effectively retains the freshness of the chicken and keeps intact its natural vitamins.

Processing of Chicken

Chickens are taken directly from the poultry farms to the processing plant where they are unloaded from their transport crates or modules, slaughtered, plucked, cleaned, cooled and graded. They are then either packaged and frozen or chilled, or processed further into various products prior to packaging and sale to distributors. Processing plants are very large, highly mechanised operations. All processing operations have a systematic preventative approaches to manage food safety risks, with approved and regularly audited Hazard Analysis and Critical Control Points (HACCP) programmes in place.

THE CHICKEN MEAT SECTOR

Consumption of chicken meat in Australia during 2006-07 is estimated to be around 811 591 tonnes which is equivalent to around 454 million birds. This is equivalent to approximately 37.4 kilogram consumption per capita or the processing of around 8.73 million broiler chickens per week. This is an increase in consumption from 2004-5, when approximately 687 960 tonnes, equivalent to around 430 million birds, were consumed. (32.7 kilograms per capita consumption or the processing of around 8.3 million broiler chickens per week). The Australian Bureau of Agricultural and Resource Economics (ABARE) figures for chicken meat are based on the formula that chicken meat consumption is 94.9 per cent of all poultry meat consumption.

Consumption was predicted to increase around 0.2 kilogram per year.

Obtaining planning approvals for new broiler farms continues to be one of the major difficulties for the chicken meat industry. This is particularly so for Victoria, NSW and Queensland. The high cost of shedding, the difficulties, delays and costs in getting permits and some limitations in getting finance all coupled with lower returns for growers is resulting in declining quality broiler shed numbers. There is, however, a trend for the general loss of farms in peri-urban areas such as the Mornington peninsular in Melbourne and loss of broiler farm contracts in the Mangrove Mountain area in NSW. Because of the issues of rural residential living new broiler farms and complexes as has been discussed above and being built on larger land holdings and more distant to the processing plants

Background

Before the 1990s, chicken meat strains were all of Australians origin and the Australian chicken meat lines (broilers) were variable in both performance and carcass quality. Liveability in growing stock was generally acceptable where operators maintained their breeding stock free of disease agents such as *Mycoplasma gallisepticum.* Fertile egg production and day old production was generally poor by international standards.

New genetic material in the form of hatching eggs imported through Torrens Island quarantine station in South Australia gave the industry an opportunity to upgrade the genetics of the Australian broiler bird.

Two key factors prompted the importation of international strains of meat chickens. One was the increasing commercial pressure on the smaller less vertically integrated companies for the supply of breeder birds, fertile eggs and day old chickens. The other was the recognition that the small Australian gene pool was limiting the rate of genetic improvement. The initial outcomes of these importations were varied. While advantages were seen in egg production, hatchability and better growth rate, the carcass conformation (particularly fat content) was not viewed favourably by some processors and customers. There was also need for improvement in both husbandry and housing if the level of performance of these new strains was to approach their genetic potential.

Two major disease episodes also dramatically affected certainty about whether new breeding stock should be imported into Australia. These were Marek's Disease (MDV) which seriously affected both imported strains and saw batch mortalities exceeding 50 per cent, and J-Leucosis which predominantly affected the Ross strain. During these times there was a move back to the utilisation of the only indigenous broiler breeder strain left, the Bartter bird.

Productivity losses were high which necessitated a total review of husbandry practices as well as the importation and registration of the type 1 Rispens Marek's vaccine. J-Leucosis was only resolved after further importation of J-Leucosis free stock. While J-Leucosis testing is not mandatory, most importing companies now test their stock for J-Leucosis.

Genetic Breeding Stock

Importation through the Torrens Island post-arrival quarantine (PAQ) facility created problems due to limited positions available to competing importers. The government-owned Torrens PAQ facility is operated under government supervision by a consortium of Australian poultry companies. Other poultry species including commercial layers, ducks and turkeys were also using Torrens Island.

The large gap of up to five years between importations meant that there was limited ability to take advantage of the continued genetic improvements of the meat chickens seen overseas. Also, when problems occurred such as

J-Leucosis, the time taken to correct this stock deficiency was prolonged. Two of the major chicken meat integrators decided to construct their own private importation facilities in line with government regulations. This allowed the more economical importation of larger numbers of great grand parent birds (GGPs) as frequently as every six months. This has enabled Australian producers to maintain their chicken meat genetic gain at a level comparable with that of other international companies to Australia.

Despite the construction of two privately owned PAQ importation facilities, and the recent reduction of the quarantine period from 12 weeks to 9 weeks for chickens and turkeys, there are limited positions in the Torrens Island quarantine station available to competing importers, with requirements allocated out until 2015. This means that the opportunities for the importation of new lines of birds, particularly those competing with existing available genetic stock are limited without the development of existing or other PAQ importation facilities.

Today there are no longer any indigenous broiler strains used by the major meat chicken producers. There are, however, remnants of these strains within alternate system producers. Invariably, either through take-overs or direct purchases of parent breeder stock, most integrators have a number of strains within their operation.

An advantage to establish business relationships with the breeder suppliers, to offset concerns about negative changes in the performance of particular strains and finally as a buffer against limited access to certain breeder stock. Limited access has occurred during previous episodes of emergency diseases such as Newcastle Disease (ND) and Avian Influenza (AI). Imported stock is brought in as GGPs usually every six to twelve months in privately owned facilities and every two or more years through Torrens Island PAQ facility. GGP and Grand parent (GP) facilities are usually located in the same region as designated hatcheries.

Day old parent breeders (PBs) are then distributed by road transport and occasionally by air transport to parent facilities located in Victoria, NSW, South Australia, Queensland and WA. There are no parent breeders in the Northern Territory and ACT. Parent broiler facilities for each integrator generally supply fertile hatching eggs to state based hatcheries from which day old chicks (DOC's) are delivered to regional broiler (grow out) farms. Historically, processing plants and grow outs were centred around and relatively close (in distance terms) to the major metropolitan cities, with outlying farms no further than 50 kilometres away. However, rural residential living and community concerns about poultry sheds have necessitated changes to the traditional location of parent breeder farms and broiler farms.

Australia is viewed favourably by the international poultry genetic companies as a location for genetic stock for the following reasons. Australia is considered politically stable, has well structured and implemented animal health programmes including quarantine and biosecurity, and is considered at a lower risk of terrorism activities (physical or biological) which can immediately close borders and restrict all movements.

With this favourable consideration of Australia, one large international breeder of poultry (including broilers, layers and turkeys) has formed a company to supply domestic and international markets. This company oversees the PAQ and breeding facilities for broiler breeders in Australia and New Zealand (NZ).

PROCESSED PRODUCTS MADE OF CHICKEN MEAT

Processed chicken is chicken meat that has either been mechanically recovered from a chicken carcass or is made of a combination of chicken meat and skin. Many different types of processing can be done on other meats, but processed chicken is primarily either mechanically recovered or is made from ground up chicken meat and formed into shapes.

Although they conjure up images of machinery and factory lines, processes can still be completed by human workers. Any meat that has gone through a process such as drying, fermenting, curing, or pre-cooking can be classified as processed meat.

The most common bits of a chicken used for food are the breasts, legs, and wings, but processing makes other parts of the chicken edible. During the processing of a full chicken carcass, the valuable cuts such as the breasts, legs and wings will be removed by a trained employee working with a knife, and then the leftover carcass is often used to mechanically recover the leftover meat. Depending on how the more valuable cuts of meat are going to be used, they may or may not be processed into another form. Foods such as chicken frankfurter are made from processed chicken, using a mixture of lean meat and chicken skin. Chicken bologna is also made from these processed parts.

Mechanical recovery is one way of making processed chicken that has attracted media attention. This method takes the chicken carcass leftover after the removal of the most valuable cuts, and then runs it through a machine. The carcass is ground up, along with cartilage, bones, and skin, in order to recover the meat that can be still garnered from the chicken. The processed chicken then comes out in a pink mousse, brimming with bacteria, waiting to be treated with ammonia to kill the microorganisms. The chicken is then re-coloured in order to make it conform to expectations of what chicken looks like and re-flavoured to remove the ammonia taste.

This mixture of processed chicken is then used in a variety of different food products in place of more expensive lean chicken. Products which make use of mechanically processed chicken include chicken ham in the US, or chicken meat balls in Asia. This process is often thought to be used in the making of chicken nuggets, but while the meat is still technically processed in most chicken nuggets, it cannot be said to be mechanically processed. Other types of processing include drying, frementing, curing, or pre-cooking.

CHOOSING A PRODUCTION SYSTEM

A producer's motivations will influence the size and type of production system chosen. Is the plan alternative poultry being a farm centerpiece or a part-time source of supplemental income? Is the plan year-round production or seasonal? Producers may choose one system for layers and another for meat birds.

Choosing a production system involves considerations such as the following:

- Intensive vs. extensive: Many large-scale operations use indoor production systems or semi-intensive systems with a yard. However, an extensive system is ideal for free-range poultry, especially combining poultry with other livestock grazing.
- Fertility implications: Does the producer want a light layer of manure spread over a large area or a heavy layer of manure over a small area? Is a goal fertility for a pasture? Or feedstock to compost for market garden or crops? Can a producer control excessive nutrients by rotating poultry land with crop production, grazing with ruminants, or making hay?

- Flexibility: Many producers start with a pasture pen since it is an inexpensive system and flexible. They can try out one batch to see whether they like raising and processing poultry and whether they can build a market. Although it is labour-intensive, the entry costs for the enterprise are low. Many producers eventually switch to a different production system as their operations grow.
- Labour and management: A fixed house is easier to service, while moving portable houses obviously takes time. Ease of access is also an issue in small pens, so many producers make pens tall enough to stand in.
- Bird welfare: Some consider the pasture pen inhumane because it may expose birds to the elements, and submissive birds have no way to escape aggressive birds in the confining quarters. Active breeds are less able to forage in a pasture pen.

Outdoor Area

Outdoor access allows poultry to express natural behaviours. Birds scratch, pursue insects, eat forage, and dust-bathe outdoors. Outdoor access provides more space and is called "extensive," which may reduce stress because the birds are less crowded. Direct sunlight, fresh air, and the elements (frosts, heat, drying) can help reduce disease. Outdoor access can enrich the lives of poultry and incorporate their activity as part of biological cycles and nutrient cycles. However, if outdoor access is poorly done, it will be a detriment for the poultry rather than a benefit.

Land should drain well and should be mainly covered with vegetation. Land with low spots may be a problem in heavy rains, and poultry may be exposed to pathogens and parasites if they drink from dirty puddles. However, waterfowl need access to bathing water. For certified organic production, there should be no synthetic chemicals applied to the land for three years.

Birds need the same services outside the house as inside. They should have access to feed and water outside so they do not have to return inside. Feeders should be protected from rain and wildlife with a shield or cover and should be easy to move to a new location. Birds also need access to shade and shelter so they don't run back to the house every time something flies overhead.

The chicken evolved from a ground dwelling forest fowl that inhabited tropical forest clearings and woodland edges and roosted in trees at night. As flightless birds from the jungle, they need protection and shade outdoors, such as trees and bush plantings. In fact, they may not venture outdoors without it. Chickens do not like full sun, strong winds, or overhead predators. European research has shown that birds will forage in the open but prefer a covered area for resting. Some free-range programs in Europe require shade/shelter in outdoor areas. Trees and bushes are multipurpose, providing shade, roosts, overhead cover, and a wind break. Man-made constructions can also be used, including roof overhangs, walls, tarps and shade panels, portable "wigwams," and strawbales with pallets on top. Tarps on wheels provide portable shade and keep manure from collecting in concentrated areas. Tall crops such as corn or sunflowers can also be planted to provide shade and additional feed. Sometimes poultry are raised close to corn fields so birds can range among the tall plants.

Poultry can be combined with trees in an "agroforestry" setting, such as an orchard or woody ornamentals. A variety of trees, shrubs, understory plants and a pasture clearing will offer a wide range of nutrition, herbs, live protein, and shelter to the birds. Elm Farm Research Centre in the U.K. has planned a poultry agroforestry system with trees, shrubs, and health-promoting herbs.

Studies of large flocks of free-range meat birds in the U.K. showed that even in summer, the maximum number of birds that came outside the house was only about 15 percent of the flock. The number of birds outside was positively correlated with the amount of tree cover on range, as well as the time of day and season of the year. Specifically, more birds ventured outside if there was tree cover. Birds were less likely to go outside in the winter or during the middle of the day. Chickens prefer areas with trees, avoid bright sun, and either stay close to the house or seek tree cover. A wide open field is not preferred habitat.

Encouraging birds to forage is important for the authenticity of free-range production and consumer confidence, and it begins with housing design. Keeping the buildings small or providing many exits enables birds to find their way outdoors. Bird-sized doorways may be used. Human doorways or opening an entire side provides additional access. Provide exits that are big enough that birds don't block the door. EU legislation requires 4 meters of pophole for every 100 square meters of house (13 feet of pophole per 1076 square feet). Maintaining vegetation or putting slat flooring by the popholes on the inside and outside helps reduce the amount of mud the birds track inside. Some programs like the Assured Chicken in the U.K. require a doormat.

Breed also plays a role in encouraging foraging. The fast-growing Cornish cross typically used for meat production in the U.S. is not as active as other breeds, especially as they get older and heavier. Some producers believe fast-growing birds in particular must be encouraged to graze by removing their concentrate feed temporarily. Sometimes fast-growing birds will go outside, but only to rest rather than forage. Slow-growing meat birds and layers are more active and may go outside and forage more. Usually birds return to the house at night due to their roosting instinct but some birds may need to be trained.

Some producers move outdoor feed and water stations away from the house to encourage foraging over a broader area and reduce stocking density near the house. The shade and shelter in the outdoor area will also encourage birds to move away from the house.

Birds go outside mainly in the morning and dusk. In hot weather, they may stay inside in the heat of the day or rest in the shade. Chickens are creatures of habit and use paths. Birds may range a considerable distance from the house depending on the production system and conditions. Active breeds may range about 100 meters (328 feet) from the house. Some producers believe that making forage available from an early age during brooding encourages birds to forage in the future.

Pasture

Chickens obtain limited nutrients from forage plants. Forage can be high in vitamins and protein; however, the nutrients in forage are not packaged well for chickens. Chickens were domesticated from wild, seed-eating jungle fowl, and have short digestive tracts. When chickens eat forage, their ceca develop microbes with the capacity to digest fiber and are much larger than the ceca of chickens that do not eat forage. Still, chickens cannot digest large quantities of fiber like ruminants can. Some other avian species, such as geese, can obtain more nutrients from forage, because they are better able to digest fiber. Poultry obtain high-quality nutrients from live protein such as worms and insects. On pasture, birds may eat enough nutrients to replace 5 to 10 percent of diet; however, when formulating rations, it may be best to assume zero contribution from pasture, because it is difficult to know what nutrients will be supplied and in what amount.

A key to pasture management for poultry is to keep the forage young and vegetative. Older plants are less digestible than young leafy plants. According to one producer, "chickens ignore vegetation over four inches high—all they will do is trample on it." In tall grass, they tend to make tunnels to feeders and not use the rest of the range. Tall grass holds moisture that may harbor parasites. Further, it can wet the birds' feathers and the moisture may be tracked into the house. Tall grass, especially when mowed, may become caught in the crop and cause digestive problems. Poultry yards should be laid out so it is easy to use a tractor to mow, plow, and plant. Ruminant grazing can help manage forage for poultry and avoid the need to mow or hay. In fact, combining sheep with poultry production is a best management practice to manage the pasture.

Pasture for free-range poultry is usually designed to be hard-wearing or is designed for ruminants. Many variables come into play in determining the "best forage" for your operation: soil type, pH, amount of rainfall, field fertility, type of tillage for seeding, size of pasture, and other planned uses of pasture, such as ruminant grazing or haying. Contact your local Extension service to discuss the best mix of cool season and warm season forages for your region. You may not need to add fertilizer because the poultry will add it in the form of manure, improving the pasture.

A perennial pasture with legumes and grasses is often suggested for ruminant pasture, because diverse species are the most reliable for a wide range of conditions, from high moisture in spring and fall to hot, dry days in summer. It may require a few years of intensive management by ruminant grazing to develop diverse pasture.

In the early part of the 1900s, scientific research examined forages and pasture management for poultry. Much of this research is still useful today; however, the modern broiler grows much faster than the meat birds of 100 years ago and needs more nutrients and feed supplementation. According to Plamondon, "Everything I've read points to oats as the ideal cool-season green feed, while ladino clover, alfalfa, and to a lesser extent other clovers are better summer feeds. My own experience with oats has been very favourable. Oats seem to do very well when broadcast by hand." According to Plamondon, the research showed that ladino clover and alfalfa remained palatable throughout the summer if mowed occasionally.

Legumes in the pasture may increase the omega-3 fatty acids in poultry meat and eggs. Chloroplast membranes of plants, where photosynthesis occurs, contain unsaturated fatty acids. The leafier the plant, the more omega-3 fatty acids it has. Clover, for example, is leafier than alfalfa, which has more stem. Research at Pennsylvania State University compared the amount of unsaturated fatty acids in three types of pasture: 1) alfalfa and grass, 2) red clover and white clover and grass, and 3) mixed grass. They found legumes had more unsaturated fatty acids. Eggs from hens raised on legumes and grass had more omega-3 fatty acids and vitamins than eggs from hens only raised on grass. Poultry can also be run on leguminous cover crops that are planted to increase nitrogen in the soil for crop production. Ruminant access to lush leguminous pasture should be restricted, especially in the spring, because they may overeat and founder (produce too much gas in the rumen).

Special pastures may be designed for poultry, including seed mixes for poultry/sheep pasture. Peaceful Valley Farm Supply offers an Omega-3 Chicken Forage Blend seed mix. There is also interest in herbs that could be beneficial for poultry health maintenance or that could improve meat quality in terms of nutrient content or flavor.

Some plants may be poisonous to poultry, including the following: castor bean (*Ricinus communis*), corn cockle (*Argrostemma githago*), daubentonia (*Daubentonia longifoli*), death camas (*Zygadenus spp.*), glottidium (*Glottidium vesicarium*), milkweed (*Asclepias spp.*), nightshade (*Solanum nigrum*), oleander (*Nerium oleander*), pokeberry (*Phytolacca americana*), potato (*Solanum tuberosum*), vetch (*Vicia spp.*), and yew (*Taxus spp.*).

Fire ants on pasture can be a concern when using pastured pens in hot climates. Care should be taken not to place young birds on fire ant mounds. However, older birds may actually eat the ants and destroy mounds. ATTRA has a publication on sustainable fire ant control.

Major parts of the western U.S. are dryland where it is difficult to keep forage in a vegetative state. Drought-tolerant plants, such as perennial and annual ryegrass, sudan grass, millet, and sorghum, can stay green during the long dry summers, but poultry may not like them as much as other forages. Much western pasture is essentially standing hay and offers little nutrients for poultry; however, live protein and other benefits of outdoor access are still important. In fact, turkeys are native to dry areas of southern North America. Low moisture on dryland reduces the danger of poultry disease and parasites, and the fertility brought by poultry is welcome. Some producers in the West raise birds on irrigated pasture.

Pasture Rotation

Rotation allows pasture to recover from grazing and reduces the buildup of excessive nutrients and pathogens. To rotate pasture, birds are moved to new pasture by moving the house or moving the birds to a new yard. Pasture should be rotated at least every two to three months, although every month is better. Pasture can be rotated after flocks of meat birds are harvested, but a layer flock should not remain in the same pasture for the entire life of the flock. The pasture must be rotated.

Mobile houses that can be moved frequently are ideal to facilitate pasture rotation. Moving portable housing creates new environments for flocks, and birds may try to return to the old location if the house is not moved far enough. If a fixed house is used, subdivide the yards into at least 4 separate yards and rotate flocks among these. Plant trees or shrubs about 30 to 60-feet away to draw birds from the house.

Free-range poultry production should not add excessive nutrients to the ground. Soil samples taken as an initial baseline and annually will monitor how much nitrogen and phosphorus is added by outdoor access or application of litter to the ground. Legislation is increasing concerning the level of nutrients that can be applied to the land from animal waste. Regulations in the U.S. vary by state. The EU does not allow more than 170 kg/N/ha/year to be added to land from livestock manure, which would be the equivalent of 580 table chickens or the equivalent of 230 hens.

Where excessive nutrients build up in the soil, pathogens are also likely to build up as well, resulting in "fowl sick" land. Although many pathogens and parasites will die after their poultry hosts are removed, some are able to survive for a long period of time and re-infect birds when they are returned to the land.

An additional consequence of not rotating pasture is that the vegetation is worn down to dirt. Mud from bare lots is tracked into the house and dirties eggs, greatly increasing egg cleaning costs and increasing moisture in the litter. Not rotating free-range yards will be a limiting factor on performance due to pathogens. If you have less than 50 birds, you probably do not need to rotate pasture. In the past, cultivation of crops or hay were rotated into poultry production to use up the nutrients and keep the soil from becoming compacted. According to Plamondon, "The old-fashioned method is to lime the pasture like mad, plow it, and replant it."

The Soil Association recommends that pastures for laying flocks be rested for 12 months between flocks, with a requirement of at least 9 months rest. For meat chickens, the Soil Association makes the following distinctions:

- Clean pasture: no poultry for three years or new pasture after crops
- Relatively safe pasture: no poultry for one year; or no poultry for six months if land has been plowed and reseeded
- Dangerous pasture: pasture that has had poultry within six months.

Many producers permit outdoor access to improve not only bird welfare but also health; however, there are concerns about birds getting diseases from wildlife. In times of extreme heightened biosecurity, birds may be temporarily confined. At the time of this writing, avian influenza is a concern, and in Europe, many free-range flocks have been confined to prevent contact with wild birds. Take measures to reduce direct contact between domestic poultry and wildlife. Keep wild birds out of range feeders so they won't eat from them or defecate in them. The Soil Association suggests a container with small slits that allows poultry to pick out only a few grains or pellets at a time. Netting over range areas reduces contact with wildlife, and covered areas can eliminate contact. Biosecurity for the Birds is a USDA project that provides information for small poultry producers on how to maintain good biosecurity.

ALTERNATE POULTRY PRODUCTION

The alternate poultry production in India is gaining momentum and attention from the farmers, entrepreneurs, professionals and researchers. It is used for food, game, fancy, pet, and also for research purposes. Here, the importance, prospects and potentials of alternate poultry production in India has been reviewed.

Quail Production

Quail is the most efficient biological machine for converting feed into animal protein of high biological value and hence is the cheapest source of animal protein for human diet. Consumption of quail began before domestication of poultry. In China, Taiwan, UK quail has been reared through centuries. During fifties its commercial production started in Italy. The CARI is the pioneer in introducing quail farming in 1974 by importing germplasm from U.S.A. It is introduced in India as an alternate avian species for growing poultry industry. M/s. AVM Hatchery and Poultry Breeding Research Centre, Coimbatore has played a major role for production on extensive scale in private sector.

Owing to the wild life act and ban on captivation of domestic quail, no worthy development and popularisation of quail production took place for last ten years. But now the ban has been lifted, it has tremendous scope to occupy a considerable portion of poultry meat market by 2010 A.D. as a profitable enterprise. Quail has unique qualities of hardiness and adaptability to diversified agro-climatic conditions. Its consumption may be referred by all, as it has no religious taboo. It has nutritive value, amasing taste, and game favour, tender, very delicious with low calorific value and high dry matter. It is rich in protein, vitamins, essential amino acid, unsaturated fatty acids and saturated fatty acids and phospholipids. It may be recommended for children and pregnant women, for speedy recovery. It is a tiny inter breeding avian species quite different from wild quail. Because of twin capacity of prolific egg production and meat yield, it attains the status of viable commercial poultry enterprises as well as rural poultry production. At present quail production is being done at Agricultural Universities or few private sectors only, but if we want to achieve our target we will have to extend our quail farming activities to rural areas where our bulk of population lives. Quail production requires less investment and gives quick returns, higher profits and hence can be adopted by rural masses quickly. A very important point is that so far benefits of quail farming have not fully reached rural masses, though quail production can generate additional income. Agriculture production can be boosted through the use of high value quail manure, as it is four times nutritive than cow dung manure.

Duck Production

Ducks are the second largest source of table eggs and there are about 23 million ducks in India. West Bengal has the highest duck population followed by Assam, Tamil Nadu, Andhra Pradesh, Bihar, Kerala, Orissa, Jammu and Kashmir and Tripura. Ducks predominantly are of indigenous type kept for egg production on natural foraging and have a production potential of about 130-140 eggs/bird/year. Duck eggs have a preference over chicken eggs in certain states and areas.Considering the importance and scope of duck rearing in our rural economy, improved strains and technologies are available in the country and the farmers are much benefited from the same.

Duck farming is primarily popular among small farmers, marginal farmers and agricultural labourers as well as poor section of the community. Ducks lays 40-50 eggs more than desi chicken. The duck egg is heavier than hen by 15-20g. Ducks require lesser attention and supplement their feed by foraging, eating fallen grains in harvested paddy fields, insects, snails, earthworms, small fishes and other aquatic materials in lakes and ponds hence incur reasonable feed cost.

Ducks have a longer profitable life and lay well even in second year. Ducks do not require elaborate houses like chicken, reducing the capital investment. Ducks are quite hardly, more easily brooded and more resistant to common avian diseases. Ducks flourish well in marshy riverside, wetland and barren moors where other types of stocks do not. Ducks have no problems of cannibalism or pugnacious behaviour. Ducks lay 95-98 per cent of their eggs early in the morning, before 9 AM, thus saves a lot of time and labour. Ducks are useful in controlling unwanted plants in ponds, lakes, and streams like green algae, duckweed, pond weed, musk grass, arrow head wild celery, etc. (5-10 ducks/ 0.405ha of water table). Ducks are good exterminators of potato beetles, grasshoppers, snails, and slugs. In areas plagued by liver flukes ducks can help correct the problem (2-6 ducks/ 0.405 ha of land). Ducks can be used to free the bodies of water form mosquito pupae and larvae (6-10 ducks/ 0.405 ha of water space).

Ducks are suitable for integrated farming systems such as duck-cum-fish farming, duck farming with rice culture, etc. In duck-cum-fish farming the droppings of ducks serve as feed for the fishes and no other feed manuring of the pond is necessary for fishes (200-300 ducks/ha of water area). Under integrated duck farming with rice culture, the ducks perform 4 essential functions, *viz.*, intertillage, weeding, insect control and manuring. The down and small body feathers of ducks are valuable as filler for pillows and as lining for comforters and winter clothing (one Pekin duck produce about 100g of down and small feathers).

The important Indian breeds are Sythet mete and Maheswari, of eastern region, Chara and Chamballi of Kerala, desi breeds of West Bengal and other states. Among improved varieties distinct breeds for egg and meat production are available. Khaki Campbell and Indian Runner are the most popular breeds for egg laying. White Pekin, Muscovy and Aylesbury are known for meat production. High-laying strains of ducks are available at the Central Duck Breeding Farm, Hessarghatta, and Bangalore. Duck units are functioning in some of the states like Assam, Tripura, Orissa, Madhya Pradesh, Andhra Pradesh, Kerala, Haryana and J & K.

Turkey Production

Turkey is mainly reared for meat and is quite popular in many western countries. It is one of the white meat choice and famous for its leanness and deliciously cooked whole turkey forms the traditional dish in Thanks giving and Christmas dinners. Turkeys are sold as whole or cut-up parts and further processed products such as sausages, patties, and nuggets. Turkey farming is still at the stage of infancy and need to be popularised among farmers to provide diversified food and employment especially in India. Rearing turkeys can be an excellent family or youth project. They are quite suitable for upliftment of small and marginal farmers as the birds can be easily reared in free range or semi-intensive system with minimal investment for housing, equipment and management. Even though turkey farming is practically non-existent in our country, few backyard birds are distributed in few areas. Also organised farms of turkeys have been maintained at Central Avian Research Institute, Izatnagar, CCS Haryana Agricultural University, Hissar, University of Agricultural Sciences, Bangalore, Rajasthan College of Agriculture, Udaipur, Kerala Agricultural University, Mannuthy and Tamil Nadu Veterinary and Animal Sciences University, Kattupakkam.

Turkeys are not difficult to raise. They require a little special care to get them off to a good start. Sometimes they are little slow in learning to eat and drink. If the farming is started with a good stock and provided optimum feed, housing and management, one can raise turkeys successfully.

There are seven standard breeds of turkeys, *viz.* Large White (Broad Breasted White), Bronze (Broad Breasted Bronze), Beltsville Small White, Bourban Red, Black, Slate and Narrgansett. The turkeys can be marketed as broiler at approximately 16 weeks of age when hens usually reach a live weight of about 8kg. Toms weigh approximately 12kg. Smaller, fryer roasters can be produced by slaughtering at an earlier age as per the market demand. Adequate research in the field of management, nutrition and disease control under tropical conditions as well as education are imperative before private entrepreneurs can be convinced for the viability of turkey enterprise in India.

Ostrich and Emu Production

Ostrich and Emu farming is now-a-days considered to be one of the most profitable agricultural projects. They are referred as 'farms of the future' due to the large variety of products and hence the high profits potential. Ostrich meat is highly nutritive and earns enormous foreign exchange. Ostriches are raised commercially for their egg, meat, feathers and hide. The increased consumer awareness of the problems of cholesterol in the blood and their possible association of heart attacks and arteriosclerosis, the demand for ostrich meat in international market began to increase. A number of beef producers in Europe, America and Canada have most recently switched to commercial ostrich farming due to higher and faster financial returns on ostrich projects. Ostrich meat is in great demand in European and American countries and is already extremely popular and available in most of the restaurants and supermarkets.

Recently Tamil Nadu Veterinary and Animal Sciences University imported 100 chicks from Malaysia. Their adaptability to climatic conditions prevailing in the state would be tested and if successful it will be recommended to the interested farmers and entrepreneurs. Considering the above aspects of alternate poultry production, our country has a great potential to develop further in this area of farm production. The NABARD and associated banks are also ready with model projects and financing of such projects through reimbursement scheme which is also a boost for future developments.

Guinea Fowl Production

An important source of traditionally raised poultry species, guinea fowl was introduced into Indian sub-continent by African ethnic migrants a few centuries back. Definite population figures are not available, it is estimated that few million birds are raised every year. Guinea fowl ranks third among the poultry birds; it is referred by different local names in different regions, *viz.*, chittra in west, china murghi in south and titari in the northern plains. Earlier attempts to raise guinea fowl intensively were made at Christian Missionary Poultry Farm, Etah (UP), Allahabad Agriculture Institute, Naini (UP), and Government Poultry Farm, Gurdaspur (Punjab) and subsequently at Military Poultry Farm. However preliminary survey of guinea fowl production in northern regions and the perusal of earlier published literature established its distinct popularity with marginal farmers, tribes and pastoralists may be attributed to its inherent hardiness and excellent foraging potentials to go as animal component of biomass-based polycultural systems. In recent years this alternate poultry species witnessed increasing emphasis for low-input grain-saving aviculture (LISA).

The primary function of guinea fowl production is to produce low-cost game flavoured meat. There are two quite distinct production systems for rising of guinea fowl. One is the modern intensive system and other is the traditional extensive system. The former is characterised by high inputs, high costs, good husbandry, hygiene and a complete supply of feed. The intensive production is largely confined to Government and public sector owned farms. Commercial farming is not much known. Traditional extensive system is the most common production system followed in rural area.

Guinea fowl holds a unique status among the other poultry species owing to its low input requirements and better forage-utilisation capacity. There are three major varieties of guinea fowl, *i.e.* Pearl, Leavender and White. Guinea fowl deserve priority research attention for helping the smallholder rural poultry production. Research and development activities should aim not primarily at designing completely new technologies to replace the traditional ones but rather understanding and strengthening them on social, ecological and economic merits.

8

Chicken Diseases

INTRODUCTION

A good history will often provide clues that will help solve a problem. Get information on the type of bird, age, feed and water source and consumption rate, growth, production, morbidity and mortality, the description of the case, previous problems, vaccination programme, medicine being used etc.

The problems may relate to management, environmental factors, and stress rather than to infection so examine the yard and housing conditions. Is the ventilation adequate? Are ammonia fumes a problem? Is it too hot or too cold? Is the litter wet or is it too dry and dusty? Is the pen too light or too dark? Are there sufficient hours of light for best production? Is the nest area darkened? Are the roosts too high? Do the birds appear comfortable? Chickens can talk and the sounds they make can indicate comfort, hunger, pain, panic, or disease.

Examination of Live Birds

Check the general appearance of the individual or group and try to determine which organ or system is involved in the illness. Note any signs or lesions that might point to a diagnosis, such as small size with poor feathering that suggests infectious stunting (malabsorption syndrome). If the birds show lameness or paralysis, is the lesion in the nervous system, bones, joints, muscles or skin? Some conditions, particularly those affecting locomotion, are easier to diagnose in live birds. Botulism which produces neck paralysis in chickens (leg and wing paralysis are more obvious in turkeys, ducks and pheasants) is an example.

Examine the skin of the head, body and legs for lice and mites, injury (particularly cannibalism), blood, mottling, swellings, anemia, cyanosis, or dermatitis. Listen for unusual breathing sounds (snicking, gurgling) and look for gasping or head-shaking that might indicate respiratory distress. Mouth-breathing (panting) is normal in chickens in hot weather. Exudate from nostrils and eyes and dirty feathers also suggest respiratory infection, or if just the eye, ammonia burn, ILTor eyeworm. Examine the droppings for evidence of diarrhea or other abnormalities. Take a blood sample for hematology or serology if indicated.

Necropsy. If a postmortem examination is to be carried out, birds that are representative of the problem in the flock must be selected. If birds have died, both sick and dead birds should be opened. Cull birds will not provide the answer. If the problem is a drop in production, try to find birds that look like they have recently stopped laying. It is important to do both an external and internal examination and to follow a specific routine to avoid missing important lesions.

- CRD -chronic respiratory disease
- IB(V) - infectious bronchitis (virus)
- ND - Newcastle diseaseAI- avian influenza
- CA(V) - chicken anemia (virus)
- EDS - egg drop syndrome
- IBH - inclusion body hepatitis
- ILT - infectious laryngotracheitis
- IBD - infectious bursal disease.

Live birds may be killed by cervical dislocation except when anemia or respiratory disease is suspected.

Examine the head, including the eyes, ears, nostrils, comb, wattles, mouth and beak.

Infected eyes and conjunctivitis are seen in CRD, sinusitis, Bordetella and Orthobacterium infection, infectious coryza and in ILT, IB and ND. Keratoconjunctivitis with central corneal ulcers suggest ammonia burn. Swollen sinuses are seen in infectious coryza (Parahaemo-philus infection) in chickens, sinusitis (mycoplasma), cryptosporidia and Bordetella infection in turkeys and pheasants. They may also be seen as the result of other infections such as influenza.

Chronic fowl cholera causes swollen wattles and sinuses in adult chickens. Fowl pox causes scabs on the comb, eyelid, and wattle, but must be differentiated from injury. Pox also occurs in turkey, pigeons, doves, canaries and other birds. If the bird has had its beak trimmed, check for proper healing, overgrowth of the lower beak or over-trimming (cut too short). Injury on the head, neck or breast or back may indicate predators. Dermatitis and scabby or crusty lesions around the mouth and eyes suggest vitamin B deficiency.

Cut across the upper beak and back into the sinuses; then through the mandible and down the esophagus into the crop. White plaques in the mouth, esophagus, or crop may be caused by capillaria worms, yeast infection (candidiasis, moniliasis), or possibly trichomoniasis or vitamin A deficiency, but most frequently by fowl pox (wet form). White plaques beside the tongue in the mouth are common in hens and turkey breeders and may be caused by mycotoxin or low humidity. Vomitoxin may produce similar lesions in young chickens and turkeys.

If the crop is enlarged and full, it may be an impacted or a sour crop (pendulous crop). The problem may be caused by excess water intake, defects in the crop itself, partial blockage of the proventriculus or gizzard or Marek's disease. Necrosis of the crop in wild birds is caused by Salmonella infection.

Examine the soft palate and larynx and cut down the trachea. Wet fowl pox lesions are seen on the roof of the mouth, pharynx and larynx.

Granulation, congestion and mucus in the trachea are seen in CRD, IB, coryza, ILT, Orthobacterium, Bordetella, and *E. coli* infection, or with dust and ammonia fumes. Hemorrhage and blood clots may occur in ILT and in ND or coryza and may cause severe gasping.

Gapes (gape worms) in pheasants, quail, and other birds is caused by Syngamus infection which also causes gasping. Cyanthastoma cause similar infection in water fowl and tracheal flukes may be found in waterfowl. Tracheal and air sac mites occur in cage birds.

Check the abdomen for lice and mites, and the vent for injury and prolapse of the oviduct. Cut down between the abdomen and the legs and dislocate the hip joints. Peel the skin off the abdomen and breast. Tightly adhering skin and dark tissues indicate dehydration. Remove the breast carefully by cutting through the abdominal muscles, ribs and coracoids.

At this point, examine the thoracic and abdominal organs, paying particular attention to the air sacs, lungs, and liver. Carefully raise the gizzard and intestines and examine the abdominal air sacs, peritoneum, spleen and the ovary in laying birds.

The air sacs are cloudy in respiratory disease such as *E. coli* infection, Mycoplasma, Aspergillus, IB or early CRD in chickens. If there is also fibrin on the liver and in the pericardial sac, suspect *E. coli* or Salmonella infection. These lesions in turkeys and other birds might also be due to Chlamydia, or in ducks Anatipestifer infection.

Pneumonia in turkeys is caused by fowl cholera (Pasteurella multocida infection), and the lungs are quite solid. Aspergillosis, ND, AI, E. coli and Ornithobacterium infection can also cause pneumonia. Peritonitis in layers is usually 'egg peritonitis' caused by *E. coli* infection from the oviduct, although acute fowl cholera also causes peritonitis.

White crystals on the heart, liver and other tissues and organs are uric acid crystals (visceral gout) and are caused by hyperuricemia from urate nephrosis secondary to water deprivation, urolithiasis or other kidney disease. Large blood clots in the abdomen or hemorrhage and hematoma on the liver are the result of trauma or fatty liver hemorrhage syndrome in chickens, or ruptured aorta in turkeys.

Tumors in or on the organs may be Marek's disease, lymphoid leukosis, or other varieties of tumors. Multiple small tumors on the organs and peritoneum in adult hens are metastasis from a carcinoma of the oviduct. This may result in ascites. Ascites may also result from heart or liver disease or from ingestion of some toxic material. Right ventricular failure occurs most frequently in meat-type chickens after 4 weeks. It occurs secondary to pulmonary hypertension causing right ventricular hypertrophy and valvular insufficiency.

Focal white lesions on the organs may be tumors or they may be tuberculosis or coli-granuloma or, if just on the liver, blackhead. Turkeys, pheasants, and peacocks are all quite susceptible to blackhead; chickens are less susceptible. There are prominent cecal cores in blackhead (Histomoniasis) and occasionally in salmonella infection or coccidiosis. In chicks, turkeys and waterfowl, examine the lungs and air sac for yellow-white foci or plaques caused by brooder pneumonia (Aspergillosis). Gasping in young birds is a sign of tracheal or bronchial epithelial injury, or obstruction and can be caused by irritating fumes or by infection (often IB plus *E. coli* or Aspergillosis). In young chicks, look for an infected navel and for yolk-sac infection or peritonitis (mushy chick, omphalitis) in which the abdomen is swollen, wet, and discoloured, and the yolk-sac is infected (due to *E. coli*, Salmonella, Staph., Proteus, etc.).

Young birds also die because they don't start to eat (starve-outs) or drink (dehydration). Deaths occur mainly at 3, 4, and 5 days. This may be a management problem (chilling, feed and water not available, etc.) or the chicks/poults may be weak or defective when hatched. Broiler chickens that die suddenly from sudden death syndrome (dead in good condition) or from heat stroke, or suffocation (piling-up) have congested, edematous lungs, a full digestive tract and congested mottled breast muscle.

Examine the circulatory and immune systems, the heart, pericardial sac, blood, spleen, bursa, thymus, and lymphoid tissue of the thigh and intestine. Birds that die from anemia are pale and the blood is watery. With CAV the thymus is small and bone marrow may be pale. Birds that bleed to death (pick-outs, ruptured fatty liver, acute cecal coccidiosis, ruptured aorta, hemorrhagic enteritis in turkeys, etc.) are also pale.

Sulfa poisoning produces anemia and widespread hemorrhage in the tissues. Chicken anemia virus (CAV) produces similar lesions and is the agent responsible for infectious anemia associated with IBH. Lead poisoning may also cause anemia. To identify anemia from parasites in blood cells (Plasmodium or leukocytozoon in ducks, turkeys and chickens), blood from a live, sick bird must be examined.

IBD (Gumboro disease) is caused by a virus that damages the bursa causing illness in 2-4 week old chickens or in younger chickens destroys part of the immune system, making birds more susceptible to other infections. Swelling, congestion and hemorrhage with or without focal necrosis in the spleen, liver and lymphoid tissue suggest septicemia (fowl cholera, fowl typhoid, streptococcosis, or erysipelas) or viremia (ND and duck virus enteritis also affect the lymphoid tissue in the intestine).

Marek's disease and lymphoid leukosis produce tumors in lymphoid tissue and organs except for the bursa which is mainly affected by lymphoid leukosis (occasional Marek's lesions may occur in the stroma of the bursa). Skin leukosis is Marek's disease virus causing viral dermatitis in the feather follicles. At processing this can be confused with scabby hip or other causes of dermatitis. Marek's disease can also cause lymphoid neoplasia in the skin.

Cut through the proventriculus and remove the digestive tract and liver. Open the proventriculus, gizzard, and small and large intestines to the cloaca. Check the cloaca carefully for evidence of picking injury. If hens are not properly beak-trimmed or are too fat, mortality from 'pick-out' is common. The whole intestine may be picked out through the cloaca. Prolapse of the vagina (and cloaca) (blow-out) may occur from excess fat or straining, secondary to injury or inflammation. Injury is common in flocks that produce large eggs before they become mature.

Examine the digestive tract for lesions and the various kinds of enteritis (hemorrhagic, necrotic, ulcerative, etc.), parasites (tetrameres, roundworms, capillary worms, tapeworms, cecal worms, and coccidia), and gastrointestinal accidents. A large proventriculus in broilers is from lack of fibre in the diet resulting in poor development of the gizzard. A thickened proventriculus sometimes with ulcers or hemorrhage may be Marek's disease or infectious proventriculitis. Green staining of the digestive tract is just bile and indicates that the bird is not eating. The liver and spleen may be small (if the bird is thin) and the gallbladder full

Salmonella pullorum (pullorum disease, bacillary white diarrhea) causes enteritis, diarrhea and death in chicks. It has been eradicated in many countries. Check the ceca, intestine and liver for lesions of blackhead, TB, coccidiosis or tumour, the liver for other varieties of bacterial, viral or protozoal hepatitis, cholangiohepatitis etc., and the pancreas for tumors.

A large liver may be lymphoid leukosis or Marek's disease, or it may be caused by bacterial hepatitis (*E. coli*, campylobacter) or fowl typhoid (Salmonella gallinarum). Hepatitis with necrosis and hemorrhage that looks like bacterial (vibrionic) hepatitis may be immune damage to veins (vasculitis) from amyloid.

A large, yellow liver may be normal fat storage in a laying bird (estrogen stimulation) but layers die from fatty liver hemorrhage syndrome. This occurs when the liver ruptures because it has become fragile due to excess fat and free radical damage from fat. A yellow or hemorrhagic liver particularly with focal necrosis may be viral hepatitis (IBH) which is seen in broilers, pigeons, raptors, owls and psittacine (but IBH does not cause infectious anemia).

Examine the testes or ovary and open the oviduct. Shrinking ova indicate illness of 2-7 days' duration or one from which the bird may be recovering. Small, sac-like ova indicate that the bird has been out of lay for a week or more and may be in a molt. Semi-solid (cooked) ova indicate bacterial infection (such as salmonella). An impacted oviduct may be secondary to vent-picking, egg-material left in the oviduct, or the bird may be egg-bound. Infection (Mycoplasma, IB, *E. coli*) can cause salpingitis as well.

A large or small fluid-filled cyst in the right abdomen beside the cloaca is the cystic remnant of the right oviduct (may be normal, but increased by IBV).

A drop in production may be related to clinical or subclinical disease (EDS, IB, MG, AE, AI, ND, etc.) or management faults (lack of light, temperature change, lack of water) or nutritional problems etc. Deformed shells suggest management faults, superovulation, EDS, IB and soft shells (higher than 1-2 per cent) calcium or vitamin D3 deficiency.

A normal-appearing dead bird with an egg in the shell gland, or just laid has likely died from acute hypocalcemia. These birds often have fragile bones (particulary the femur), lack of medullary bone and rib infolding (osteoporosis, osteopenia, osteomalacia). Hard (fibrotic) or swollen testes indicate bacterial infection (salmonella).

Examine the kidneys and ureters. Swollen, pale or white spotted kidneys indicate hyperuricemia from urate nephrosis and may be due to lack of water or other kidney disease. Swollen. pale kidneys are also seen in IBH, IBD and fatty liver and kidney disease. Ureters plugged with hard stony material (urolithiasis) indicates a previous low phosphorus diet.

Swollen kidneys and nephritis may be due to IBV (nephrotrophic strain) or *E. coli* infection and usually causes death from dehydration. Newcastle's disease causes lympholytic foci in the kidney in pigeons.

Examine the skin, integument, muscles, bones and joints. Emaciation, along with small organs, suggests malnutrition, stunting syndrome, beak injury (poor trimming), peck order (psychological) problems, chronic disease (coccidiosis), bumblefoot or other lameness, or chronic poisoning (lead, insecticide, etc.).

Muscular degeneration due to vitamin E-selenium deficiency can cause lameness, particularly in ducks. Ionophore toxicity causes muscle damage and paralysis in turkeys. Granulomas in the breast muscle are usually a vaccine reaction.

Sarcosporidial cysts produce small, white lesions in the muscle of water fowl. Examine bones and joints for abnormality and deformity. Angular bone (valgus-varus) deformity of the intertarsal joint is caused by lateral or medial bending of the tibio-tarsal and metatarsal bones and is a common problem in meat-type poultry. It has a variety of possible causes (nutritional, rapid growth, management, etc.). Tibial dyschondroplasia causes backward bending or fracture of the top of the tibia. Slowing growth in young birds will help prevent leg deformity.

Other types of hock and stifle lameness and ruptured tendons are frequent in heavy roaster and turkeys and may be mainly due to injury as the result of heavy weight and fast growth, but some respond to added selenium or B vitamins.

Check for poor bone-breaking strength (osteoporosis) and, in young birds for rubbery bones, soft beaks, and beaded ribs which indicate calcium or Vit. D3 deficiency (rickets). Cage layer fatigue because of fragile bones may be due to phosphorus deficiency. Calcium and Vit. D3 deficiency also cause fragile bones (osteoporosis) in adults, but the most common cause is continuous high production. Infectious stunting syndrome (malabsorption syndrome, fragile bones, osteoporosis) in young broilers is caused by intestinal damage from viral infection in young chicks. The chickens are small, poorly feathered and there is poorly digested food in the lower intestine. Osteomyelitis also causes fragile bones.

Curly-toe paralysis in young birds may be riboflavin deficiency, but in older birds and turkeys may be genetic or due to lack of roosts. Cracked feet and foot dermatitis may be pantothenic acid or biotin deficiency, but scaly leg is caused by mites.

Footpad dermatitis and hock lesion are often caused by poor litter conditions. Toe injury in young birds may be cannibalism or mechanical injury. Arthritis in the feet or hocks or other joints suggests infectious synovitis (Mycoplasma synoviae) or *E. coli* or Staph. infection often with osteomyelitis.

Infection in the wing joints in pigeons is usually due to salmonella. In broilers, roaster and broiler breeders viral arthritis (reovirus infection) may cause lameness or ruptured tendons. Ruptured tendons are usually caused by rapid growth and large body size (heavy weight) and there is usually thickening of the tendon above the hock.

If growing birds are lame, and there is no evidence of infection or rickets, cut into the proximal tibia and look for necrosis caused by osteomyelitis or dyschondroplasia and split the spine at T4 to look for spondylolisthesis (kinky-back), a plug of cartilage impinging on the cord or consider Marek's disease.

Necrotic dermatitis is caused either by staph. or clostridium infection and is associated with immuno-suppression (usually by CAV or IBD). Scabby-hip is usually from overcrowding, poor litter conditions, poor feathering or scratches. Dermatitis or granulation in the neck may be a vaccine reaction, or contaminated vaccine.

Disturbances of the nervous system may cause incoordination, staggering, paralysis, walking backwards (with wings flapping for balance), tremors, stargazing, and other odd behaviour. In case of lameness, paralysis, or incoordination, examine the sciatic nerves, spinal cord, and brain. Histologic examination will be required for diagnosis.

ND may produce CNS disturbances in pigeons as well as nervous, respiratory, intestinal and reproductive lesions in chickens, pheasants, turkeys, and wild and cage birds of all ages. Range paralysis is a form of Marek's disease affecting the peripheral and central nervous system causing lameness, incoordination and paralysis. Marek's can also cause botulism-like paralysis and transient paralysis.

Vitamin E deficiency (avian encephalomalacia) causes soft, dark areas of hemorrhage in the cerebellum which may be visible grossly. B vitamin deficiency (thiamine and other) may also cause nervous signs. Avian encephalomyelitis (AE) (epidemic tremor) affects birds up to 3-4 weeks old from non-immune parents.

Arsenilic acid and other feed additives and toxins (botulism, lead) may cause CNS disturbances, while others like the ionophores and coffee weed seeds (Cassia) cause nerve or muscle damage. Bacterial infection (pasteurella, pseudomonas, salmonella, staph. etc.) and fungi (aspergillus, etc.) also cause meningoencephalitis, occasionally in outbreak proportions.

METABOLIC AND NUTRITIONAL DISEASES

These are conditions caused by a disturbance of normal metabolic functions either through a genetic defect, inadequate or inappropriate nutrition or impaired nutrient utilisation. These include Fatty Liver Syndrome, Perosis (or slipped tendon), Rickets and Cage Layer Fatigue.

Infectious Diseases

An infectious disease is any disease caused by invasion by a pathogen which subsequently grows and multiplies in the body. Infectious diseases are often contagious, which means they can be spread directly or indirectly from one living thing to another.

These include Avian Encephalomyelitis, Avian Influenza, Avian Tuberculosis, Chicken Anaemia Virus Infection (or CAV), Chlamydiosis, Egg Drop Syndrome (or EDS), Fowl Cholera (or Pasteurellosis), Fowl Pox, Infectious Bronchitis, Infectious Bursal Disease (or Gumboro), Infectious Coryza, Infectious Laryngotracheitis, Lymphoid Leukosis, Marek's Disease, Mycoplasmosis, Necrotic Enteritis, Newcastle Disease, Salmonellosis

Parasitic diseases

Parasitic diseases are infections or infestations with parasitic organisms. They are often contracted through contact with an intermediate vector, but may occur as the result of direct exposure. A parasite is an organism that lives in or on and takes its nourishment from another organism. A parasite cannot live independently. These include Coccidiosis, Cryptosporidiosis, Histomoniasis, Lice and Mites, Parasitic Worms (or Helminths), Toxoplasmosis, Trichomoniasis.

Behavioural diseases

Abnormal behavioural patterns can lead to injury or ill health of either or both of the abnormally behaving bird and its companions. These include Cannibalism (or aggressive pecking).

FOWLPOX IN CHICKENS AND TURKEYS

Fowlpox is a slow-spreading viral infection of chickens and turkeys characterized by proliferative lesions in the skin (cutaneous form) that progress to thick scabs and by lesions in the upper GI and respiratory tracts (diphtheritic form). It is seen worldwide.

Etiology and Epidemiology

The large DNA virus (an avipoxvirus, family Poxviridae) is highly resistant and may survive for several years in dried scabs. Field and vaccine strains have only minor differences in their genomic profiles, although the strains can be differentiated to some extent by restriction endonuclease analysis, and immunoblotting. Recently, molecular analyses of vaccine and field strains of fowlpox viruses have shown some significant differences. The virus is present in large numbers in the lesions and is usually transmitted by contact through abrasions of the skin.

Skin lesions (scabs) shed from the recovering birds in poultry houses can become a source of aerosol infection. Mosquitos and other biting insects may serve as mechanical vectors. Transmission within flocks is rapid when mosquitos are plentiful. Some affected birds may become carriers, and the disease may be reactivated by stress (*e.g.*, moulting) or by immunosuppression due to other infections. The disease tends to persist for extended periods in multiple-age poultry complexes.

Clinical Findings

Only a few birds develop lesions at one time. Lesions are prominent in some birds and may significantly decrease flock performance. The cutaneous form is characterized by nodular lesions on various parts of the unfeathered skin of chickens and on the head and upper neck of turkeys. Generalized lesions of feathered skin may also be seen. In some cases, lesions are limited chiefly to the feet and legs. The lesion is initially a raised, blanched, nodular area that enlarges, becomes yellowish, and progresses to a thick, dark scab. Multiple lesions usually develop and often coalesce. Lesions in various stages of development may be found on the same bird. Localization around the nostrils may cause nasal discharge. Cutaneous lesions on the eyelids may cause complete closure of one or both eyes.

In the diphtheritic form, lesions develop on the mucous membranes of the mouth, esophagus, pharynx, larynx, and trachea (wetpox or fowl diphtheria). Occasionally, lesions are seen almost exclusively in one or more of these sites.

Caseous patches firmly adherent to the mucosa of the larynx and mouth or proliferative masses may develop. Mouth lesions interfere with feeding. Tracheal lesions cause difficulty in respiration and may simulate infectious laryngotracheitis in chickens. Laryngeal and tracheal lesions in chickens must be differentiated from those of laryngotracheitis.

Often, the course of the disease in a flock is protracted. Extensive infection in a layer flock results in decreased egg production. Cutaneous infections alone ordinarily cause low or moderate mortality, and these flocks generally return to normal production after recovery. Mortality is usually high in the generalized or diphtheritic form.

Diagnosis

Cutaneous infections usually produce characteristic gross and microscopic lesions. When only small lesions are present, it is often difficult to distinguish them from abrasions caused by fighting. Microscopic examination of affected tissues stained with H&E reveals eosinophilic cytoplasmic inclusion bodies. Cytoplasmic inclusions are also detectable by fluorescent antibody and immunohistochemical methods.

The elementary bodies in the inclusion bodies can be detected in smears from lesions stained by the Gimenez method. Viral particles with typical poxvirus morphology can be demonstrated by negative-staining electron microscopy as well as in ultrathin sections of the lesions. The virus can be isolated by inoculating chorioallantoic membrane of developing chicken embryos, susceptible birds, or cell cultures of avian origin. Chicken embryos (9-12 days old) are the preferred and most convenient host for virus isolation.

Field isolates and vaccine strains of fowlpox virus can be compared by restriction endonuclease analysis of viral genomes. This method is useful for comparing closely related DNA genomes. However, because of the large size of the genome, minor differences are difficult to detect by this method. Detailed genetic analysis reveals differences between vaccine strains and field strains responsible for outbreaks of fowlpox in previously vaccinated chicken flocks.

While vaccine strains of fowlpox virus contain remnants of long terminal repeats of reticuloendotheliosis virus (REV), most field strains contain full-length REV in their genome. Nucleic acid probes derived from cloned genomic fragments of fowlpox virus can also be used for diagnosis. This procedure is especially useful for differentiation of the diphtheritic form of fowlpox (involving the trachea) from infectious laryngotracheitis.

PCR can be used to amplify genomic DNA sequences of various sizes using specific primers. This procedure is useful when an extremely small amount of viral DNA is present in the sample. PCR has been used effectively to differentiate field and vaccine strains of fowlpox virus. Recently, 2 monoclonal antibodies that recognize different fowlpox virus antigens have been developed. These monoclonal antibodies can be used for strain differentiation by immunoblotting. The complete sequence of the fowlpox virus genome has been identified recently and is useful in comparing the sequences of selected genes of other avian poxviruses.

Prevention and Treatment

Where pox is prevalent, chickens and turkeys should be vaccinated with live-embryo or cell-culture-propagated virus. The most widely used vaccines are attenuated fowlpox virus and pigeonpox virus isolates of high immunogenicity and low pathogenicity. A turkeypox vaccine has been developed to control pox in turkey flocks in which fowlpox vaccine has been ineffective.

This virus appears to be immunologically different from fowlpox virus. In high-risk areas, vaccination with an attenuated vaccine of cell-culture origin in the first few weeks of life and revaccination at 12-16 week is often sufficient. Health of birds, extent of exposure, and type of operation determine the timings of vaccinations.

Because the infection spreads slowly, vaccination is often useful in limiting spread in affected flocks if administered when <20 per cent of the birds have lesions. Because passive immunity may interfere with multiplication of vaccine virus, progeny from recently vaccinated or recently infected flocks should be vaccinated only after passive immunity has declined. Vaccinated birds should be examined 1 week later for swelling and scab formation ('take') at the site of vaccination. Absence of 'take' indicates lack of potency of vaccine, passive or acquired immunity, or improper vaccination. Revaccination with another serial lot of vaccine may be indicated.

Naturally infected or vaccinated birds develop humoral as well as cell-mediated immune responses. Humoral immune responses can be measured by ELISA or virus neutralization tests.

Infectious Bronchitis

Infectious bronchitis is an acute, rapidly spreading, viral disease of chickens characterized by respiratory signs, decreased egg production, and poor egg quality. Some strains of the causative virus, infectious bronchitis virus (IBV), are nephropathogenic. The latter strains produce interstitial nephritis resulting in significant mortality. Infectious bronchitis is of major economic importance to commercial chicken producers worldwide.

Etiology and Epidemiology

IBV, a coronavirus, is worldwide in distribution and has numerous serotypes. Two or more serotypes may be seen simultaneously in one geographic region. IBV is shed by infected chickens in respiratory discharges and feces. The highly contagious virus is spread by airborne droplets, ingestion of contaminated feed and water, and contaminated equipment and clothng of caretakers. Naturally infected chickens and those vaccinated with live IBV may intermittently shed virus for many weeks or even months. Virus infection in layers and breeders occurs cyclically as immunity declines or on exposure to different serotypes.

Clinical Findings

Signs occur after an incubation period of 18-48 hr. Spread to other birds is rapid, and morbidity may be nearly 100 per cent. The nature and severity of the disease are influenced by the age and immune status of the flock and virulence of the causal strain. Young chickens cough, sneeze, and have tracheal rales for 10-14 days. Wet eyes and dyspnea may be seen, and facial swelling may also occur ccasionally, particularly with concurrent bacterial infection of the sinuses. In broiler chickens, IBV infection is a major cause of poor feed conversion, reduced growth rate, and condemnation of meat at processing. Nephropathogenic strains can produce interstitial nephritis with high mortality (up to 60 per cent) in young chickens. In most outbreaks, however, mortality is 5 per cent, although secondary bacterial infections may cause higher losses.

In layers, egg production may drop 5-50 per cent, and eggs are often misshapen, thin-shelled, and contain watery albumen. Egg production and egg quality generally return to near normal levels in most birds on recovery.

Lesions

Respiratory tract lesions include mucoid exudate in the trachea and bronchi, generally without hemorrhage. Caseous plugs may be found in the trachea of young birds. Air sacs are thickened and opaque. Secondary bacterial infections in meat-type birds, especially with coliform bacteria, produce caseous airsacculitis, perihepatitis, and pericarditis. Nephropathogenic strains produce swollen, pale kidneys, with tubules and ureters distended with urates. In layers, urolithiasis is associated with virus infection and certain dietary factors.

Diagnosis

Diagnosis cannot be based solely on clinical signs because of similarities to mild respiratory forms of Newcastle disease, laryngotracheitis, and infectious coryza.

Seroconversion or a rise in IBV antibody titer shown by ELISA, hemagglutination inhibition, or virus neutralization tests can be used for diagnosis given a history of respiratory disease or reduced egg production. A definitive diagnosis is generally based on virus isolation and identification.

Virus can be isolated by inoculation of bacteria-free tissue homogenates of trachea, cecal tonsils, and kidneys into 9-to 11-day-old chicken embryos. Several blind passages of the virus may be necessary for isolation of some field strains.

The virus produces embryo stunting, curling, and urate deposits in the mesonephros, with variable mortality. Because the virus exhibits great antigenic variation, the serotype should be identified if possible.

Serotypes are conventionally identified with the aid of known serotype-specific chicken antisera in the virus neutralization test. However, the virus neutralization test is expensive, time consuming, and not readily available; therefore, it is not commonly used. A limited number of serotype-specific monoclonal antibodies (MAb) have been developed for serotyping purposes.

However, direct application of MAb-based immuno-histochemical procedures for detection of viral antigen in infected chicken tissues is not considered dependable because of the low concentration of the antigen in the tissues.

The MAb have been best used after the virus is propagated by passage in chicken embryos, in which case the virus can be detected in the cells associated with the chorioallantoic membranes by immunofluorescence or immunoperoxidase staining, or in the allantoic fluid by ELISA.

Analyses of the viral genome for the purpose of identifying the virus serotype are now commonly used. These methods are based on the application of reverse transcriptase PCR (RT-PCR), using-specific oligonucleotide primers, to produce DNA copies of IBV genes, usually of the S1 part of the spike glycoprotein gene. Subsequently, the RT-PCR product is subjected to restriction fragment length polymorphism (RFLP) or analysed by nucleotide sequencing. For RFLP, the RT-PCR product is digested with a set of specific restriction endonucleases, and the digested nucleic acid fragments are separated by gel electrophoresis. The specific pattern of their separation in the gel is compared with those of the standard strains for identification.

Control

No available medication alters the course of the disease, although antibiotic therapy may reduce mortality due to secondary infections. Increasing the temperature in the poultry house and under the hover by 5-10°F (3-5°C) may lower mortality. Attenuated vaccines used for immunization may produce mild respiratory signs. Live vaccines are initially given to chicks 1-14 days old by spray, drinking water, or eyedrop. Revaccination is common. Live or adjuvanted killed vaccines are sometimes used in breeders and layers to prevent egg production losses.

Many serotypes are recognized, and a number of new or variant serotypes have been reported, which pose problems in immunization and diagnosis. If possible, selection of vaccine should be based on knowledge of the prevalent serotype(s) on the premises. The most commonly used live vaccines in the USA contain strains of IBV serotypes Massachusetts, Connecticut, and Arkansas. Vaccination with selected variant serotypes is practiced in some areas. Outbreaks with mortality due to nephritis have been associated with several variant strains in Australia and the USA. Infection with standard as well as variant serotypes have been associated with egg production losses in vaccinated layer flocks.

DIFFERENT TYPES OF RESPIRATORY DISEASES

Fowl Pox

Fowlpox is a worldwide disease of poultry caused by viruses of the family *Poxviridae* and the genus *Avipoxvirus*. The viruses causing fowlpox are distinct from one another but antigenically similar, possible hosts including chickens, turkeys, quail, canaries, pigeons, and many other species of birds. There are two forms of the disease. The first is spread by biting insects (especially mosquitoes) and wound contamination and causes lesions on the comb, wattles, and beak. Birds affected by this form usually recover within a few weeks. The second form is spread by inhalation of the virus and causes a diphtheritic membrane to form in the mouth, pharynx, larynx, and sometimes the trachea. The prognosis for this form is poor.

Vaccines are available for fowlpox (ATCvet code: QI01AD12). Chicken are usually vaccinated with *pigeonpox virus*. Turkeys are also routinely vaccinated.

Synonyms: chicken pox (not to be confused with chicken pox in humans; the human disease does not affect poultry and vice versa), sore head, avian diphtheria, bird pox

Species affected: Most poultry — chickens, turkeys, pheasants, quail, ducks, psittacine, and ratites — of all ages are susceptible.

Clinical signs: There are two forms of fowl pox. The dry form is characterized by raised, wart-like lesions on unfeathered areas (head, legs, vent, etc.). The lesions heal in about 2 weeks. If the scab is removed before healing is complete, the surface beneath is raw and bleeding. Unthriftiness and retarded growth are typical symptoms of fowl pox.

In laying hens, infection results in a transient decline in egg production. In the wet form there are canker-like lesions in the mouth, pharynx, larynx, and trachea. The wet form may cause respiratory distress by obstructing the upper air passages. Chickens may be affected with either or both forms of fowl pox at one time.

Transmission: Fowl pox is transmitted by direct contact between infected and susceptible birds or by mosquitos. Virus-containing scabs also can be sloughed from affected birds and serve as a source of infection. The virus can enter the blood stream through the eye, skin wounds, or respiratory tract. Mosquitos become infected from feeding on birds with fowl pox in their blood stream. There is some evidence that the mosquito remains infective for life. Mosquitos are the primary reservoir and spreaders of fowl pox on poultry ranges. Several species of mosquito can transmit fowl pox. Often mosquitos winter-over in poultry houses so, outbreaks can occur during winter and early spring.

Treatment: No treatment is available. However, fowl pox is relatively slow-spreading. Thus, it is possible to vaccinate to stop an outbreak. The wing-web vaccination method is used for chickens and the thigh-stick method for turkeys older than 8 weeks.

Prevention: Fowl pox outbreaks in poultry confined to houses can be controlled by spraying to kill mosquitos. However, if fowl pox is endemic in the area, vaccination is recommended. Do not vaccinate unless the disease becomes a problem on a farm or in the area. Refer to the publication PS-36 (Vaccination of Small Poultry Flocks) for more information on fowl pox vaccinations.

Newcastle Disease

Newcastle disease is a contagious bird disease affecting many domestic and wild avian species. First found in Newcastle, United Kingdom in 1926, then by Burnet in 1943 in Australia in connection with laboratory infection where the virus was isolated from a ocular discharge of a patient to show the specific antibody titre in the patient's blood. Newcastle has a negative sense single stranded genome which codes for a RNA directed RNA polymerase, hemagglutinin- neuraminidase protein, fusion protein, matrix protein, phosphoprotein and nucleoprotein in the 5' to 3' direction. Its effects are most notable in domestic poultry due to their high susceptibility and the potential for severe impacts of an epizootic on the poultry industries. It is endemic to many countries. Newcastle disease was discovered in Newcastle upon Tyne, England in 1926 (Doyle), but also at this time slightly different strains were found in other parts of the world.

Exposure of humans to infected birds (for example in poultry processing plants) can cause mild conjunctivitis and influenza-like symptoms, but the Newcastle disease virus (NDV) otherwise poses no hazard to human health. Interest in the use of NDV as an anticancer agent has arisen from the ability of NDV to selectively kill human tumour cells with limited toxicity to normal cells. No treatment for NDV exists, but the use of prophylactic vaccines and sanitary measures reduces the likelihood of outbreaks.

Causal Agent

Description: The causal agent, Newcastle disease virus, is a negative-sense single-stranded RNA virus. Transmission occurs by exposure to faecal and other excretions from infected birds, and through contact with contaminated feed, water, equipment and clothing.

Strains: NDV strains can be categorised as velogenic (highly virulent), mesogenic (intermediate virulence) or lentogenic (nonvirulent). Velogenic strains produce severe nervous and respiratory signs, spread rapidly and cause up to 90 per cent mortality. Mesogenic strains cause coughing, affect egg quality and production and result in up to 10 per cent mortality. Lentogenic strains produce mild signs with negligible mortality.

Use as an anticancer agent: In 1999, promising results were reported using an attenuated strain of the Newcastle virus, codenamed MTH-68, in cancer patients by researchers who had isolated the strain in 1968. It appears the virus preferentially targets and replicates in certain types of tumor cells, leaving normal cells almost unaffected. In 2006, researchers from the Hebrew University also succeeded in isolating a variant of the NDV, codenamed NDV-HUJ, which showed promising results in 14 glioblastoma multiforme patients.

History of NDV in cancer therapy: Even if the oncolytic effect of the Newcastle Disease Virus (NDV) was documented already in the 1950s, the main advances of viruses in cancer therapy came with the advent of reverse genetics technologies (Flanagan *et al.* 1955 in Mullen and Tanabe 2002, Vigil *et al.* 2007). With these new possibilities, studies of modified NDV strains with enhanced cancer treatment properties have been put on the agenda. This was demonstrated by Vigil *et al.* (2007) where the engineered Hitcher B1 NDV/F3aa strain was modified to express a highly fusogenic F-protein in combination with immunostimulatory molecules such as IFN-gamma, interleukin 2 or tumor necrosis factor alpha. Promising results was discovered with proteins associated to the adaptive immune system which paved the way for possibilities to use NDV to create a tumor-associated antigen. Another study showed how NDV/F3aa could be modified to express NS1, an influenza virus protein with capability to modulate with the innate immune response, for example, by suppressing the induction of the cellular interferons (Zamarin *et al.* 2009b).

NDV, pros and cons in cancer therapy: NDV possesses many unique anti-cancer properties and thereby provides an excellent base in virotherapy research. NDV has selectivity on oncogenic cells, were it replicate without, or in a less pronounced way, harming normal cells (Elankumaran *et al.* 2006, Fábián *et al.* 2007). It binds, fuse into and replicate within the infected cells' cytoplasm independent of cell proliferation (Elankumaran *et al.* 2006). One of the main issues using NDV in treatment is the host/patient immune response against the virus itself, which prior to the time of the reverse genetics technology decreased the applicability of NDV as a cancer treatment (Mullen and Tanabe 2002, Kuruppu and Tanabe 2005).

NDV-induced mechanisms leading to tumor cell death: The precise way in which the presence of NDV induce tumor cell death remains to be clarified and may show variation both regards strains of NDV and to which type of cancer is targeted. Elankumaran *et al.* (2006) showed that NDV triggers apoptosis in a wide range of cancer cell types via the mitochondrial/intrinsic pathway, through loss of membrane potential and thereby inducing release of cytochrome c in the tumor cell. The results of Elankumaran *et al.* (2006) also indicate that the extrinsic pathway is activated by TNF-related apoptosis-inducing ligand (TRIAL)-induced NDV-mediated apoptosis in a late stage. Altomonte *et al.* (2009) studied a hyperfusogenic NDV/F3aa(L289A) with refined abilities to fusing into somatic cells. NDV has aggregating properties causing syncytia formations of tumor cell which, apart from amplifying immune based cell killing, also result in necrosis of cells. This pathway was believed to lead to a considerable boost of immune activation and potentially an antitumor response, which was supported by observations of a significant accumulation of NK-cells and neutrophils following the infusion of NDV/

F3aa(L289A) in Hepatocellular Carcinoma cells. In addition, Vigil *et al.* (2008) demonstrated an increase of CD4+ and CD8+ T-cells within the tumor cells when inducing NDV/F3aa recombined with the cytokine interleukin-2 (IL-2). Also Zamarin *et al.* (2009a) show that a NDV/F3aa-IL-2 strain induced the immune system, giving a cytotoxic effect on the tumor cells. A 15-year study on patient with malign melanoma showed increased numbers of oligoclonal CD8+ T-cells in the blood, suggesting that the vaccination with NDV oncolysates was associated with prolonged survival among the patients and that CD8+ T-cells played an important role (Batliwalla *et al.* 1998).

Use as a biological weapon: Newcastle disease was one of more than a dozen agents the United States researched as potential biological weapons before the nation suspended its biological weapons programmes.

Transmission: NDV is spread primarily through direct contact between healthy birds and the bodily discharges of infected birds. The disease is transmitted through infected birds' droppings and secretions from the nose, mouth, and eyes. NDV spreads rapidly among birds kept in confinement, such as commercially raised chickens.

High concentrations of the NDV are found in birds' bodily discharges; therefore, the disease can be spread easily by mechanical means. Virus-bearing material can be picked up on shoes and clothing and carried from an infected flock to a healthy one.

NDV can survive for several weeks in a warm and humid environment on birds' feathers, manure, and other materials. It can survive indefinitely in frozen material. However, the virus is destroyed rapidly by dehydration and by the ultraviolet rays in sunlight. Smuggled pet birds, especially Amazon parrots from Latin America, pose a great risk of introducing NDV into the US. Amazon parrots that are carriers of the disease but do not show symptoms are capable of shedding NDV for more than 400 days.

Clinical findings

Symptoms: Signs of infection with NDV vary greatly depending on factors such as the strain of virus and the health, age and species of the host. The incubation period for the disease ranges from two to 15 days. An infected bird may exhibit the following signs:

They can include respiratory signs (gasping, coughing), nervous signs (depression, inappetence, muscular tremors, drooping wings, twisting of head and neck, circling, complete paralysis), swelling of the tissues around the eyes and neck, greenish, watery diarrhea, misshapen, rough- or thin-shelled eggs and reduced egg production.

In acute cases, the death is very sudden, and, in the beginning of the outbreak, the remaining birds do not seem to be sick. In flocks with good immunity, however, the signs (respiratory and digestive) are mild and progressive, and are followed after seven days by nervous symptoms, especially twisted heads.

Synonyms: pneumoencephalitis

The highly contagious and lethal form of Newcastle disease is known as viscerotropic (attacks the internal organs) velogenic Newcastle disease, VVND, exotic Newcastle disease, or Asiatic Newcastle disease. VVND is not present in the United States poultry industry at this time.

Species affected: Newcastle disease affects all birds of all ages. Humans and other mammals are also susceptible to Newcastle. In such species, it causes a mild conjunctivitis.

Clinical signs: There are three forms of Newcastle disease – mildly pathogenic (lentogenic), moderately pathogenic (mesogenic) and highly pathogenic (velogenic). Newcastle disease is characterized by a sudden onset of clinical signs which include hoarse chirps (in chicks), watery discharge from nostrils, labored breathing (gasping), facial swelling, paralysis, trembling, and twisting of the neck (sign of central nervous system involvement). Mortality ranges from 10 to 80 percent depending on the pathogenicity. In adult laying birds, symptoms can include decreased feed and water consumption and a dramatic drop in egg production.

Transmission: The Newcastle virus can be transmitted short distances by the airborne route or introduced on contaminated shoes, caretakers, feed deliverers, visitors, tires, dirty equipment, feed sacks, crates, and wild birds. Newcastle virus can be passed in the egg, but Newcastle-infected embryos die before hatching. In live birds, the virus is shed in body fluids, secretions, excreta, and breath.

Treatment: There is no specific treatment for Newcastle disease. Antibiotics can be given for 3-5 days to prevent secondary bacterial infections (particularly *E. coli*). For chicks, increasing the brooding temperature 5°F may help reduce losses.

Prevention: Prevention programmes should include vaccination, good sanitation, and implementation of a comprehensive biosecurity programmes.

DISEASE PREVENTION AND CONTROL

General Considerations

- Three industries:
  - o Broilers
  - o Turkeys
  - o Layers.

- Meat production in broilers and turkeys will be discussed primarily.

Disease prevention management:

- Vertical Integration (VI) plays a vital role in disease prevention
  - o Company controls housing, breeds and breeders, feed, live production, live-haul, and processing
  - o Contract growers and company owned farms
  - o Over 95+% production in broilers (VI)
  - o Over 85% of the production in turkeys (VI)

Production parameters:

- Broilers:
  - o 45 to 56 days of age weighing 5 – 7 pounds
    - * Straight run; sexes raised separately
  - o Feed conversion 1.90 – 2.10 pounds of feed per pound of gain
  - o Livability 95%
  - o Condemnations < 1%
  - o Cost per pound of production 20-25 cents
    - * Add processing cost per pound
  - o Two-thirds of cost in feed.

Production parameters:

- Turkey hens:
  - o 14 – 16 weeks of age weighing 15 – 18 pounds
  - o Feed conversion: 2.20 pounds of feed per pound of gain
  - o Livability: 94%
  - o Condemnations less than 1.5%
  - o Cost per pound of production 32 cents per pound
    - * Add processing cost per pound.

Production parameters:

- Turkey toms:
  - o 16 – 22 weeks weighing 32 – 45 pounds
  - o Feed conversion: 2.6 pounds of feed per pound of gain
  - o Livability 90%
  - o Condemnations less than 2%
  - o Cost per pound of production 35 cents per pound
    - * Add processing cost per pound.

Disease Prevention Management:

- Housing:
  - o Environmental control houses; temperature and ventilation control (power ventilation)
    - * Curtain sided houses

- o Closed water system in broilers (nipple drinkers).
- All-in-all-out production results in same age of flock on farms
  - o Broilers – 100%
  - o Broilers chicks all placed on a farm at same time (within days)
  - o Broilers all processed at the same time (within days)
  - o Zone raising in geographic areas.

Disease Prevention Management:

- Two Stage production in turkeys
  - o Brooder house placement of poults
    - * Cleaned and disinfected after each flock
  - o Moved to grow-out facilities on same farm at approximately 5 weeks of age
  - o There are single stage farms (brooder versus grow-out).

Disease Prevention Management:

- Biosecurity
  - o Traffic control to and from farm
  - o Wild bird and rodent control
  - o Protective clothing (coveralls, boots, head coverings)
  - o Dead bird disposal
  - o Farm isolation
  - o Farm clean-out and disinfection, down time.
- Best management practices/guidelines.

Disease prevention management:

- Vaccination
  - o Breeders: 10 – 12 diseases (22-25 serotypes) in chickens: 8 – 10 diseases (18 – 20 serotypes) in turkeys
    - * Breeder health
    - * Egg production
    - * Maternal antibodies to chicks/poults
  - o Blood testing standard for disease monitoring.

PPT Slide:

- Meat birds. 5 diseases (10 serotypes) in chickens: 1-3 diseases in turkeys
  - o Health
  - o Production
  - o Processing health
- Blood testing standard for disease monitoring
- Problems are not in diseases we can vaccinate for!

Antimicrobial Use:

- Therapeutic

- Disease prevention/growth promotion
- Day old injection/In-ovo administration.

Therapeutic Antimicrobial Use

- E.coli infection is the #1 cause for use of therapeutic antimicrobials
    - o Clostridia spp. and pasteurellosis are also treated
- Secondary bacterial infection is due to primary respiratory and/or enteric disease
    - o E. coli is troublesome; Does not lend itself to vaccine development; E. coli is ubiquitous
    - o Infectious bronchitis as example of primary infection
- E. coli primarily treated via water
- Feed grade therapeutic antibiotics uncommon.

Therapeutic antimicrobial use:

- We currently have 12 antibiotics used as intervention strategies for bacterial disease
- Most commonly used
    - o Tetracyclines, streptomycin, neomycin, bacitracin,
- Less commonly used
    - o Lincomycin, spectinomycin, tylosin, erythromycin, sulfonamides, penicillin
- Fluoroquinolone are held in reserve because:
    - o Importance to poultry and humans
    - o Cost
    - o Currently represents the only consistent treatment for E. coli.

Therapeutic antimicrobial use:

- Guidelines established by AAAP/AVMA are used in the decision making process
- Diagnostic work-up initiates intervention strategies
- Management and supportive therapy considered prior to antimicrobial therapy.

Therapeutic antimicrobial use:

- Antimicrobial use based on diagnostics, mortality and morbidity, age of flock, farm history, susceptibility patterns
- Antimicrobials use must be approved by veterinarian, live production specialist, or other health service technician before use
    - o Extra-label and fluoroquinolone use ordered and prescribed by veterinarian.

Therapeutic antimicrobial use:

- Records kept and utilized

- Most important to therapeutic antimicrobial use are the diagnostics performed to identify the primary agent involved to initiate preventative strategies and avoid future therapeutic interventions
- Currently no vaccine or antimicrobial for improper management.

Disease prevention:

- 4 antimicrobials are used for the prevention of clostridial (necrotic) enteritis
- "Sub therapeutic" vs. low level prophylaxis
    - o Levels are lower than that used in an acute outbreak of disease
    - o Anticoccidial feed additives are generally static and not cidal; proliferation of low numbers of coccidia predisposes the intestines to infection
    - o Virginiamycin, bacitracin, lincomycin, tylosin, bambermycin*
- Other antimicrobials used in therapy are not used for growth promotion.

Mechanisms of action for low level antimicrobial use:

- Some are known and some unknown
- Virginiamycin*, bacitracin*, lincomycin*, tylosin, bambermycin (chickens vs. turkeys)
    - o Not tetracycline, erythromycin, penicillin, sulfonamides
- Necrotic enteritis control
- Increased hot and chilled carcass weights
- Increased breast meat yield
- Protein sparing effects.

Antimicrobial use benefits:

- Maintains intestine tensile strength and integrity
    - o Very important at processing (automation)
- Reduces feed needed for a pound of gain
    - o Reducing feed conversion from 2.00 to 1.99 represents 40,000,000 pounds of feed (chickens only) (89 million pounds – turkeys)
    - o Reduces utility costs, and less contamination to the environment with nitrogen and phosphorus.

Day-old injection – In-ovo:

- We deal with a biologic environment impossible to sterilize ……….. However ………..
- Hatcheries have stringent disinfection and sanitation programs including microbiologic monitoring for fungi and bacteria (sanitation of eggs??)
- In the incubation period, the yolk is drawn into the abdominal cavity at 19 and 25 days of incubation for chicks and poults respectively.

Day-old injection – In-ovo:

- The egg is a closed system and the potential for small numbers of bacteria to rapidly increase in numbers because of the incubation temperature
- The in-ovo system provided a unique opportunity to prevent bacterial proliferation in the yolk within the egg
- Gentamicin and ceftiofur are most commonly used
- Sarafloxacin is the only approved In-ovo antimicrobial and IS NOT and HAS NEVER USED.

Other Considerations:

- Competitive exclusion products
- Volumetric versus mg/kg dosing (AMDUCA)
- Processing (antibacterial rinses); irradiation
- Antimicrobial therapeutic use is a salvage procedure
- No Vaccine for bad management and no drug for it either
- Industry continuously evaluates what it does.

EXTERNAL AND INTERNAL PARASITISM

External Parasitism

Mites: Feather mites (family *Analgesidae*) often show specific preferences for different locations on the feathers or for specific types of feather. Quill mites (*Syringophilus, Dermoglyphus*) burrow into the feather shaft resulting in a powdery-white appearance. After the feather has been eaten away the calamus remains within the follicle which may fail to regenerate normal feathers. The mites can be demonstrated amongst the powdery debris squeezed out of an affected feather shaft.

Many species of *Cnemidocoptes* mites cause mange in birds. The most common are *C. mutans* of poultry and *C. pilae* in budgerigars (and many other parrots) and canaries. The mites spend their entire life on the bird. The lesions can occur on any featherless part of the skin and are characterised by raised honeycombed encrustations on the cere, beak, eyelids and feet. Occasionally it becomes generalised and affects feather follicles. Cnemidocoptic mange is easily controlled with 2 treatments of moxidectin or ivermectin (200 ìg/kg) 4 weeks apart. The drug can diluted and administered directly to the skin or in the drinking water.

Dermanyssus gallinae and *Ornithonyssus sylvarium* are large mites which attack poultry and other bird species. They are blood sucking mites which may be found on or off the host. *Dermanyssus* lay eggs off the host, *Ornithonyssus* on the host. Their life cycle is completed in 7 days. Heavy infection causes irritation and anaemia. Both mites may infect humans causing pruritis. Wild birds (particularly sparrows and starlings) nesting in houses are sometimes the source of mites which attack humans.

Mites are probably the most common ectoparasite that affect birds. They are usually smaller than 2 mm and transmit many diseases

Feather Mite: *Dermanyssus gallinae* (red mite):

- White when fasting, red when eating
- Can affect all birds, not so much raptors and psittacine birds
- Does not live on bird-visits at night
- Feeds at night. Female lays eggs 12 hours after a feed, hatch in 48 hours
- Adults survive 8-12 months without feeding
- Not common on raptors and psittacine birds.

Northern Mite: *Ornithonyssus sylvarum:*

- Life cycle entirely on host
- Can survive only a few days off host
- Most bird species susceptible
- Direct transmission
- Ornithonyssus sp commonly found on nestling psittacine birds.
- Mites can survive up to 4 weeks off the host (Arends, 1997).

Quill Mites: *Syringophilus bipectinatus, Dermoglyphus elongates:*

- Live inside quills-body narrow and elongated
- Not host-specific
- Many birds suit
- Skin Mites: *Epidermoptes bilobatus, Michrolichus avus*
- Small mites, affect most birds
- Life cycle on host.

Visceral Mites: *Sternostoma tracheacolum* (rhinonyssid mites):

- Affects many birds
- Canaries commonly affected
- Gouldian finch – species not known.

Subcutaneous Mites: *Laminosioptes cysticola and Hypodectes sp:*

- Look like small white grains of rice
- Mites are usually dead and surrounded by connective tissue
- Eventually calcify
- Life cycle unknown.

Skin Mites: Epidermoptes bilobatus and *Michrolichus avus* (epidermoptic mites):

- Soft, rounded body
- ound on many birds

- Life cycle unknown, probably on host
- Lesions can become secondarily infected.

Trombiculid mite larvae:

- Can infect the skin of canaries, pigeons, and psittacine birds.
- Affected birds are usually non-pruritic
- Oedematous skin of the leg (dorsal to the hocks) and abdomen.
- Secondary infections often occur.

Cnemidocoptic Mites: *Cnemidocoptes pilae* and *Cnemidocoptes mutans:*

Domestic Fowl: *C mutans*

- Transmission direct and indirect
- Scaley face in budgerigar
- Scaley leg in domestic chicken
- Raised white-yellow honeycomb-like encrustations on the cere, beak and around the eyes
- Elbows, legs and skin around the cloacal opening
- The lesion can look like flour on the skin, especially in SCC
- Eventual deformity in the budgerigar
- Malocclusion of the beak
- Treatment moxidectin 200 micrograms/kg once a week.

Canary: Tassle foot, also featherless parts of skin.

Sulphur Crested Cockatoo: may look like flour. Disfigurement of beak.

Domestic Fowl: *C mutans*

- Scaley leg
- Burrows under scales of legs, inducing a rough, raised, powdery appearance
- Proliferation of the scales of the legs and digits
- Lameness or loss of skin may result.

Control of Mites

Applying a pyrethrum spray (Avian Insect Liquidator concentrate (Vetafarm products)) to the birds, their nest material, nest box and the walls of the aviary. The insecticide should be applied to the skin, not the feathers, as this is where the mites reside. The insecticide should be applied weekly for three times (ie, over 2 weeks). Mites can spread on people and other fomites.

Prevention of Mite Infection

Regular monitoring of the aviary and nestboxes for evidence of mites. Treatment of adult birds prior to breeding.

New nest boxes each year, treated with pyrethrum spray and allowed to dry before being used for breeding.

Moxidectin administered to each bird at 200 ìg/kg will kill blood sucking mites.

Lice

Many species of lice can affect the skin of birds usually without feather damage. Lice are larger than mites and are usually apathogenic although they may cause a mild pruritis. Dull, damaged feathers, presence of eggs.

- Very common external parasites of birds-larger than mites.
- Dorso-ventrally flattened body.
- No wings, legs have hooks at the end
- Eggs laid on feathers
- Heaviest infections on sick birds
- They tend to be *HOST*-specific-transmission direct
- Pruritis, damaged feathers, dull plumage
- Lice can be seen with eyes – but do you observe them????
- Presence of eggs – some look like wasp nests around calamus
- Treatment-once a week, 2-3 times:
    * pyrethrin-based insecticides
    * Ivermectin/moxidectin for BITING lice
    * Lice cannot survive away from the host so treatment of the environment is not absolutely essential.

Ticks (*Argasidae, Ixodidae*):

- Oval flattened body when fasting, round after eating.
- *Argas persicus* – the fowl tick. Can affect many bird species by causing blood loss and is a vector for avian spirochaetes. In tropical areas they can be the most important ectoparasites of poultry.
- The life cycle may be completed within 8 weeks in warm weather. In temperate climates the ticks remain inactive off the bird in crevices during cold weather. Nymphs live up to 15 months without a feed and adults can survive many years off the host!
- Pale yellow to grey 15mm long – adults 8 legs, larvae 6 legs
- Shelter in dark in day, feed at night
- Larvae stay on fowl in day
- Transmits *Borrelia anserina,* the cause of tick fever
- The presence of these ticks is an aid to diagnosis.

Ixodes ticks have been reported as a cause of paralysis but are more likely to cause anaemia due to blood loss.

Fleas (*Ceratophyllus gallinacea, Echidnophagia gallinacea* [the "stick-fast flea"]):

- Small insects with laterally flattened body
- Adults have no wings – they can run and jump
- Fix mouth to skin and suck blood
- Poultry and nesting birds
- Vectors of infectious diseases
- Seen mainly in free range poultry in tropical areas.
- The mouthparts of the adults are buried in the skin which prevents them from moving around.
- Eggs drop off and the developing stages are found in the soil.

Hippoboscid flies live between the feathers in many species. They fly out briefly and then dart back into the plumage. They are non-pathogenic but may transmit *Haemoproteus* and viral pathogens.

Mosquitoes can irritate nestlings. It may be necessary to control mosquitoes in specific situations to prevent the transmission of poxviruses (and other viruses) and blood parasites. Mosquito netting, Shelltox ministrips and mossie zappers may be necessary.

Many filaroids inhabit the subcutaneous connective tissue of birds often without causing an inflammatory response.

Avioserpens taiwana infects ducks in Asia, and induces granulomas in the skin of the submandibular area and thighs.

Skin flukes (*Collyriclidae*) produce granulomas and fibrous cysts around the cloaca of many bird species.

DIFFERENT TYPES OF POULTRY DISEASES

Amyloidosis

A Coronavirus infection of chickens with a morbidity of 50-100 per cent and a mortality 0-25 per cent, depending on secondary infections.

Infection is via the conjunctiva or upper respiratory tract with an incubation period of 18-36 hours. The infection spreads rapidly by contact, fomites or aerosol. Some birds/viral strains can be carriers for up to 1 year.

The virus, which may survive 4 weeks in premises, is sensitive to solvents, heat (56°C for 15 mins), alkalis, disinfectants (Formal 1 per cent for 3 mins). Poor ventilation and high density are predisposing factors.

Signs

- Sudden death.
- Muscular shivering.
- Otherwise as for standard IB.

Post-mortem Lesions

- Oedema of pectoral muscles and subcutaneously on abdomen, lesions progress to necrosis and scarring of deep pectorals in convalescence.
- In layers the ovules may be intensely congested.
- Other lesions of 'classical' IB may be encountered.

Diagnosis

3-5 passages in CE allantoic cavity, HA-, typical lesions, FA, ciliostatic in tracheal organ culture, cell culture (Vero, CK) only after adaptation Serology: HI, Elisa (both group specific), SN (type specific), DID (poor sensitivity, short duration, group specific).

Treatment

Sodium salicylate 1gm/litre (acute phase) where permitted-antibiotics to control secondary colibacillosis (q.v.).

Prevention

Live vaccines of appropriate sero-type and attenuation, possible reactions depending on virulence and particle size.

Aspergillosis

A fungal infectious disease, caused by *Aspergillus fumigatus,* in which the typical sign is gasping for breath, especially in young chicks. Sometimes the same organism causes eye lesions or chronic lesions in older birds.

The fungus can infect plant material and many species of animals including birds and man. Occasionally similar lesions are produced by other species of *Aspergillus* or even other fungi such as *Penicillium, Absidia* etc.

It affects chickens, turkeys, ducks, penguins, game birds, waterfowl, etc., worldwide.

The infection has an incubation period of 2-5 days. Morbidity is usually low, but may be as high as 12 per cent. Mortality among young affected birds is 5-50 per cent.

Transmission is by inhalation exposure to an environment with a high spore count; there is usually little bird-to-bird transmission. Spores are highly resistant to disinfectants.

Signs

- *Acute form:*
- Inappetence.
- Weakness.
- Silent gasping.
- Rapid breathing.
- Thirst.
- Drowsiness.
- Nervous signs (rare).
- *Chronic Forms:*
- Ocular discharge (ocular form only).
- Wasting.

Post-mortem Lesions

- Yellow to grey nodules or plaques in lungs, air sacs, trachea, plaques in peritoneal cavity, may have greenish surface.
- Conjunctivitis/keratitis.
- Brain lesions may be seen in some birds with nervous signs.

Diagnosis

This is usually based on the signs and lesions and microscopic examination for the fungus, preferably after digestion in 10 per cent potassium hydroxide.

It may be confirmed by isolation of the fungus, typically by putting small pieces of affected tissue on Sabouraud agar.

Growth occurs in 24-48 hours and colonies are powdery green/blue in appearance.

Differentiate from excessive exposure to formalin or vaccinal reactions in day olds and from heat stress in older birds.

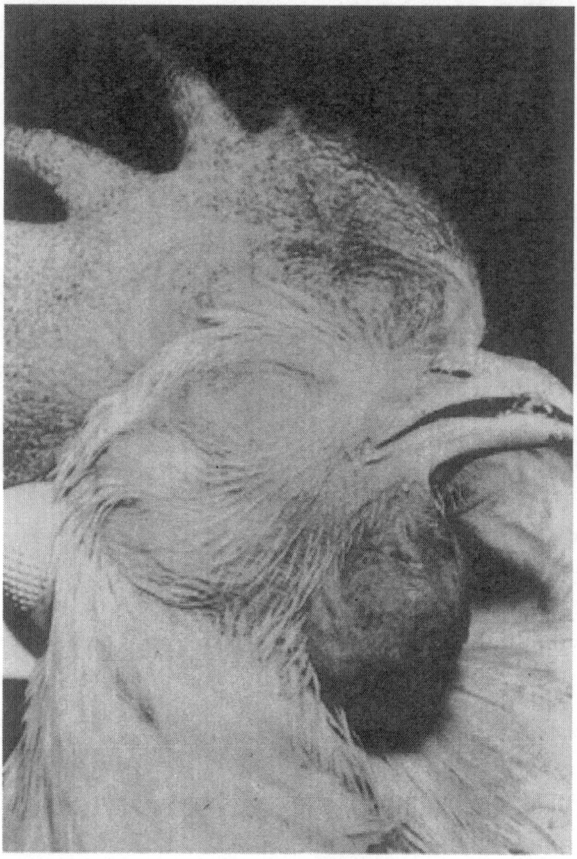

Treatment

Usually none. Environmental spraying with effective antifungal antiseptic may help reduce challenge. Amphotericin B and Nystatin have been used in high-value birds.

Prevention

Dry, good quality litter and feed, hygiene, Thiabendazole or Nystatin has been used in feed.

Anatipestifer Disease, New Duck Syndrome, Duck Septicaemia

An acute or chronic septicaemic disease caused by *Riemerella anatipestifer*, syn *Pasteurella*, or *Moraxella* a. It affects ducks of any age, sometimes turkeys, and may also be isolated from chickens, game birds and wild waterfowl. Mortality is 2-75 per cent in young ducks. Transmission is mainly direct, bird-to-bird, via toenail scratches, especially of the duckling foot, or through respiratory epithelium during respiratory disease. It can also be by faecal contamination of feed, water or the environment where survival of the infectious agent may be prolonged. Adverse environmental conditions and pre-existing disease are predisposing factors.

Signs

- Weakness.
- Neck tucked in.
- Head/neck tremor.
- Ataxia.
- Disinclined to walk.
- Incoordination.
- Dyspnoea.
- Ocular and/or nasal discharge.
- Hyperexcitability.

Post-mortem Lesions

- Perihepatitis without much smell or liver damage.
- Pericarditis.
- Airsacculitis.
- Enlarged liver and spleen.
- Occasionally fibrinous meningitis.
- Salpingitis
- Purulent synovitis.
- Chronic arthritis, sometimes with erosions of the joint cartilage.

Diagnosis

Lesions, isolation and identification of organism-blood or chocolate agar in candle jar or 5 per cent CO_2. Differentiate from duck viral enteritis, duck viral hepatitis, fowl cholera, colibacillosis, coccidiosis, chlamydiosis.

Treatment

Sulphonamides and potentiated sulphonamides are the products most commonly recommended for drinking water application. Subcutaneous injections of penicillin + dihydrostreptomycin, or streptomycin + dihydrostreptomycin are also highly effective.

Prevention

Good husbandry and hygiene, rigid depopulation and disinfection, adequate protection, 'hardening off', correct house relative humidity, sulphonamides in feed. Inactivated and attenuated vaccines available in some countries. Autogenous bacterins sometimes used.

Arizona Infection, Arizonosis

Caused by the bacterium *Arizona hinshawii*, renamed *Salmonella Arizonae.* It affects turkeys, mainly in North America, and is not present in the UK turkey population. Mortality is 10-50 per cent in young birds, older birds are asympto-matic carriers. Transmission is vertical, transovarian, and also horizontal, through faecal contamination of environment, feed etc., from long-term intestinal carriers, rodents, reptiles.

Signs

- Dejection.
- Inappetence.
- Diarrhoea.
- Vent-pasting.
- Nervous signs.
- Paralysis.
- Blindness, cloudiness in eye.
- Huddling near heat.

Post-mortem Lesions

- Enlarged mottled liver.
- Unabsorbed yolk sac.
- Congestion of duodenum.
- Cheesy plugs in intestine or caecum.
- Foci in lungs.
- Salpingitis.
- Ophthalmitis.
- Pericarditis.
- Perihepatitis.

Diagnosis

Isolation and identification, methods as per *Salmonella* spp. Differentiate from salmonellosis, coli-septicaemia.

Treatment

Injection of streptomycin, spectinomycin, or gentamycin at the hatchery is used in some countries. Formerly in-feed medication with nitrofurans was also used.

Prevention

Eradicate from breeder population, fumigation of hatching eggs, good nest and hatchery hygiene, inject eggs or poults with antibiotics, monitor sensitivity.

Avian Leukosis, Lymphoid Leukosis, Leukosis/Sarkoma Group

A complex of viral diseases with various manifestations such as lymphoid leukosis, myeloblastosis, erythroblastosis, osteopetrosis, myxosarcomas, fibrosarcomas, other tumours. It affects chickens worldwide with susceptibility varying considerably among different strains and types of stock-egg layers are generally more susceptible to lymphoid leukosis.

Morbidity is low but mortality high. Mortality tends to be chronically higher than normal for a prolonged period. Egg production is somewhat reduced.

There may be increased susceptibility to other infectious diseases due to damage to the immune system. Vertical transmission is most important by infection of the egg white in infected breeders (who are long-term carriers), lateral transmission is poor but infection may occur by the faecal-oral route, especially in young birds. In lymphoid leukosis the incubation period is about 4-6 months; it may be as short as 6 weeks for some of the other manifestations. The causative viruses are rapidly inactivated at ambient temperature and on exposure to most disinfectants.

Signs

- Depression.
- Emaciation.
- Loss of weight.
- Persistent low mortality.
- Enlargement of abdomen, liver or bursa.
- Many are asymptomatic.

Post-mortem Lesions

- Focal grey to white tumours, initially in the bursa, then liver, spleen, kidney etc. Liver may be very large.
- Microscopic-cells lymphoplastic

Diagnosis

History, age, lesions, cytology. Differentiate from Marek's disease, coligranuloma.

Prevention

Good hygiene, all-in/all-out production, control arthropods, eradication-checking of antigen in the albumen is a basis for eradication.

Avian Rhinotracheitis 'Swollen Head Syndrome'

A viral disease of chickens, turkeys, guinea fowl and possibly pheasants seen in Europe, Africa, South America and North America. It is caused by a pneumovirus of the Paramyxoviridae family, first isolated from poults in South Africa in 1978. Two subgroups have been identified on the basis of the G-protein sequence: A (original UK isolates) and B (original southern Europe isolates). There is rapid lateral transmission with infection by aerosol through the respiratory route; vertical transmission is uncertain. As for many infections, fomites can be important in moving infection between farms. The incubation period is 5-7 days, morbidity is 10-100 per cent and mortality can be 1-10 per cent.

Signs

- Decreased appetite, weight gain and feed efficiency.
- Facial and head swelling (though this can occur in other conditions).
- Loss of voice.
- Ocular and nasal discharge.
- Conjunctivitis.
- Snick.
- Dyspnoea.
- Sinusitis.

Post-mortem Lesions

- Serous rhinitis and tracheitis, sometimes pus in bronchi. If secondary invasion by *E. coli* then pneumonia, airsacculitis and perihepatitis.
- Congestion, oedema and pus in the air space of the skull occurs in a proportion of affected birds due to secondary bacterial infections.

Diagnosis

Clinical signs, serology, isolation of ciliostatic agent. Differentiate from Infectious Bronchitis, Lentogenic Newcastle disease, low virulence avian influenza, *Ornithobacterium rhinotracheale*. Serology-Elisa normally used, not all commercial kits are equally sensitive to response to both A and B challenge viruses.

Treatment

Antibiotic not very effective. Control respiratory stressors, chlorination of drinking water, multivitamins.

Prevention

All-in/all-out production, vaccination (degree of cross protection between

A and B types remains to be established). Live vaccines can reduce clinical signs and adverse effects, inactivated vaccines may be used in breeders prior to lay.

Beak Necrosis

A condition seen in chickens and turkeys caused by excessively fine mashed feeds.

Signs

- Feed accumulates along edges of lower beak leading to distortion and necrosis of horny tissue.
- Has been associated with curled tongue in turkeys in the past.
- This may also be associated with ulcers in the roof of the mouth (palate) which can be confused with some forms of mycotoxicosis.

Diagnosis

Clinical signs, exclusion of other causes of similar signs.

Treatment

Not usually sufficiently severe to justify medication. Mild water sanitation may help control secondary infections in the affected tissues.

Prevention

Check feed particle size by granulometry, grind less finely.

9

Egg Packaging, Transport and Storage

PACKAGING OF SHELL EGGS

Nature has given the egg a natural package-the shell. Despite its relative strength, the egg is an extremely fragile product and even with the best handling methods, serious losses can result from shell damage. Economical marketing generally requires that eggs be protected by the adoption of specialized packaging and handling procedures.

Functions of Packaging

Packaging is an important component in delivering quality eggs to buyers. It embraces both the art and science of preparing products for storage, transport and eventually sale. Packaging protects the eggs from:

- micro-organisms, such as bacteria;
- natural predators;
- loss of moisture;
- tainting;

- temperatures that cause deterioration; and
- possible crushing while being handled, stored or transported.

Eggs also need to breathe, hence the packaging material used must allow for the entrance of oxygen. The material used must be clean and odourless so as to prevent possible contamination and tainting. Authentic egg packaging materials can be reused, but careful attention must be paid to possible damage, odours and cleanliness. The packaging must be made to withstand handling, storage and transport methods of the most diverse kind and to protect the eggs against temperatures that cause deterioration and humidity. Finally, consumers like to see what they are buying, especially if it concerns fresh produce. An egg package should be designed so that the customers not only recognize the product as such, but can also see the eggs they are buying. Many factors must be taken into consideration for packaging eggs. It is important to obtain information regarding the necessary requirements for a particular market, such as:

- quality maintenance;
- storage facilities;
- type of transport;
- distance to be travelled;
- climatic conditions;

- time involved; and
- costs.

EGG PACKAGES

There are many different types of egg packages, which vary both in design and packaging material used.

Type 1: Packing eggs with clean and odourless rice husks, wheat chaff or chopped straw in a firm walled basket or crate greatly decreases the risk of shell damage. The basket has no cushioning material such as straw and therefore damage to the eggs may occur more easily. This kind of packaging may be fit for short distance transport.

Type 2: A very common form of packaging is the filler tray. The fillers are then placed in boxes or cases.

Filler trays are made of wood pulp moulded to accommodate the eggs. They are constructed so that they can be stacked one on top of the other and can also be placed in boxes ready for transport.

Filler trays also offer a convenient method for counting the eggs in each box, without having to count every single egg. Usually the standard egg tray carries 36 eggs. Therefore, if a box holds five trays, for example, the box has a total of 180 eggs (36 x 5 = 180).

The cases used may be made of sawn wood; however, they are more commonly made of cardboard. When using cardboard cases, special care must be taken in stacking so that excessive weight is not placed on a case at the bottom of a stack.

The advantages of using plastic egg fillers are that they can be reused and are washable. The fillers can be covered with plastic coverings and be used as packages for final sale to the buyer. More importantly, however, plastic transparent fillers allow for the inspection of eggs without handling or touching the eggs.

Type 3: Eggs can also be packed in packages that are smaller and specific for retail sale. Each package can hold from two to twelve eggs.

It is also possible to pack eggs in small paperboard cases and cover them with plastic film. Egg cases have also been developed from polystyrene. The advantages of using polystyrene are superior cushioning and protection against odours and moisture. The package is also resistant to fungus and mould growth.

The use of small cases is restricted by availability and cost considerations. However, small cases are good for retailers and customers. They are easy for the retailers to handle and customers are able to inspect the eggs.

Labelling

Labels are a source of important information for the wholesaler, retailer and consumer and not just pieces of paper stuck onto cartons or boxes. The important facts on the label contain information for buyers concerning the eggs, their size and weight and quality/grade description-AA, A or B. Labels may also indicate the producer, when the eggs were laid, how to store them and their expiration date.

Persuading the buyer to purchase the product without tasting, smelling or touching is another function of labelling.

Labels can be either printed directly on cartons or attached to the cartons. The cost of labelling must be taken into consideration.

Costs of Packaging

When calculating the costs of packaging, expenses must be considered for:

- packaging materials;
- labelling;
- labour;
- additional working capital required;
- changing existing facilities (if applicable); and
- packaging machinery (if applicable).

Storage of Eggs

The storage of shell eggs during the main laying season, in order to conserve them for consumption when they are scarce, has been practised for many centuries.

For the successful storage of eggs, the following conditions must be met.

- The eggs placed in storage must be clean; they must not be washed or wet.
- Packaging material used should be new, clean and odourless.
- Loss of water due to evaporation should be reduced to a minimum.
- The storage room must be free from tainting products and materials and should be cleaned regularly with odourless detergent sanitizers.
- The storage room must be kept at a constant temperature and humidity must be checked.
- There should be air circulation in the storage room.
- Eggs should be stored so that they are allowed to breathe.
- As far as possible, interior quality should be monitored; there should be a good proportion of thick white, the yolk should stand up well, and the flavour of white and yolk should be good.

If all of the above requirements are to be met, refrigerated storage is necessary.

COLD STORAGE OF EGGS

In the tropics, eggs can deteriorate very quickly unless they are stored at low temperatures. The ideal temperature for storage in such climates is 13°C or lower (usually between 10° and 13° C). Here refrigeration is a necessity for successful commercial storage; however, it may be unavailable or the costs too high.

The most important factors in successful cold storage are as follows.

- The selection and packaging of eggs.
- The equipment and preparation of the cold store.
- Proper temperature, humidity and air circulation.
- Periodic testing for quality.
- The gradual adjustment of eggs to higher temperatures when removed from storage.

The Selection and Packaging of Eggs for Storage: Eggs for storage must be clean, of good interior quality and have a sound shell. If they are to be stored for more then a month, they should be equivalent to the U.S. grade A. Therefore, it is best to candle all eggs before storage. It may also be advisable to take a sample and to break out these eggs as a further quality check. The period of time between laying and storage should not be more than a few days. The eggs should be kept cool during that time.

Packaging materials used for storage should be new, clean, odourless and free from damage. When packaging material is reused, it is extremely important that it is clean, odourless and free from damage. It is important that the material used allow the eggs to "breathe" and to be free from tainting odours. It should also be sturdy in the event that the cases have to be stockpiled on top of one another.

The Equipment and Preparation of the Cold Store: The storage room should have a concrete floor that is washable. Walls and ceilings must also be washable. Wooden buildings have been found to be satisfactory, provided they do not impart foreign odours or flavours to the eggs. The room should be scrubbed thoroughly with hot water and soap or an odourless detergent sanitizer before being used. A final rinse with a hypochlorite solution will help greatly in deodorizing the storeroom. A liberal application of freshly slaked lime to unpainted plaster surfaces will also help. The storage room should be aired and dried out thoroughly after cleaning, then closed up and the refrigeration turned on. It is best to allow several days for the temperature and humidity to stabilize before introducing the eggs.

Proper Temperature, Humidity and Air Circulation: Careful and accurate control of the air condition is essential. A temperature between-1.5° and-0° C is recommended. At a temperature of-2.5° C eggs freeze. The room should be well constructed and insulated and the refrigeration should be capable of maintaining an adequate uniform temperature in all areas. The cases of eggs should be separated by wood-strips and kept well away from the walls so as not to obstruct air circulation. Aisles left for the convenience of handling specific egg cases also help air circulation. Periodic ventilation of the storage room is advisable to promote air exchange.

The relative humidity should be between 80 and 85 percent at a cold storage temperature of-1° C. At cold storage temperatures of about 10° C the relative humidity should be between 75 and 80 percent. In such instances, on average, egg weight loss should not exceed 0.5 percent per month. During the early stages of storage when the packaging material is absorbing moisture at a high rate, the floors should be sprinkled with clean water several times a day. If forced-air circulation is feasible, a controlled temperature water-spray air washer may be used. If the humidity becomes excessive, part of the air can be cycled through a unit containing calcium chloride. Where eggs have been oiled less attention can be paid to the humidity level.

Periodic Testing for Quality: Periodic quality checks are essential if the risk of heavy egg losses is to be avoided. Every month or so a sample of eggs should be selected from the various lots and tested. Usually a sample of about 1 percent of all eggs in storage may be sufficient. For example, if 3 000 eggs are kept in storage, 30 eggs sampled from various egg cases will enable a good estimation of the general quality level of the eggs. If there is evidence of excessive deterioration, it is best to dispose of the eggs quickly, after eliminating those that are unfit for consumption.

The Gradual Adjustment of Eggs to Higher Temperatures: Care must be taken in removing eggs from storage to avoid the condensation of moisture on shells. This is minimized by raising the temperature slowly or by moving the eggs through rooms with intermediate temperatures. If condensation occurs, the eggs should be held under conditions that allow the moisture to evaporate within a day or so.

As indicated earlier, eggs should not be stored with products that may taint them. For the long term, eggs are best stored alone, while for the short term they may be kept with dairy products such as milk and mild-flavoured cheese. The average storage life for eggs is between six and seven months.

ECONOMICS OF COLD STORAGE

There is a tendency to underestimate the difficulties involved in providing good cold storage facilities and to recommend their installation without adequate investigation of their cost and potential economic return. The following factors should be considered when contemplating cold storage.

- Refrigeration is a complex and highly technical business.
- Capital investment and operating costs must be estimated.
- Potential available business must be appraised.

The potential available business must be appraised as well as its distribution over the different seasons of the year and the costs involved. Egg storage to even out the availability of supplies is likely to provide business for only a part of the year. The average-not maximum-price difference between the plentiful and scarce seasons must be calculated. If projected returns do not significantly exceed the costs envisaged for storage, there is little incentive for egg traders to make use of storage.

It must be considered that some egg producers, according to their circumstances and possibilities, maintain yearly production through special breeding and feeding programmes and by providing illumination in the hen laying houses. This may even out the rate of egg production throughout the year and hence long-term storage should not be considered.

Layout of Packaging and Storing Facilities for Shell Eggs

A model layout of a packaging and storing room for shell eggs is seen below:

1. Eggs enter the packing/storage facility
2. Temporary store room
3. Candling room
4. Weighing/cleaning room
5. Packaging area
6. Long-term storage
7. Eggs ready for transport.

The layout for the packaging and storing facility is of great importance for efficient and effective management. The various rooms should be kept clean, well ventilated and, where necessary, refrigeration provided. All personnel working in the facility should wear clean outer garments, use caps or head bands and wash their hands when handling eggs and equipment. All equipment used should be clean.

Eggs Enter the Packing/Storage Room: Eggs from production are brought into the packing/storage facility. Eggs can be brought in by hand or by conveyor belt. In intensive egg production, the birds lay eggs that roll out of the cage onto conveyor belts, which transport the eggs directly to the packing/storage facilities.

Temporary Storage Room: Here eggs are stored temporarily before they are moved to the candling room.

Candling Room: Eggs are brought into the candling room, where candlers verify the interior and external quality of eggs. The small squares represent candling benches.

Cleaning/Weighing Room: After candling, eggs are transported by conveyor belts to the cleaning/weighing room. Here eggs are cleaned with abrasives, where possible, and sorted by weight. Usually the size indicates which category eggs should fall into-small, medium or large. This can be done by hand; however, automated weighing machinery is available.

Packaging Area: After weighing, the eggs are taken to the packaging area. Packaging can be done either by hand or automatically by machinery.

Each machine is set to pack only predetermined egg weights. For example, machine No.1 packs only 60-gram eggs. If the eggs are below that weight, they will be conveyed to machine No. 2. The eggs are then packed automatically.

After packing, eggs may either be kept in long-term storage or may be ready for immediate transport.

POINTERS FOR HIGHER EGG PRODUCTION

Quality Birds

Choose the strain that will perform best and is known to have good livability under reasonable environmental conditions. Good chicks may cost more but they will perform better and pay more too.

Housing

There should be ample fresh air, free from drafts. Air must be circulating. High levels of non-desirable gases decrease growth rate and increase flock's susceptibility to respiratory disease. Ensure that the litter is dry. A well managed litter helps the birds in putting on feathers and improve feed conversion. It also reduces coccidiosis problem.

Crowding

Overcrowding increases mortality, stress, as well as production cost.

Feeding

Always ensure adequate fresh feed. Birds that are without feed for six hours will record a drop in production and a 12 hour starvation will result in moult of wing feathers. There should be adequate feeder space for the birds. Guard against feed wastage. Maintain records of daily feed consumption. It will enable to determine feed utilisation and bird's performance.

Watering

Provide plentiful and clean disinfected water. This management factor, although obvious, is commonly violated. Water restriction is a quick way to accidentally force the flock to moult. Ensure that the waterers are so placed that they are easily accessible to birds.

Lighting

The duration of light should be 16 hours per day, but not beyond 17 hours. No advantage is obtained by exceeding this limit. The amount of light given to the flock in one day should never be less than that given the day before. A decreasing day length can prematurely cause hens to go out to production. One 40 watt electric bulb is sufficient for 200 sq.ft. area.

Vaccination

Ensure that all birds are vaccinated for Marek's Disease and Ranikhet Disease. Birds not vaccinated are highly susceptible to these disease.

Debeaking

Follow correct debeaking programme. Poor debeaking can adversely affect egg production.

Culling

Unsuitable and uneconomic birds should be timely culled.

Health

Watch for early signs of disease for its timely treatment before it flares up in a big way. Some of the symptoms that indicate the onset of disease problems are : Drop in egg production and feed consumption: increased morbidity and mortality: inactivity and lack of vigour: droopy ruffled appearance and respiratory distress. Look for any sudden change in egg quality.

Sanitation

Sanitary measures are of vital importance in poultry operation. Keep roundworms, tapeworms and caecal worms under control. External parasites are a serious farm hazard, and can reduce production if unchecked. Deworming at regular intervals should be practised.

Egg Quality

Respiratory and intestinal diseases should be kept under control for the maintenance of quality of egg shells. Indiscriminate use of sulpha drugs can affect the egg shell quality. The use of tetracycline can, however, improve it.

Records

A daily record of feed consumption, egg production, mortality, income and expenditure is essential to help improve farming efficiency and pinpoint troubles and their solutions.

Routine Checking

Critical items of management should be listed on a daily, weekly or seasonal check list. Every item must be checked. It helps to locate the cause of trouble when it occurs. Routine checks are: Cleaning and refilling of waterers and feeders: cleaning the house and spraying insecticide; stirring the litter; dusting; culling of birds; egg collection, etc.

EGG WHITE FOAM

Creating an Egg Foam

The physical stress of beating the egg white can create a foam. There are two types of physical stress caused by the beating of the egg whites with a whisk, the first being that the whisk drags the liquid through itself creating a force that unfolds the protein molecules . This process is called denaturation. *The second stress* comes from the mixing of air into the whites which causes the proteins to come out of their natural state. These denatured proteins gather together where the air and water meet and create multiple bonds with the other unraveled proteins and thus becomes a foam holding the incorporated air into place. This is because the proteins consist of amino acids; some hydrophilic (attracted to water) and some hydrophobic (repelled by water). This process is called coagulation, because it is like blood clotting.

Stabilizing Egg White Foam for Culinary Purposes

Copper Bowl: Copper bowls have been used in France since the 18th century to stabilize egg foams. The copper in the bowl assists in creating a tighter bond in reactive sulfur items such as egg whites. The bond created is so tight that the sulfurs are prevented from reacting with any other material. A silver plated bowl will have the same result as the copper bowl or a pinch of powdered copper supplement from a health store used in a glass bowl will yield the same result as well. Drawbacks of the copper bowl include the expense of the bowl itself, as well as the fact that the bowls are difficult to keep clean. Copper contamination from the bowl is minimal as a cup of foam will contain a tenth of one's daily normal intake level.

Adding an Acid

Cream of tartar (potassium bitartrate) is an acidic salt that can be used to change the pH of the egg white to an acidic range by boosting the number of free-floating hydrogen ions in the egg white. This has the effect of stabilizing the foam, and is therefore an alternative to using a copper bowl. 1/8 teaspoon/ 0.5g cream of tartar should be used per one egg white to create this effect. 1/2 teaspoon/2ml of lemon juice can also be used to create the same results.

Health Issues

Although egg whites are prized as a source of low-fat, high-protein nutrition, a small number of people cannot eat them. Egg allergy is more common among infants than adults, and most children will outgrow it by the age of five. Allergic reactions against egg white are more common than reactions against egg yolks. In addition to true allergic reactions, some people experience a food intolerance to egg whites.

Yolk

An egg yolk is a part of an egg which feeds the developing embryo. The egg yolk is suspended in the egg white (known more formally as albumen or ovalbumin) by one or two spiral bands of tissue called the chalazae. Prior to fertilization, the yolk together with the germinal disc is a single cell; one of the few single cells that can be seen by the naked eye. As a food, yolks are a major source of vitamins and minerals. They contain all of the egg's fat and cholesterol, and about one-fifth of the protein.

If left intact while cooking fried eggs, the yellow yolk surrounded by a flat blob of whites creates the distinctive sunny-side up form of the food. Mixing the two components together before frying results in the pale yellow form found in omelettes and scrambled eggs.

The yolk in a newly laid egg is round and firm. As the yolk ages it absorbs water from the albumen, which increases its size and causes it to stretch and weaken the vitelline membrane (the clear casing enclosing the yolk). The resulting effect is a flattened and enlarged yolk shape.

Yolk color is dependent on the diet of the hen; if the diet contains yellow/ orange plant pigments known as xanthophylls, then they are deposited in the yolk, coloring it. A colorless diet can produce an almost colorless yolk. Farmers may enhance yolk color with artificial pigments, or with natural supplements rich in lutein (marigold petals are a popular choice), but, in most locations, this activity is forbidden.

Uses:

- It is sometimes separated from the egg white and used in cooking (for mayonnaise, custard, hollandaise sauce, crème brûlée, *avgolemono*, and *ovos moles*).

- It is used in painting as a component of traditional egg-tempera.
- It is used in the production of egg-yolk agar plate medium, useful in testing for the presence of *Clostridium perfringens.*
- Egg yolks also contains spermcells antibody called antiglobulin (IgY). The antibody transfers from the laying hen to the egg yolk by passive immunity to protect both embryo and hatchling from microorganism invasion.
- Egg yolk can be used to make liqueurs such as Advocaat, or mixed drinks such as Eggnog.

Composition of Chicken Egg Yolk

The yolk makes up about 33% of the liquid weight of the egg; it contains approximately 60 calories, three times the caloric content of the egg white.

One large egg (50 grams in weight, 17 gram yolk) contains approximately: 2.7g protein, 210 mg cholesterol, 0.61g carbohydrates and 4.51g total fat. (USDA National Nutrient Database)

All of the fat soluble vitamins, (A, D, E and K) are found in the egg yolk. Egg yolks are one of the few foods naturally containing vitamin D.

The composition (by weight) of the most prevalent fatty acids in egg yolk is typically as follows:

- Unsaturated fatty acids:
    - o Oleic acid 47 %
    - o Linoleic acid 16 %
    - o Palmitoleic acid 5 %
    - o Linolenic acid 2 %.
- Saturated fatty acids:
    - o Palmitic acid 23 %
    - o Stearic acid 4 %
    - o Myristic acid 1 %.

Egg yolk is a source of lecithin, an emulsifier and surfactant.

The yellow color is caused by lutein and zeaxanthin, which are yellow or orange carotenoids known as xanthophylls

Double-yolk Eggs

Double-yolk eggs occur when ovulation occurs too rapidly, or when one yolk becomes joined with another yolk. These eggs may be the result of a young hen's productive cycle not yet being synchronized. Some hybrid breeds of hens also produce double yolk eggs by default. Such eggs are produced in West Bengal, India and in particular by Arambagh Hatcheries in Arambagh.

Some hens will rarely lay double-yolked eggs as the result of unsynchronized production cycles. Although heredity causes some hens to have a higher propensity to lay double-yolked eggs, these occur more frequently as occasional abnormalities in young hens beginning to lay. Usually a double-yolked egg will be longer and thinner than an ordinary single-yolk egg. Double-yolked eggs usually only lead to observed successful hatchlings under human intervention, as the unborn chickens would otherwise fight each other and die.

Yolkless Eggs

Eggs without yolk are called "dwarf" or "wind" eggs. Such an egg is most often a pullet's first effort, produced before her laying mechanism is fully ready. In a mature hen, a wind egg is unlikely, but can occur if a bit of reproductive tissue breaks away, stimulating the egg producing glands to treat it like a yolk and wrap it in albumen, membranes and a shell as it travels through the egg tube. This has occurred if, instead of a yolk, the egg contains a small particle of grayish tissue. An archaic term for a no yolk egg is a "cock" egg. Since they contained no yolk and therefore can't hatch, it was traditionally believed that these eggs were laid by roosters. This type of egg occurs in many varieties of fowl. They have been found in chickens, both standard and bantams, guineas and coturnix quail.

Bibliography

Alexander, D.: *Poultry Diseases,* Elsevier, 2007.

Anton, M. & Schade, R.: *Bioactive Egg Compounds,* Springer, Delhi, 2007.

Ball, W.: *Egg Quality Guidelines for the Australian Egg Industry,* AECL Publication, UK, 2004.

Bell, D.D & Weaver, W.D. & North, M.O.: *Commercial Chicken Meat and Egg Production,* Kluwer, USA, 2001.

Berton, V. and Mudd, D.: *Profitable Poultry: Raising Birds on Pasture,* USDA's Sustainable Agriculture Network (SAN), Washington, DC, 2001.

Blackbourn, David: *The Long Nineteenth Century: A History of Germany,* Oxford University Press, New York, 1998.

Boorman, K.N.: *Poultry Feedstuffs, Supply Composition and Nutritive Value,* CABI Publishing, UK, 2002.

Chenoweth, H.: *Free-Range Poultry,* Free-Range Poultry Production and Marketing, Creola, Ohio, 2001.

Clark, Christopher: *Iron Kingdom: The Rise and Downfall of Prussia,* Cambridge, The Belknap Press of Harvard University Press, Massachusetts, 2006.

Cotterill, O.J.: *Egg Science and Technology,* Food Products Press, Imprint of Haworth Press, New York, London, 1995.

Coutts, J.A. & Wilson, G.C. & Fernandez, S. & Rosales, E. & Weber, G. & Hernandez, J.: *Optimum Egg Quality: A Practical Approach,* 5M Publishing, U.K, 2007.

Coutts, J.A. & Wilson, G.C.: *Egg Quality Handbook,* NSW DPI, MT, 1990.

Cramer, C.: *Sustainable Farming Connection: Where Farmers Find and Share Information,* Sustainable Farm Publishing, US, 1997.

Deeming, D.C. & Ferguson, M.W.J.: *Egg Incubation, Its Effects on Embryonic Development in Birds and Reptiles,* Cambridge University Press, UK, 1991.

Dekkers, J.C.M., H.H. Zhao, and RL. Fernando: *Linkage Disequilibrium Mapping in Livestock,* Belo Horizonte, Brazil, 2006.

Dekkers, J.C.M.: *Methods and Strategies for QTL Mapping,* University of Wisconsin, Madison, 2005.

Donald, E. Green: *A History of the Oklahoma State University Division of Agriculture,* Oklahoma State University, Stillwater, 1990.

Elson, H.A.: *Poultry Production Systems, Behaviour, Management and Welfare,* CAB International, NY, 1992.

Fanatico, A.: *Pastured Poultry: A Heifer Project International Case Study Booklet,* Little Rock, AR, 2000.

Foreman, P.: *The Chicken Tractor: The Permaculture Guide to Happy Hens and Healthy Soil-All New Straw Bale Edition,* Good Earth Publications, USA, 2002.

Fumo, A & Mata, B & Young, M.: *Controlling Newcastle Disease in Village Chickens,* ACIAR, US, 2002.

Gillespie, J.R.: *Modern Livestock and Poultry Production,* Thomson Delmar Learning, 2004.

Glatz, P & Bourke, M.: *Beak Trimming Handbook for Egg Producers,* Landlinks, UK, 2006.

Glatz, P.C.: *Poultry Welfare Issues: Beak Trimming,* Nottingham University Press, UK, 2005.

Hunton, P.: *Poultry Production,* Elsevier, 2007.

Leclercq, B.: *Nutrition and Feeding of Poultry,* Nottingham University Press, U.K., 1994.

Mead, G.: *Food Safety Control in the Poultry Industry,* Woodhead Publishing Limited, Abington Hall, Abington, Cambridge, 2006.

Mead, G: *Poultry Meat Processing and Quality,* CRC Press, USA, 2004.

Mudd, D.: *Profitable Poultry: Raising Birds on Pasture,* USDA's Sustainable Agriculture Network (SAN), Washington, DC, 2001.

Nakai, S & Guenter, W.: *Egg Nutrition and Biotechnology,* CABI Publishing, NY, 2000.

North, M.O.: *Commercial Chicken Meat and Egg Production,* Kluwer, USA, 2001.

Nowland, W.J.: *Modern Poultry Management in Australia,* Rigby, 1978.

Saif, Y.M.: *Diseases of Poultry,* Iowa State Press, USA, 2003.

Salnsbury, D.: *Poultry Health and Management,* Blackwell Scientific, London, U.K., 1992.

Tullett, S.G.: *Poultry Science Symposium Number 22.* Butterworth-Heinemann, NJ, 1991.

Weber, G. & Hernandez, J.: *Optimum Egg Quality: A Practical Approach,* 5M Publishing, U.K, 2007.

Weeks, C & Butterworth, A.: *Measuring and Auditing Broiler Welfare,* CABI, UK, 2004.

Whitehead, C.C.: *Bone Biology and Skeletal Disorders in Poultry,* Carfax Publishing Company, U.K., 1992.

Wiseman, J. & Garnsworthy, P.C.: *Recent Developments in Poultry Nutrition,* University Press, India, 1999.

Index

N

P

R

S

T

U

❑❑❑